Bruce E. Shields

THE TÜBINGEN SCHOOL

Tübingen about 1825

THE
TÜBINGEN
SCHOOL

by

HORTON HARRIS

CLARENDON PRESS · OXFORD
1975

Oxford University Press, Ely House, London W.1

GLASGOW NEW YORK TORONTO MELBOURNE WELLINGTON
CAPE TOWN IBADAN NAIROBI DAR ES SALAAM LUSAKA ADDIS ABABA
DELHI BOMBAY CALCUTTA MADRAS KARACHI LAHORE DACCA
KUALA LUMPUR SINGAPORE HONG KONG TOKYO

ISBN 0 19 826642 1

Printed in Great Britain by
William Clowes & Sons, Limited, London, Beccles and Colchester

Preface

'If you write', requested George Henry Lewes[1] of Eduard Zeller, 'pray let it be in the Latin character, the German Handschrift being very puzzling to me.'[2] George Henry Lewes was not alone in his difficulties of deciphering the old German handwriting. The author of this book spent innumerable hours labouring through many hundreds of pages of handwritten correspondence comprising the extant letters of the eight members of the Tübingen School. But only by utilizing the personal letters can a true and living portrayal of the School be obtained. For the Tübingen School consisted not just of theological views and hypotheses, but of persons; and if we would learn to understand the School, then it is essential to learn to know its members.

The Tübingen School was not of merely minor importance for theology. It was *the most important theological event in the whole history of theology from the Reformation to the present day*. Within the two decades of its existence the whole course of Biblical and especially New Testament criticism was fundamentally changed. Indeed, it would not be too much to say that all modern exegesis and interpretation of the Bible find their roots and origins in the Tübingen School.

One's first reaction to such statements will probably be that such claims are undoubtedly exaggerated. But the fact is that so little is known of the School and its influence upon succeeding theological generations that its enormous importance has never been fully perceived. Present-day descriptions are usually confined to a few meagre lines about the head of the School, Ferdinand Christian Baur, occasionally with brief mention of Eduard Zeller and Albert Schwegler. But such descriptions are invariably so general that almost nothing of worth can be learned, while oftentimes the representations are inaccurate or even erroneous. Within the last one hundred years no book dealing with the School has been written. The first and finest investigation of the Tübingen School was contained in an article by Gerhard Uhlhorn in 1858,[3]

---

[1] The husband of the novelist George Eliot (Mary Ann Evans).

[2] 17 Jan. 1868; UBT, Md 747, Ks. 22.

[3] 'Die älteste Kirchengeschichte in der Darstellung der Tübinger Schule', *JDT*, III (1858), pp. 280–349.

two years before Baur's death. Baur replied in his brochure 'The
Tübingen School' published in the following year and his
son-in-law Eduard Zeller also composed an apology for the
School in 1860, which sparked off a debate with Albrecht Ritschl
—the apostate member of the School. In 1863 the Englishman
R. W. Mackay published his *The Tübingen School and its Antecedents*. This was a poor book. It was far too superficial in its
approach and dealt more with the antecedents of the School than
with the School itself. Of higher calibre was the representation
of the Frenchman Samuel Berger,[4] but this book, too, added
nothing to what had been written previously. Finally, in 1864
came a long article by Heinrich Beckh,[5] carefully written, but
lacking the conciseness and trenchancy of Uhlhorn's portrayal.
None of these representations portrayed the members of the
School themselves; nor was it possible to take into consideration
their private correspondence.

After Baur's death in 1860 the Tübingen School as a School
was gradually forgotten. Attention became focused on Ritschl
and the Ritschlian School so that by the end of the century the
Tübingen School belonged to the past. Where interest still
remained it centred on Baur rather than on his School. In the
course of a century only one lone monograph stands out as
significant: Gustav Fraedrich's study of Baur,[6] which was
published in 1909. After the First World War the dialectical
theology of Barth, Brunner, and Bultmann held the stage, and not
until the publication of Wolfgang Geiger's 'Speculation and
Criticism'[7] in 1964 did any other work of major importance on
Baur appear.

Geiger's book which dealt with the development of Baur's
theological views was followed two years later by Peter C.
Hodgson's more comprehensive portrayal of Baur's life and
theology.[8] Hodgson took account of Baur's letters and sermons,
and his careful and painstaking application to details provided an

---

[4] *F. C. Baur: les origines de l'école de Tubingue et ses principes, 1826–1844* (Strasbourg,
1867).
   [5] 'Die Tübinger Schule kritisch beleuchtet', *Zeitschrift für Protestantismus und
Kirche*, N.F. LXXIV (1864), pp. 1–244.
   [6] *Ferdinand Christian Baur* (Gotha, 1909).
   [7] *Spekulation und Kritik* (Munich, 1964).
   [8] *The Formation of Historical Theology: A Study of Ferdinand Christian Baur* (New
York, 1966).

example for all to follow. But Hodgson's presentation of Baur's theological views was almost diametrically opposite to Geiger's, so much so that the poor reader has to decide which picture of Baur he should accept—Baur the rationalist and atheist (Geiger) or Baur the pious, if heterodox, Christian believer (Hodgson).[9] Thus it was not surprising that Klaus Penzel, in his review of both books,[10] made the appeal: 'Will the real Ferdinand Christian Baur please stand up?'

An investigation of the Tübingen School really requires a voluminous work running into many hundreds of pages. The literature which must be considered in any representation of the School is vast, and no one is more aware than the author how much more could have been written. However, it was felt that to go into more detail would blur or even destroy the over-all picture of the School, which was the author's aim. And anyway, who today has time to read voluminous works? Therefore, this book sets out to provide a clear and concise account of the eight personalities who constituted the Tübingen School, their theological views and the history of the School—its rise, its decline, and its end. The source material available for producing a coherent and interesting account of the personal lives of Baur and his disciples turned out in some cases to be rather meagre. This has meant scraping the bottom of the barrel and in some parts the content may appear rather thin. I can only apologize for this and say that I have tried to do my best with the material at my disposal. To keep the book at a reasonable size has also meant omitting all that was considered of secondary importance in order to concentrate on the essential points. This was especially the case in the chapter on the Rise and Decline of the School, where I have not attempted to provide answers to the complex historical questions but have simply outlined the problems involved and the Tübingen endeavours to resolve them. Nevertheless, I hope that the specialist too may find sufficient information to occupy his interest and that the *real* Ferdinand Christian Baur will have finally stood up.

[9] This contrast is certainly over-simplified but it does express the *fundamental* difference between the two presentations. Hodgson in his later reply to Geiger [*Ferdinand Christian Baur on the Writing of Church History*, edited and translated by Peter C. Hodgson (New York, 1968), pp. 6–8] refrained from discussing the really essential point of divergence between them. See chapter 11.

[10] *Journal of Religion*, XLVIII (1968), pp. 310–23.

Apart from three books by Baur and Zeller's commentary on Acts none of the theological writings of the Tübingen School have ever been translated into English. Nor have the greater part of the excerpts from the letters ever before been published, either in German or in English. Details as to the location of the letters are contained in the bibliography. Although in a few instances an older translation of the German passages exists, all quotations have been newly translated by me. On the assumption that the reader who knows no German will be more interested in understanding the title of books and articles than in simply seeing the original words, I have generally adopted the procedure of translating the German titles and placing them in inverted commas. Titles in English or translated into English have been italicized. The original title has often been printed in the footnotes and a selected bibliography has been included for the specialist.

Two points concerning translations: 1. The word 'catholic' has been left uncapitalized when referring to the Church universal of the first three centuries, and capitalized only when it refers to the Roman Catholic Church. 2. The German word *Geist* (Spirit) when used as referring to Hegel's Infinite Spirit has been treated as an impersonal Spirit of neuter gender. Thus when the Spirit is regarded as being synonymous with God, there will sometimes be a disagreement of masculine and neuter pronouns. However it has been thought better to allow this anomaly to remain, rather than to confuse the intrinsic meaning of the two words.

My thanks are due to *Oberbibliotheksrat* Dr. F. Seck and *Oberbibliotheksrätin* Dr. D. Blieske for help in deciphering letters and providing information; to Wendy and my father for reading the manuscript; Anne for typing it; Anneliese for typing the bibliography; Professor F. F. Bruce and the Revd. Professor T. F. Torrance for reading parts of the typescript; and to all others, too numerous to mention by name, who have helped along the way.

HORTON HARRIS

1973–4

Contents

List of Illustrations

PLATES

MAPS

Abbreviations

ADB	*Allgemeine Deutsche Bibliographie*
AW	Baur's *Ausgewählte Werke*
BWKG	*Blätter für Württembergische Kirchengeschichte*
DJWK	*Deutsche Jahrbücher für Wissenschaft und Kunst*
EKZ	*Evangelische Kirchenzeitung*
ET	English Translation
HJ	*Hallische Jahrbücher*
HN	Hilgenfeld's *Nachlass*
HZ	*Historische Zeitschrift*
JBW	*Jahrbücher der biblischen Wissenschaft*
JDT	*Jahrbücher für deutsche Theologie*
JG	*Jahrbücher der Gegenwart*
JWK	*Journal für wissenschaftliche Kritik*
OR	Otto Ritschl, *Albrecht Ritschls Leben*, vol. I (1892)
PJ	*Preussische Jahrbücher*
PK	*Protestantische Kirchenzeitung*
RE	Herzog's *Realencyklopaedie* (3rd ed.)
SBB	Staatsbibliothek Berlin
SMM	Schiller-Nationalmuseum Marbach
SMSK	*Schwäbische Mercur, Schwäbische Kronik*
TJ	*Theologische Jahrbücher*
TSK	*Theologische Studien und Kritiken*
TZT	*Tübinger Zeitschrift für Theologie*
UBH	Universitätsbibliothek Heidelberg
UBT	Universitätsbibliothek Tübingen
VA	Zeller's *Vorträge und Abhandlungen*
WLS	Württembergische Landesbibliothek Stuttgart
ZBZ	Zentralbibliothek Zürich
ZKG	*Zeitschrift für Kirchengeschichte*
ZTK	*Zeitschrift für Theologie und Kirche*
ZWT	*Zeitschrift für wissenschaftliche Theologie*

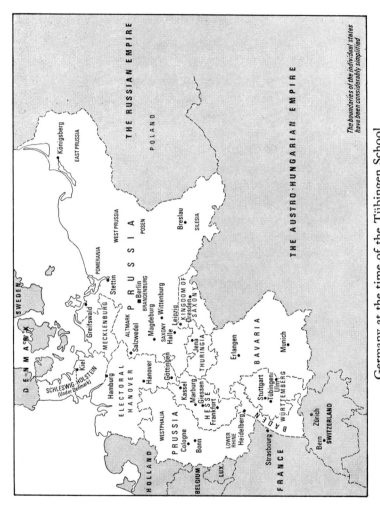

Germany at the time of the Tübingen School

The boundaries of the individual states have been considerably simplified

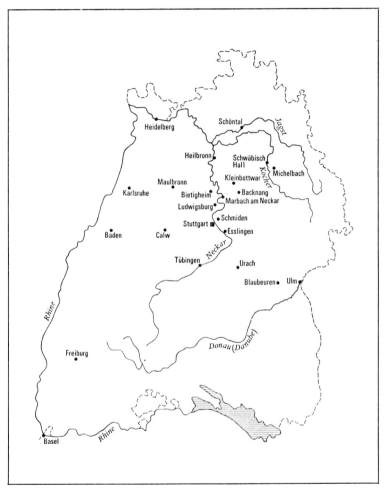

Baden-Württemberg

1. Introduction

No single event ever changed the course of Biblical scholarship as much as the appearance of the Tübingen School. All New Testament criticism and, derivatively, much Old Testament criticism from the mid-nineteenth century onwards finds its origin, consciously or unconsciously, in this School. For almost twenty years the Tübingen School dominated the whole *avant-garde* investigation of the New Testament, and the reverberations in this field set up a corresponding reaction in the realm of Old Testament study. It is no exaggeration when we say that the Tübingen School constituted the central point of nineteenth-century Biblical research.

When one speaks about the Tübingen School in Protestant theological circles today, that School connected with the name of Ferdinand Christian Baur is immediately recognized as being meant. But this was not always the case and in the early nineteenth century there were two other Tübingen Schools—the Catholic Tübingen School[1] which was influenced by Schleiermacher's theology, and the Old Tübingen School[2] which advocated a rational supernaturalism. In this latter School the divine inspiration and authority of the Bible were still upheld, while an intelligent and reasoned investigation of it was not forbidden. The School represented a critical approach to Scripture but still within a strictly orthodox framework, and since its founder G. C. Storr had been a bulwark of orthodoxy and the younger Bengel was a grandson of the famous Johann Albrecht Bengel, it was generally regarded as belonging to an orthodox point of view. The new Tübingen School did not originate out of the Old Tübingen School, but in direct antithesis to it; for it represented a direct repudiation of the supernatural presuppositions of the Old School. What the new Tübingen School desired was the right to a purely historical, scientific investigation of the New Testament, untrammelled by considerations of a supernatural or miraculous nature. Baur's student days and early academic career were lived in the atmosphere of the Old Tübingen School and not until 1835

[1] See p. 137f. [2] See p. 23f.

did he publicly express his disagreement with its supernatural viewpoint. It is interesting to note that following Baur's criticism of Schleiermacher's theology in 1827–8, Schleiermacher himself mistakenly reckoned Baur as a member of the Old School.

We may distinguish three separate periods in the history of the new Tübingen School.

I. THE PERIOD OF PREPARATION AND EMERGENCE, 1835–41

The beginning of the Tübingen School may be dated from the appearance of Strauss's *Life of Jesus* in 1835. It may at first sight seem strange that a School whose head was Baur should begin with Strauss, but this fact must be emphasized: The Tübingen School begins with Strauss and not Baur. For it was Strauss's book which marked the break between the old conservative School of Storr and Bengel and the new radical anti-supernatural viewpoint first put forward publicly by Strauss. It is true that Baur had laid the foundations for his total-view of early Christian history in his article on the church at Corinth,[3] but this caused no radical stir in the theological world of the day. It did not touch the burning issue which divided the Old Tübingen School from the new—the denial of the supernatural and miraculous element in Christianity. Baur's investigation of the Corinthian church was simply one more article in a theological journal, unorthodox enough to cause perhaps a few raised eyebrows among the more perceptive readers, but certainly containing nothing remarkable enough to create a whole new school. Strauss's book, on the other hand, changed Tübingen almost overnight from a centre of orthodoxy into a centre of heresy. Only after the *Life of Jesus* had rocked the whole theological world to its foundations did Baur come to be placed in the same category as his notorious pupil. Baur's 'Christian Gnosticism' which appeared in that same fateful year (1835) was immediately branded as Hegelian and his investigation of the Pastoral Epistles (1835) was seen as a denial of the divine inspiration and authority of the Scriptures. In 1837 Strauss's 'Polemical Writings' stirred up more dust and in the succeeding years Baur devoted himself to his long treatises on the Atonement

---

[3] 'Die Christuspartei in der korinthischen Gemeinde...', *TZT*, 1831: IV, pp. 61–206.

(1838) and the Trinity (1841–3), both of which were written from a Hegelian viewpoint that could not be disguised. And finally, in 1840–1 came Strauss's 'Doctrine of the Christian Faith' which represented a complete denial of all the traditional Christian doctrines.

Thus in this initial period the name of Tübingen was coupled not primarily with Baur, but was rather synonymous with unbelief, the most notorious representative of which was Strauss, with Baur being regarded as a close second and even more dangerous in that, unlike Strauss, he did not openly confess his atheism. Small wonder that the students from Tübingen who journeyed to Berlin to further their theological studies should be suspected of having been led astray by the anti-Christian Strauss and the heretical Dr. Baur. Schwegler, who arrived in Berlin during the autumn of 1841, well portrayed the situation there.

I arrived here on 3 October after a very happy journey but entered the city with a bad omen in that on just the second day I sprained my ankle so badly that I had to be handed over to the doctor, who tortured me with leeches, poultices, and the like and forbade me to walk for several days. Scarcely recovered, I had the same misfortune a second time. Thus as yet I have been unable to make any visits. Apart from the Hegelians there is absolutely no theologian I can approach, for among the orthdox party there reigns a boundless animosity against Tübingen. Dr. Baur is the *bête noire* of the pietists here, hated even more than Strauss. Whoever comes here from Tübingen is *a priori* looked upon as an unbeliever unless he legitimizes himself by outbreaks of hatred against heresy; even poor old Belser who is certainly least to blame for Israel's troubles had to listen to Twesten[4] saying: one doesn't rightly know where one is with the Tübingen doctors who come here; at least 'seven-eighths of the theology students in Tübingen are cracked!'[5]

2. THE PERIOD OF FORMATION AND CONSOLIDATION, 1842–6

At the beginning of the 1840s a circle of young lecturers used to meet each evening in one of the Tübingen inns (the 'Neckar Tyranny') under the leadership of Friedrich Theodor Vischer, friend of Strauss and lecturer in the philosophical faculty at Tübingen. The group, which among others included Eduard

[4] Professor of dogmatics and New Testament exegesis at Berlin.
[5] To Zeller, 21 Oct. 1841.

Zeller, Albert Schwegler, Karl Christian Planck, Karl Griesinger, and Johannes Fallati, was portrayed for us by Zeller.

In Tübingen about this time there were a number of young men of liberal views and scientific mind who worked as lecturers in the various faculties and also as authors sought to make known their views, some in their own periodicals. A few of these had already been appointed to salaried lectureships, most, however, as unsalaried lecturers had to struggle for many years and against strong opposition for the position which they all subsequently found inside or outside of Württemberg. Some came from the Hegelian School of philosophy, others had busied themselves with empirical investigation; but just as the former sought to supplement the philosophical speculation through criticism and historical investigation, the latter strove for a scientific connection and interpretation of the facts. Yet, with all the diversity of academic faculties and viewpoints the great majority of us were generally agreed about the necessity to think scientifically. In addition there were various personal associations, friendships made at the university, and an equality of academic and social relations. It was natural that under these circumstances the greater part of the group entered into a closer personal intercourse; others joined in, likewise mostly younger men in varying positions in society; now and again came strangers who stayed in Tübingen for a longer or shorter time and a gay and lively circle with a changing periphery thus formed. This, however, still had its well-defined middle-point in those who would meet every evening, and sometimes also at midday, at a local inn, in order to relax in cheerful discussion after the day's work had been completed. Then there was usually an animated conversation in which literary and personal news, philosophical and political discussion, good and poor jokes were all mixed up. Our opponents were not spared; whatever new had happened in the little university town was sure to be discussed here. The tone was most unconstrained; we expressed ourselves frankly, indeed even inconsiderately and bluntly; but because in general we had a high regard for each other and got on well together, disagreements were easily overcome and good-natured humour would usually atone for any offensive behaviour and enable us to overlook the unpleasant experiences which most of the participants could relate. We spent a joyful time together, a second blossoming of our university years which was certainly not unfruitful; it was a time rich in aspirations and plans, in hopes, disappointments, and successes.[6]

From this group, which we may call the Tübingen circle, emerged the Tübingen School under the leadership of Zeller.

[6] 'Albert Schwegler' in Schwegler's *Römische Geschichte*, vol. III, pp. xxiii–xxiv.

The patron and head of the School was Baur, but the leader and guiding force in these early years was undoubtedly Zeller who founded and edited the literary organ of the School, the *Theologische Jahrbücher*, by which the Tübingen views were propagated throughout the land. The School was established around this journal and without it it is doubtful whether or not the School would ever have come into being.

Previous to 1842 articles from Tübingen had usually been sent to the radical *Hallische Jahrbücher* edited by Arnold Ruge in Halle. However, the journal had fallen more and more into the hands of Bruno Bauer who had taken a special dislike to Strauss and his friends at Tübingen. The members of the Tübingen circle were therefore unanimous in their desire to publish their own journal which would aim at pursuing a scientific investigation of the Bible while avoiding the wild extravagances of Bruno Bauer and his radical followers. Zeller was the obvious editor and the launching of the new journal heralded the beginning of the Tübingen School as a School. The first issue appeared in 1842 with Zeller having to write all the book reviews himself; but slowly more contributions began to arrive and even the blustering Ewald was only too willing to help. However, the new journal found readers only slowly. 'What sort of a sensation has the *Theologische Jahrbücher* caused in Württemberg?', wrote Schwegler to Zeller from Berlin early in 1842. 'Here they are fairly quiet about it; the Hegelians are pleased, but on the other hand it seems that no one *wants* to take much notice of it, i.e. until we compel them to.'[7] And a few months later he reported[8] that the only one in Halle to subscribe to the *Jahrbücher* was Tholuck, the pietist professor of theology.

The Tübingen standpoint was expounded not only in the theological journal: in 1843 Schwegler founded the *Jahrbücher der Gegenwart*, the political companion to the *Theologische Jahrbücher*, and this provided a platform from which the members of the Tübingen circle could express their opinions on historical and political issues, past and present. And there were also books: Schwegler's 'Montanism' (1841), Köstlin's 'The Teaching of the Gospel and Letters of John' (1843), Baur's *Paul, the Apostle of Jesus Christ* (1845), and Schwegler's 'Post-apostolic Age' (1846).

[7] To Zeller; undated letter about January 1842.
[8] To Zeller, 25 July 1842.

In 1845 Vischer was suspended for two years from his new professorial position on account of his outspoken remarks about Christianity. Against considerable opposition he had been appointed a professor in the philosophical faculty in 1844, for in his *Kritische Gänge* published in that same year he had made an insulting attack on the pietists.

I have called pietism a scab, a suppuration of the best juices of the spirit, and I have been persecuted for this statement with that rage which I know, but do not fear ... Pietism is therefore the born and sworn enemy of true scientific thinking ... The madness of pietism lies in the peculiarity of its interest in religion ... The pietist is religious as if religion is his trade, the pietist is he who goes around professing his religion, the pietist is the man who smells for religion ... A pietist must be a hypocrite ...[9]

Now, in his inaugural address he confessed himself a pantheist and promised his enemies 'a fight without quarter', 'my full, unmitigated hostility, my open and utter hate'. This was the final straw for the orthodox and pietists who raised a loud clamour throughout Württemberg for his dismissal. Among those writing pamphlets against him was a young Swabian literary critic, Dr. Heinrich Merz, who had once been friendly with Schwegler and had been asked by Schwegler to contribute to the *Jahrbücher der Gegenwart*. Since that time, however, Merz had professed his conversion to Jesus Christ and completely broken with the Tübingen principles. Zeller now wrote a personal attack on Merz which Merz answered in a brochure attacking not only Zeller, Schwegler, and Vischer, but the whole Tübingen perspective and especially the Tübingen evaluation of the books of the New Testament.

But where can one find a living historical picture of the Redeemer after having been critically 'liberated' for four years long? Matthew, Mark, Luke?—historical poetry! John?—didactic poetry! Acts?—ecclesiastical-political novel! Romans?—diplomatic document between Jewish and Gentile Christianity! the last two chapters unauthentic. Ephesians?—unauthentic! Philippians?—unauthentic! Colossians?—unauthentic! Thessalonians?—the second letter at least unauthentic! Timothy, Titus, Philemon?—all unauthentic! 1 and 2 Peter?—unauthentic! The letters of John?—unauthentic if Revelation is

[9] *Kritische Gänge* (Tübingen, 1844), pp. xx ff.

authentic! Hebrews?—unauthentic? Jude?—unauthentic! The Revelation of John?—authentic! authentic Jewish, authentic Ebionite! authentic unevangelical! That was our Biblical-theological school-bag from Tübingen; that was our sustenance for heart and soul in the inn of speculative criticism. 'Or what man of you, if his son asks him for a loaf, will give him a stone?' And shall we then thank these intellectual foster-fathers of ours after we have finally perceived that they gave us, at most, rotten fish?[10]

The whole controversy over Vischer's address, however, simply discredited the Tübingen School in the eyes of the orthodox even more. And there was a heavy price to pay: promotion was withheld. The King of Württemberg refused his consent to Zeller's nomination for a professorial chair; Schwegler, whose *Jahrbücher der Gegenwart* had infuriated the Church authorities, was not appointed as tutor in the Tübingen seminary; Planck and Köstlin both had to struggle for teaching positions as did all those who were known to be sympathetic to the Tübingen viewpoint.

The year 1846 marked the high-point of the School, which was reached not in the works of Baur, but in Schwegler's 'Post-apostolic Age'. With prose of crystal clarity—Schwegler was undoubtedly the finest prose-writer in the School—and a masterly organization of the material, Schwegler's work summed up all the previous investigations of the School and presented the Tübingen perspective in its most concise, comprehensive, and representative form. In no other work, before or after, was the Tübingen total-view applied so consistently to the whole of the New Testament.

3. THE PERIOD OF DECLINE AND DISSOLUTION, 1847–60

In a military campaign the initial assault is often that part of the campaign where the greatest progress is made. Afterwards the going becomes stiffer; the troops are forced to dig in and defend the captured positions. So it was with the Tübingen School. The first five years had been occupied in attacking the traditional theology and establishing the new Tübingen total-view—its most developed exposition being found in Baur's *Paul, the Apostle of Jesus Christ* (1845), Schwegler's 'Post-apostolic Age' (1846), and Baur's 'Critical Investigation of the Canonical Gospels' (1847). Now it was time to defend the new perspective against attacks not only from outside the camp, but also from within. There were

---

[10] *Die Jahrbücher der Gegenwart und ihre Helden* (Stuttgart, 1845), p. 16.

two main factors responsible for the break-up of the School: the dissolution of the Tübingen circle and the internal disagreement within the School itself.

From 1847 the Tübingen circle began to fall apart. Zeller followed a call to Bern and Schwegler abandoned theology; the old Tübingen circle was never again the same. 'Things here', wrote Schwegler, 'are what they were like before the good old days; the social relationships have almost collapsed; we see one another at midday coffee but not otherwise. Griesinger, Vischer, and I have withdrawn from the "Tyranny" . . .'[11] In 1854 Planck resigned from his position and departed from Tübingen for Ulm; in the following year Vischer left for Zürich, and in 1857 Köstlin crossed over to the philosophical faculty. The three North-German members of the School did not reside in Tübingen. Ritschl had spent a semester there in 1845/6, but Hilgenfeld neither set foot in the town nor met Baur personally, and Volkmar, who on account of his political activities had been forced to leave his native Hesse, found a refuge in Zürich, from where he contributed his articles to the *Theologische Jahrbücher*. These three newer members of the School provided its new blood but also the seeds of its destruction. For they all had their own individual views and could not be content with a merely uncritical acceptance of the views which had been previously put forward by Baur, Zeller, and Schwegler. Thus during the 1850s the Tübingen viewpoint was subjected to a fresh examination which led to a continual disagreement between Baur, Ritschl, and Hilgenfeld, with Volkmar, as ever, continuing to follow his own peculiar path. These differences and disagreements within the School finally became so acute that Ritschl broke with Baur, and Hilgenfeld distanced himself as much as possible from the name of Tübingen.

But all this forms the substance of the following pages in which we first learn to know the individual members of the School and then its history—its rise, its decline, and its end.

---

[11] To Zeller, 30 Apr. 1847.

PART I

THE MEMBERS OF THE TÜBINGEN SCHOOL

PLATE I

Ferdinand Christian Baur (1826)

PLATE II

1. F. C. Baur (1859)

2. Eduard Zeller

3. Albert Schwegler

4. Karl Christian Planck

PLATE III

1. Karl Reinhold Köstlin

2. Albrecht Ritschl

3. Adolf Hilgenfeld

4. Gustav Volkmar

PLATE IV

Ferdinand Christian Baur (1859)

2. Ferdinand Christian Baur

It may be said, that as Levi was in the loins of his ancestor Abraham (Hebrews 7:10), so Baur's association with Tübingen began long before the time of his birth, for his grandfather Christian Valentin Baur was a physician in that town and from his marriage to Maria Dorothea Wittelin came a son, Baur's father Christian Jacob Baur, born at Tübingen in 1755. Christian Jacob Baur received his early education at a private school in the town until his fourteenth year, when along with thirty other boys of the same age he entered the lower seminary at Blaubeuren. In the most congenial and charming surroundings, he spent what he himself described as 'two joyful and happy years', following which the class was transferred to the higher seminary in the former Cistercian monastery at Bebenhausen, three miles north of Tübingen. After two further years he was now ready to enter the University and in 1773 he took up residence in the Tübingen seminary (the Stift). Here he studied philosophy for two years, gaining his Master's degree in 1775; this was followed by a further three years' theological study. After graduation in 1778 he was appointed curate to the church in Holzelfingen where he remained for the next twelve years, until in 1790 an important event marked his life. In this year he married Eberhardine Gross, the daughter of the Superintendent in Urach, and following the wedding he brought his bride home to the little village of Schmiden, where he had recently been appointed vicar.[1]

In some respects the town of Schmiden has scarcely changed from the quiet little country village which it was at the end of the eighteenth century. It has, naturally, grown in size, but the old houses are still there and it does not take much imagination to picture how the village would have appeared almost two centuries ago. Lying three miles north-east of Stuttgart it is now practically a suburb of that continually expanding city. Traffic roars and rumbles in a steady stream along the main road which runs

---

[1] Personal testimony of Christian Jacob Baur (UBT, Md 750, IX).

through the centre of the town and on work-days a virtually never-ending volume of noise from the modern means of conveyance—so different from the old horse and coach—fills the air. On the side of a low hill, slightly above and overlooking the village, stands the church, a typical country church with no distinctive features. The original building dates from medieval times, although the body of the church was later rebuilt. Of the original building only the sanctuary remains, its interior walls decorated with a number of badly faded frescoes dating from a pre-Renaissance period. Nothing impressive is to be seen; no stained-glass windows greet the eye and the only attractive feature is the beautifully carved crucifix which stands on the altar table. The parsonage, a plain and modest house, is situated directly by the church and the first child of the young couple was born here on 21 June 1792—a boy, who received the names Ferdinand Christian.

Of the young Ferdinand's childhood we know practically nothing, except that he was well brought up by his parents, who demanded of him obedience, diligence, and conscientiousness. His mother was described as a capable woman, somewhat prone to depression, while his father was a man of great devotion to his work and possessed of an untiring energy—a characteristic also inherited by his son. His theological views are difficult to determine on account of the sparsity of information, but we do know that he was decidedly opposed to the philosophy of Kant and Fichte, which he regarded as atheistic and contrary to the Christian faith. Nor did he have any time for rationalism, although he knew that reason had its place in making the Christian doctrines understandable, as long as this was not at the cost of revelation. Even so, it is doubtful whether in the last analysis his view of Christianity amounted to more than an intellectual understanding of the Christian faith, combined with the conviction that Christianity offered the best and most reasonable means of moral enlightenment.

In his earliest years the young Ferdinand was absorbed in his books and had little desire to play games with the other boys in the village. It was therefore not surprising that he had no friends or comrades and it was probably a relief to him when, in 1800, the family shifted to Blaubeuren where his father had been appointed Superintendent of the district.

At the foot of the Swabian Alb, twelve miles north-west of Ulm, the rustic little town of Blaubeuren nestles snugly on a flat, plateau-like area of land at the head of the Blau valley. The village is surrounded on three sides by steep thickly wooded hillsides from which jut out jagged pinnacles of grey rock, towering above the trees. The monks who founded the monastery here at the end of the eleventh century immediately perceived the suitability of the site, for directly behind the monastery a spring of fresh, clear water gushes upwards from a subterranean source into a pool of water possessing a beautiful ultramarine-blue colour. From this colour the pool derives its name of 'Blautopf' or 'Blue-pot'. The town itself grew up slowly outside the monastery walls and some of the houses date back to the sixteenth, and even the fifteenth, century. Over valley and town a serene and tranquil atmosphere prevails and here Ferdinand Christian spent the remaining years of his childhood. His education during this time was supervised by his father who gave him a thorough grounding in Greek, Hebrew, and Latin until in 1805, at the age of thirteen, following in the footsteps of his father, he entered the doors of the monastery to begin his study in the lower seminary.

In the second half of the fifteenth century the old monastery was almost completely rebuilt in the late-Gothic style, and during the Reformation it was taken over by the Lutherans as a pre-paratory school for future pastors. The boys would spend two years in a lower seminary and a further two years in a higher seminary, each intake being known as a *Promotion*. Shortly after Baur had finished his seminary training the whole system was reorganized: the higher seminaries were abolished and each *Promotion*, consisting of thirty to forty boys, now spent the whole four years at one of the four lower seminaries in Württemberg— at Blaubeuren, Maulbronn, Schöntal, or Urach.

When Baur's *Promotion* entered the Blaubeuren seminary, the staff there consisted of three teachers—an *Ephorus*, or head of the seminary, and two senior teachers called professors. The *Ephorus*, Prelate H. D. Cless, was 'a fat, little, apathetic man who, when announcing a punishment, peered at the boys with an affected sternness from his thin-slit eyes over the rims of his spectacles'. Of the two professors, J. F. Wurm, and C. D. Heermann, we know very little. The *Ephorus* was responsible for the religious instruction and the two professors divided the academic subjects between them, Wurm being responsible for Latin, Greek, the poets, rhetoric, and mathematics while Heermann taught Hebrew, Latin, history, and philosophy. The days were always full with lectures while the rest of the time was mostly taken up with private study and homework. Physical exercise in those times played a very minor role, although when weather permitted there were often walks along the valley. Sunday was always piously observed with morning worship and periods of religious instruction, the day closing with singing and prayer.

Exams were held at the end of each semester with complicated passages of German to be translated into Latin, Greek, and Hebrew. Baur was fourth in the class. The first three pupils, according to the reports, were more talented and received higher marks in logic, history, mathematics, and German style, but in later years they never attained the same heights as did Baur. The report which Baur received on graduating from the seminary ran as follows: 'Talent: good. Diligence: persistent and punctual. Manners: sedate and modest. Religion: very good. Latin: very good. Rhetoric: very good. History: good. Mathematics: good. German style: good.' and K. L. Bauer commented: 'If at this time he did not attain the highest marks in the subjects which were later his main interest, then it is simply a sign for us that he developed slowly and steadily and did not belong to those whose talents ripened early.'[2]

Encouraged by the king of Württemberg, an experiment was attempted in 1807 when two *Promotions* were brought together in the Maulbronn seminary under the tuition of four professors. One *Promotion* was from Blaubeuren, and thus it came about that Baur spent the two following years in Maulbronn. Of this period little is known except that, according to Zeller, the teaching was of a higher standard and the professors more friendly. Two other points of interest should also be noted: first, that the Superintendent of the Church in Maulbronn was Prelate J. F. Schelling, the father of the great philosopher; thus Baur's attention would probably have been drawn to the prelate's son even before Baur began his university study. Secondly, in his second year at the seminary Baur met his friend Ludwig Friedrich Heyd and formed a friendship which remained firm until Heyd's death in 1842.

[2] Karl Bauer, 'Zur Jugendgeschichte von Ferdinand Christian Baur (1805–1807)', *TSK*, XCV (1923/4), p. 313.

Contrary to Zeller's opinion that the 'monkish life' in the seminary constricted Baur's personality, one may fairly say that the routines of scholarly study would have been just what Baur most of all desired; certainly he never uttered a single word of regret or criticism about the years he had spent behind the seminary walls. Indeed, the greatest pleasure which Baur found in life was in his study, and when we read the words of his brother-in-law, Robert von Mohl: 'Of all the men I ever met Baur was the least worldly-wise, the least experienced or even capable of judgement in the practical issues of daily living, a true child in everyday life',[3] then it becomes evident that Baur was in fact unsuited for any other life but that of a scholar.

UNIVERSITY YEARS IN TÜBINGEN

Twenty-five miles south of Stuttgart, Tübingen on the river Neckar is one of the most charming and fascinating university towns in Germany. Now a large and important university centre, in the early years of the nineteenth century the population numbered only 6,000. The town itself grew up during the Middle Ages, at the foot of the castle which was built about A.D. 1050 by the Palatine count of Tübingen and rebuilt in the sixteenth century. The other building which dominates the town is St. George's Church, commonly known as the *Stiftskirche* or Seminary Church, a late-Gothic building dating back to A.D. 1470, its choir a place of burial for the dukes of Württemberg. Along the river bank, below the old houses which back on to the river and which once formed part of the old city wall, runs a path leading to the tower where Hölderlin spent the last thirty-six years of his life. But perhaps the most enchanting corner of the whole town is the almost triangular market-place. Surrounded by the old houses with their pretty gables and colourful panelling, the sloping cobble-stone pavement is dominated on its west side by the magnificent council house, erected in 1435 and remodelled in the Renaissance style of the sixteenth century. Here on market-day the farmers' wives still gather to sell their produce.

But Tübingen is famous most of all for its University, founded by Duke Eberhard in 1477. Melanchthon had studied and taught here before travelling north to Wittenberg, and when Württemberg went over to the Reformation a few years later, the Lutheran

[3] *Lebenserinnerungen* (Stuttgart, 1902), I, p. 192.

seminary (the Stift) was established in the old Augustinian monastery. A number of students who were to make their mark in the world had passed through its doors: Kepler (1589–93), Hölderlin (1788–93), Hegel (1788–91), and Schelling (1790–5), and in 1809 Baur also entered the seminary, which was to become his home for the next five years. The first two years were devoted to a study of philosophy and he appears to have derived little profit from the lectures of A. H. Schott, 'neither a deep nor stimulating thinker', and J. F. Abel—a man of little importance. Indeed, it was generally agreed that the professors in the theological faculty had a better knowledge of philosophy than those in the philosophical faculty. Nevertheless, Baur would have had time to immerse himself in Plato, Aristotle, and the more modern philosophers—Kant, Fichte, and Schelling—who at that time were arousing great interest in Tübingen, so that the two years could not have been entirely without value.

Much more important in regard to Baur's theological development were the three years spent in the theological faculty from 1811 to 1814. During the first two decades of the nineteenth century the Old Tübingen School was at its height and although the founder of the School, Gottlob Christian Storr, had died in 1805, his work had been carried on by the brothers J. F. and K. C. Flatt, F. G. Süskind, and Ernst Gottlieb Bengel, the grandson of the famous Biblical expositor, Johann Albrecht Bengel. Storr's aim had been to substantiate the authority of the Bible through historical investigation and reasoned argument, but after his death an emphasis appeared in his successors which went far beyond his original intention. In the writings of the younger members of the School the divinity of Jesus now received a rather secondary place. The truth of Jesus' teachings was now emphasized independently of his Person, and his divinity tended to be derived from the greatness of his life, character, and teaching. Jesus was divine in that he revealed divine truths to mankind. This new emphasis reached its peak in the writings of the younger Bengel (so called to distinguish him from his grandfather), who portrayed Jesus as a great ethical teacher, 'the highest educator of humanity', the supernatural element in Jesus' life and work being discreetly pushed into the background. Not that any of the old traditional doctrines were explicitly denied; but Jesus was now regarded as divine in consequence of the divine truths which he taught; his divinity was ascribed to him rather than being inherent in his Person.

Of all Baur's teachers it was Bengel who exercised the greatest influence upon him during this period and in Baur's review of Kaiser's book on Biblical theology, which Baur wrote in 1817, we can perceive a loosening of those ties which had hitherto bound Baur to the old traditional orthodoxy in which he had been reared and educated.[4]

PROFESSOR IN BLAUBEUREN

On graduating from the University in the summer of 1814, Baur served as a curate, first in Rosswaag and then in Mühlhausen. For a short time he was tutor in the lower seminary at Schöntal before being called to teach as tutor in the Tübingen Stift from 1816 to 1817. His mother had died in 1815 and two years later came another hard blow when the death of his father left the family in sore need. Baur as the eldest of the six children now undertook the responsibility of looking after the household, and the Church authorities, being sympathetic to his situation, appointed him to one of the two professorships which had recently fallen vacant in the lower seminary at Blaubeuren.

While holidaying in Kirchheim in the summer of 1820, he made the acquaintance of Emilie Becher, daughter of the Stuttgart Court-physician Gottlob Benjamin Becher. Now a bachelor of twenty-eight with a good position and steady income, Baur saw in the eighteen-year-old Emilie a prospective counterpart to his taciturn and unpractical nature. A few seasonable words from his sister appear to have met with a favourable response and Baur wasted no time in writing to her father.

Honoured Sir,

Were it not for an inexorable compulsion in my heart, I would not have had the courage to come before you with the matter which I now dare to bring forward . . . While spending a few days of my vacation in Kirchheim recently I met your youngest daughter Emilie and the impression which she made upon me did not allow me to leave Kirchheim without confiding to my sister something of the unpreten-

---

[4] A more comprehensive account of the main influences contributing to Baur's theological development—the Old Tübingen School, Schelling, Schleiermacher, and Hegel—is contained in chapter 10.

tious desire which had been stirred up in my heart . . . If I am not to be followed throughout my whole life with the reproach, that when the time was right I let the happiness which seemed to meet me slip through my fingers, then I am left with no other choice than to turn directly to you with the request—if I may hope that my affection for your youngest daughter may meet with a corresponding inclination from her side—that the fatherly and motherly consent may be given to the object of my desire.

Short, I admit, is the time of my acquaintance with your daughter, but what is noble expresses itself unmistakably, even in a short time, in noble dispositions, and in vain must I have dedicated my life to scientific investigation if anything else should have a higher place in my eyes than the priorities of heart and soul . . .

And so may these lines—which I feel contain so much of infinite significance for my future life, infinitely more than I can or will express —reach you accompanied by my most fervent wish, that a letter which will decide the future and have bearing on eternity may be guided by a higher hand . . .[5]

The father gave his permission and the young couple were married at Stuttgart in the following spring (30 April 1821). Little is known of the marriage but it was apparently very happy, and for Baur the death of his wife in 1839 after a long period of illness was an immeasurable loss. Five children were born during these years: Emilie Caroline (1823–1904), the eldest, married Eduard Zeller in 1847; Ferdinand Friedrich (born 1825), following in the footsteps of his father, became a professor in the lower seminary at Maulbronn from 1866 to 1874; a daughter, Marie Pauline, was born in 1829 and lived until 1920; a third daughter Fanny Elise, born in 1831, lived only one month; and Albert Otto (born 1834), the most talented of all the children, died in 1868 aged only thirty-four, after having already made a name for himself through his research into zoology and anatomy.

In Blaubeuren the brunt of the teaching was borne by Baur and his colleague Friedrich Heinrich Kern (1790–1842), Baur's close companion. Baur lectured on the classical prose-writers Herodotus, Thucidides, Livy, Tacitus, and others, while Kern concentrated on the poets, Homer, Sophocles, Virgil, etc. In addition Baur lectured on ancient history and mythology, while in his spare time he translated two books of Thucidides' 'History

---

[5] To Emilie Becher's father, 21 Oct. 1820.

of the Peloponnesian War' into German; his translation, however, was too literal for the publishers and was not accepted.

During these years at Blaubeuren Baur busied himself with Schelling's philosophy, although it would appear that he was little influenced by Schelling's ideas. It was otherwise with Schleiermacher's *The Christian Faith* which Baur first read during the spring and summer of 1823. 'No theological work has yet attracted me in so many respects as this', he wrote to his brother. Even so, Schleiermacher's influence upon Baur was limited. Baur perceived that Schleiermacher's theological views were pantheistic, and while he admired the greatness of Schleiermacher's achievement in writing the first Dogmatics interpreting the Christian faith from a non-supernatural standpoint, he also saw clearly the faults and defects in Schleiermacher's system which Schleiermacher had not been able to eradicate. In Baur's first book, the three-volume 'Symbolics and Mythology' which appeared in 1824/5, the influence of Schleiermacher is easily perceptible, but Baur was never in any danger of surrendering his independence of thought.

The book itself is an investigation into the essence of religion, which Baur defined in Schleiermacherian terminology as 'the consciousness (or feeling) of dependence upon God'. Baur suggested a division of the self-consciousness into a higher and lower level, the lower level being the sensual consciousness or feeling (which may also be described as the consciousness of things around us), the higher consciousness being the religious consciousness by which one becomes aware of God as the absolute cause of all being. It is this higher consciousness which differentiates man from the animal world, while its harmonious unity with the lower consciousness (feeling) creates the pure feeling of dependence upon God. This religious consciousness manifests itself in the various religions through symbols and myths, which are the vehicles by which this mediation takes place. Baur viewed the essence of every religion as lying in the higher religious consciousness, in the consciousness of the higher supra-sensual sphere, in the feeling of absolute dependence upon a power existing outside of natural and sensual perception. This feeling of dependence has its seat in the religious consciousness and finds its expression in the various myths and legends of the many national cultures. Revelation is not to be thought of as supernatural communication from an other-worldly source, but is manifested in history as a general revelation of God, a divine process of education for mankind.

Baur's academic talent, which was evidenced in the writing of the book, did not pass unnoticed, but for the orthodox the book possessed a very suspicious pantheistic ring which caused considerable concern in the higher ecclesiastical circles. One incident which Baur related in a letter to his friend Heyd, reveals that even in the mid-1820s there was a widespread distrust of Baur's views on Christian doctrine.

> By the way, I must also tell you that during the vacation Süskind began an argument with me, which lasted two hours, over my philosophical views. He called me a pantheistic idealist and declared that with such views all the foundations of religion and morality would be overturned. To be sure, he said this sparingly and mildly and without taking the matter to its logical conclusion, but he did say it, although it doesn't worry me at all. It is simply a proof of his obdurate dogmatic nature![6]

THE CALLING TO TÜBINGEN

The younger Bengel died on 23 March 1826 and the necessity arose of appointing a new professor who would be able to bring some fresh life to the somewhat pedantic faculty. It was hoped that the famous Church historian Neander might be induced to leave Berlin and come south, but he was apparently not interested and attention therefore turned to those in Württemberg itself. On account of his dogmatic studies Baur appears to have been the first choice, although Süskind and Steudel opposed him on account of his known pantheistic leanings. The Ministry of Education requested a reference concerning Baur from the theological faculty; this described him as a learned 'investigator, possessing original views, an excellent philosophical spirit, and a perceptive gift of analysing and organizing copious amounts of historical material', but also added: 'even though he may estimate the worth of Christianity very highly, the faculty can give no assurance that the ideas which he expresses could be everywhere brought into agreement with the pure view of Christianity as a

---

[6] To Heyd, undated but probably autumn 1825.

revelation of God to man, prepared through special divine intervention in history.'[7]

The students took Baur's part and a petition signed by 124 theological students, including the whole Blaubeuren *Promotion*, was presented, calling for Baur's appointment. However a confidential report from Süskind and Schmid counselled that a scholar 'who has adopted the new ideas of a mystic-pantheistic rationalism' should not be appointed.

This theological view which in consequence of Schelling's nature-philosophy is at the present time propagated especially by the writings of the Berlin theologian Schleiermacher and finds its greatest acceptance among the youth particularly, sounds extremely pious and mystic according to its words. On the one hand it also contains a true mysticism, but on the other hand it not only binds itself to rationalism, in that it permits no faith in the authority of Christ's divine instruction, but is itself in a logical way destructive to genuine practical religion, indeed, to even the foundations of morality; for it identifies God and the world, accepts no God who is separated from the world, but allows all things to exist in God, in the divine substance itself.[8]

The appointment hung in the balance during the summer recess and Baur expressed the current state of affairs in a letter to Heyd.

The Tübingen affair against all expectation is still dragging on. . . . The external factors as far as I hear—for I know nothing yet from an authoritative source whether the discussion concerns me alone—are favourable for me. The faculty proposed Osiander and me; in Stuttgart, too, they seem to be kindly disposed towards me. The only one not in favour is Süskind who is supposed to have used his influence on behalf of my colleague Kern, although he has not actually been proposed. The incident with the students was in many respects disagreeable to me and had I had even an inkling of it I would have taken trouble to stop it. Steudel let me know his mind about it, which makes it all the more inconceivable how the faculty could have proposed me. At any rate, from what I hear, the relations in Tübingen and especially in the theological faculty must be such that in this respect also I probably cannot look forward to very much which promises to be pleasurable. And yet can I reject the appointment if it is offered me? Shall I renounce a situation that still assures me of a better future than my present position—which in many respects is so monotonous—on account of difficulties and relations which, on the other hand, I hope to be able to

---

[7] E. Schneider, *Ferdinand Christian Baur in seiner Bedeutung für die Theologie* (Munich, 1909), pp. 9–10.   [8] Ibid., p. 10.

overcome? I'm sorry that I started on this matter straight away, but I really need to be able to say these things to you, as I have so little opportunity to talk about them. Even Kern has recently avoided all mention of the matter and yet I have done not the slightest to forward it in any way at all, and will do nothing.[9]

The Ministry of Education decided that the faculty needed some young blood and both Baur and Kern were appointed full professors along with Christian Friedrich Schmid who was promoted from the position of assistant professor. Steudel now became the head of the faculty. Baur's fears concerning relations within the faculty were not realized, as we see from a letter to Heyd in September of the same year. 'In Tübingen we were well received; only Steudel expressed his mind to me in a letter, saying he hopes that in the hitherto so-united faculty two kinds of God and two kinds of Christ will not be taught, and that there will be also a foundation upon which he will be able to build with me.'[10]

Coupled with Baur's appointment to the professorial chair was the obligation to preach ten times a year in the *Stiftskirche*. This office of morning preacher, which Baur shared with other members of the theological faculty, was discharged by Baur until 1848, when the office was separated from the professorial chair and Baur was thus relieved of his responsibility.

Steudel, Kern, Baur, and Schmid were the four full professors comprising the theological faculty until Steudel's death in 1837. The various subjects were divided among them in the following way: Old Testament exegesis was taught by Steudel with additional tuition from Julius Mohl, professor of Oriental literature in the philosophical faculty; New Testament exegesis was Baur's department; dogmatics and apologetics were covered by Steudel and Kern; Christian ethics by Kern and Baur; Church history and the history of dogma by Baur; and homiletics, the Catechism, and Christian education by Schmid.

Relations among the four professors seem to have been amicable enough and Schmid had not yet set himself in opposition

[9] To Heyd, 19 Aug. 1826. University appointments were made by the Ministry of Education in consultation with the faculty concerned. But as the Minister was appointed by the Crown the Crown always had the final say. Theological appointments were always the most difficult in that theological viewpoints were always of primary significance. Thus the tact and ingenuity of the Minister were often tested to the full in trying to please or appease the faculties, the Church authorities, and the ruling powers.

[10] To Heyd, 19 Sept. 1826.

to the newer Biblical criticism, as he did after the appearance of Strauss's *Life of Jesus* in 1835. Only one argument appears to have disrupted the good relationships within the faculty; this was Baur's disagreement with Steudel in 1831 concerning an article which Baur had written for the *Tübinger Zeitschrift für Theologie*, the theological journal which Steudel, in co-operation with the other members of the faculty, had founded in 1828. But we shall allow Baur himself to relate exactly what took place.

During the summer I handed over to Steudel, at his own request, an article for the journal, an investigation into the original significance of the Passover and the rite of circumcision,[11] whereby here and there I had to express a few doubts about the literal reality of a few of the narratives in Genesis and Exodus. On the following day I received a letter saying that my article could not be accepted for the journal because it ran too much against the basic principle of the journal, that Holy Scripture contains a divine revelation. In the case of its being accepted, Steudel as editor would hold himself obliged *as a matter of conscience* to append a refutation of a large part of my assertions. Along with this there naturally flowed all kinds of other misunderstandings in Steudel's whole conception of my views. I simply could not take this sitting down and believed myself compelled to tell him exactly what I thought. I thereupon wrote Steudel an answer, the like of which he has probably rarely received, and told him that he would certainly be deceiving himself if he thought that I would set myself under his authority and allow myself to be inspected by him at every step. I had to exchange three letters with him on the matter and had full opportunity to express openly to him everything that I had on my heart. The result was that we became completely reconciled with one another and also since that time have stood in the best relation with one another. However, I remained by my declaration which I gave him at the beginning—that I would have nothing more to do with a journal of such a spirit.[12]

THE CLASH WITH MÖHLER

With a relaxation of tension between Protestants and Catholics in early nineteenth-century Württemberg, the Catholic University which had been founded at Ellwangen in 1812 was transferred to Tübingen as the Catholic faculty of theology. The leading spirit

[11] The article appeared in the following year, *TZT*, 1832: I, pp. 40–124.
[12] To Heyd, 1 Oct. 1831. Not 1832. Baur's original letter bears the date 1831; Zeller, however, in copying the letter misread the last numeral. This date is also to be corrected in Hodgson, *Formation of Historical Theology*, p. 12, n. 45.

in the new faculty was Johann Sebastian Drey (1777–1853). Drey, who had been greatly influenced by the romantic movement, above all by the writings of Schlegel and Schelling, was widely suspected of being tainted with the heretical views of the rationalists. Similar criticism was mounted against his two colleagues Johann Baptist Hirscher (1788–1865) and J. G. Herbst (1787–1836).[13] In the first ten years of the new faculty a freer and more critical spirit was certainly blowing, a spirit very much in tune with the romanticism of the times and one not prepared to submit meekly to the papacy. To what extent Drey and his colleagues had dispensed with the traditional and central doctrines of the Church over against a merely outward observance, is difficult to determine,[14] but certainly the Tübingen Catholic professors aroused the animosity of the conservative elements in the Church and were distinctly out of favour at Rome.[15]

In 1823 the Catholic faculty gained a new lecturer with the appointment of the twenty-seven-year-old Johann Adam Möhler (1796–1838).[16] Möhler also had fallen under the influence of the romantic movement and had been especially attracted by the theology of Schleiermacher. Realizing that Protestant and Catholic Churches had much in common he sought to bridge the gap between them with his book on the unity of the Church (1825), a treatise which evoked much interest among Protestants and Catholics alike. At this period, however, Möhler's views were obviously far too Schleiermacherian to have any hope of winning Catholic approval, and as opposition from the Catholic conservatives stiffened, Möhler slowly retreated from his former liberal views. In 1832 he published his work on the basic differences separating the two Confessions. Baur was both intrigued and displeased. 'I have not got round to any real literary work this winter as I have been continually busy with the revision of my

[13] Other members of the School—the so-called second generation—who taught later were Franz Anton Staudenmaier (1800–56) and the Hegelian-influenced Johannes Kuhn (1806–87).
[14] Catholic theologians are divided in their estimates of the School. The two opposite viewpoints are summed up in the works of H. J. Brosch, *Das Übernatürliche in der Katholischen Tübinger Schule* (Essen, 1962), and J. R. Geiselmann, *Die Katholische Tübinger Schule* (Freiburg, 1964).
[15] Drey was denounced to the Pope and Hirscher's book on the Mass was placed on the Index.
[16] On Möhler, see H. Fels, *Johann Adam Möhler, Der Weg seines geistigen Werdens* (Limberg, 1939).

lectures on the history of dogma. Also the reading of Möhler's "Symbolics" engages my time as this winter I am lecturing on symbolics. Perhaps I shall yet write something against this learned but malevolent opponent of Protestantism.'[17]

Baur's answer which appeared in the autumn of 1833[18] was a careful investigation of the essential principles upon which both Churches were founded, and in particular the doctrines of original sin, justification by faith, the sacraments, the Church, and finally, the difference between the two Churches in general. It can be fairly said that the work was a firm but polite rebuttal of Möhler's theological arguments. Möhler, however, took it as a personal rebuff and in his reply he made a bitter attack on Baur who returned the compliment in a second and smaller monograph.

From my former frequent reading of Herr Möhler's writings I have, to be sure, not been able to gain a very high opinion of my opponent's dialectical perception and speculative talent. But I could scarcely have expected such an empty, superficial, and exceedingly trivial treatment of such an important speculative question as the one which lies before us, nor such incapacity to emphasize and penetrate into its essential moments and to think oneself into the whole standpoint which the disputed view demands.[19]

The clash of views caused great bitterness between the two combatants and from that time forth they had nothing more to do with each other. It was thus a great relief to Baur when in 1835 Möhler accepted a call to Munich. The farewell gathering marking his departure from the University was attended by professors from the various faculties. Baur deliberately stayed away.

BAUR AND THE HEGELIAN PHILOSOPHY

In the face of the enthusiasm shown by his former Blaubeuren students, Strauss, Märklin, and Vischer, for the new Hegelian philosophy, it was inevitable that Baur's attention should be directed to the fresh speculative breeze blowing from Berlin. Along with Wilhelm Hoffmann, Strauss and his friends used to meet twice a week during their last two years in the Stift (1829–30) to study Hegel's writings. Whether or not Baur at this time remained simply an interested onlooker or whether he actually

[17] To Heyd, 1 Feb. 1833.
[18] 'Der Gegensatz des Katholicismus und Protestantismus ...', TZT, 1833: III, IV, pp. 1–438. Published as a book in 1834 and reprinted in 1836.
[19] *Erwiderung auf Herrn Dr. Möhlers neueste Polemik* ... (Tübingen, 1834), p. 107.

concerned himself with the new fascination of his pupils is not known, but probably he did not take the speculative ideas too seriously, and perhaps regarded them as something of a novelty which in time would slowly fade away. Strauss had spent the winter of 1831/2 in Berlin where he had met Hegel just a few days before Hegel's death from cholera. Somewhat dispirited by this new turn of events Strauss thought of leaving Berlin, but decided to stay on and hear the other Hegelian lecturers, Michelet, Ganz, and Henning. On returning to Tübingen Strauss lectured on the speculative philosophy to packed auditoriums, and the great success of his lectures must have convinced Baur that the new novelty was not to be taken lightly. We know that by 1833 Baur had espoused the speculative ideas as his own viewpoint for in this year, in his long refutation of Möhler's book, Baur explicitly confessed himself a Hegelian: 'It is in general the Hegelian method which the author of this article employs in order to provide a solution to the task he has set himself.'[20] In the work itself, however, there is little to indicate a convinced adoption of the Hegelian viewpoint and it would appear that not until the winter of 1834/5, in the process of writing his book on Gnosticism, did Baur really make an intensive study of the speculative philosophy. He refers to Hegel in a letter to his brother dated 15 February 1835, where he comments that he hopes to have his new book on Gnosticism completed by Easter.

The title is: 'Christian Gnosticism, or the Christian Philosophy of Religion in its Historical Development'. The last section deals with the newer philosophy of religion—J. Böhme, Schelling, Schleiermacher, Hegel. Hegel's 'Philosophy of Religion' has especially engaged me this winter and in many ways attracted me. I shall probably also give offence[21] since I cannot find the atrocities in it which are usually supposed to burden it.[22]

---

[20] *TZT*, 1833: IV, p. 421.
[21] Baur means that the orthodox will be offended with his favourable treatment of the speculative philosophy. Hodgson's translation of the final sentence: 'Thus I am likely to come up against the fact that I am not able to find in it the atrocities commonly attributed to it' (op. cit., p. 23) is incorrect, because he followed the false transcription of Lang. Hodgson's explanation that the handwriting is unclear is inadmissible; the words are in fact quite plain and run: 'Ich stosse wahrscheinlich dadurch auch an, da ich die Atrocitäten, die man ihr gewöhnlich aufbürdet, nicht in ihr finden kann.' It would appear that Lang deliberately altered the original wording because he could not understand its meaning.
[22] To F. A. Baur, 15 Feb. 1835.

From this time on, Baur set himself under the banner of Hegel, and there were few whose understanding of the Master surpassed his own.

STRAUSS'S LIFE OF JESUS

In 1835 Strauss's epoch-making *Life of Jesus* shook the theological world of his day. Years afterwards Baur, who had actually discussed the content of the book with Strauss during its composition, portrayed the sensation which the work had produced on its appearance.

One must oneself have lived through the period in which Strauss's book appeared in order to have any conception of the reaction which it caused. Seldom has a work of literature produced such a great sensation so quickly and so universally, and summoned the forces of war with great excitement to a battleground on which the most varied parties opposed each other and raised the ardour of the conflict to the most intense passion. The Straussian *Life of Jesus* was the glowing spark by which the already long-collected tinder burst into blazing flame.[23]

For the first few months after its publication, during which time Strauss was dismissed from his position in the Stift, Baur said and did nothing. He wanted to be a 'passive spectator' and was content to wait and see what would happen. The earliest expression of his opinion which we possess is found in a letter to his brother in December 1835.

You will doubtless soon be ready to read the second volume of Strauss's book, which you can likewise have from me. I find it—as far as I have been able to read up till now—just as interesting as the first volume; the whole work has been executed with great logicality. Recently Heyd wrote me his opinion of the first volume; it was more favourable than I would have believed: these critical views, he remarked, are unmistakably true. I hear little more about the matter here as Steudel has taken up such an attitude to Strauss that it would be against discretion to speak of Strauss's work in Steudel's presence. Also with regard to my Pastoral Epistles, I have not heard from any side a verdict which I find particularly interesting. What's your opinion of the book?[24]

[23] *Geschichte der christlichen Kirche*, V, p. 363.   [24] To F. A. Baur, 4 Dec. 1835.

In Tübingen at that time there was a Protestant fraternity consisting of the professors in the theological faculty, clergymen, and some laymen. In December, just subsequent to the appearance of the second volume of the *Life of Jesus*, Steudel proposed a discussion on the question: 'What attitude the Protestant Christian should take to the present danger confronting the Christian faith, caused by new publications in the realm of theological science, especially in so far as a knowledge of these publications, which is increasing among the people, threatens to destroy their faith.' It would appear that this was a manœuvre intended to force Baur to take a personal stand in the matter, for as yet he had said nothing openly. Baur accepted the responsibility of writing a paper on the subject[25] and performed his task in such a masterly way, avoiding all the crucial questions, that he provided no opportunity for any accusation to be made against him on the grounds that he held the same views as Strauss. As a matter of fact, in the whole ten and a half pages of closely written Baurian minuscule, Strauss is scarcely mentioned, and certainly not defended. That Baur was sympathetic to Strauss's plight is not in question, but it cannot be said that Baur openly and actively supported the views in which he had formerly acquiesced. It is only fair to add that from Baur's standpoint the price of defending Strauss would have been too high, for Strauss's fate was sealed from the moment his book appeared in print and nothing that Baur might have said or done could have helped him. By December his dismissal from the Stift was already a *fait accompli*, and Baur would have gained nothing and lost everything had he aligned himself with Strauss.

One further important point should be noted here. Years afterwards, when the publication of Strauss's *Life of Jesus* had faded into the background, Baur attempted to diminish the influence which Strauss's book had had on his own historical investigations. He had struck out on his own particular path, he maintained, before the publication of the *Life of Jesus*, and was in no way dependent upon Strauss for his views. Zeller could not completely agree with this judgement and in his 'Reminiscences', written in 1904, he gave an enlightening account of a visit to Baur during the winter preceding the appearance of Strauss's book, which

[25] UBT, Md 750, V, 7.

revealed just how short a distance Baur had travelled in his historical investigations up until that time.

In visits to the serious-minded man who was always deeply immersed in his investigations, it was often somewhat difficult for us to enter freely into conversation with him if we did not ask him about some theological topic. We therefore eagerly looked around for conversation material before we went to him. One day (it would have been in the winter of 1834/5) I pressed my friend Bockshammer into accompanying me to Baur; I had something for him. As we came to the professor I explained that the representation of the so-called apostolic council in the fifteenth chapter of Acts seemed to me incompatible with that of Paul in Galatians; what was *his* view of the matter? After he had looked over both passages for a moment Baur answered me that this observation had up until the present escaped his notice; but he held it for well grounded and immediately confirmed it through a discussion of how the alteration of the historical situation here would connect with the whole tendency of Acts. I found this approach extremely instructive and it showed me clearly what difference there is between an isolated— even if true—observation and a comprehensive historical perspective. But I found it even more remarkable that Baur had not noticed the incompatibility of the two narratives long previously. At that time his criticism of the New Testament was just in its beginnings and only years later did it dare to take bolder strides, after the appearance of Strauss's *Life of Jesus* and the completion of Baur's own great works on the history of dogma.[26]

THE CALLING OF BAUR TO BERLIN AND HALLE

1. The Calling to Berlin

The death of Schleiermacher on 12 February 1834 was an inestimable loss for the Berlin theological faculty and the question of his successor was therefore of the highest importance. The appointment was rendered more difficult in that not only was Schleiermacher famous as a University professor, but he was also renowned as First Preacher at the Trinity Church in Berlin, the preaching office at that time being coupled with his theological professorship.

The negotiations involved in the appointment lay in the hands of Johannes Schulze, a Hegelian in his views and the right-hand man of Altenstein, the Minister of Education. Some

[26] Zeller, *Erinnerungen eines Neunzigjährigen* (Stuttgart, 1904), pp. 93–4.

thirteen years previously Schulze had made a journey through the Danish province of Holstein and in Kiel he had been impressed by the revivalist preacher Claus Harms. On the same visit he had also met the young theologian August Twesten, at that time professor of theology in Kiel, and had expressed the hope that this 'extremely fine teacher' should one day be won for a Prussian university. By 1834, however, Schulze was attempting as far as possible to pursue a liberal path, and was fully in favour of calling Baur to the vacant chair.

The Berlin theological faculty was divided on the appointment. Hengstenberg, Marheineke, and G. F. Strauss proposed Hermann Olshausen from Königsberg, while Neander was solidly in support of Twesten. In this situation Schulze perceived the chance of securing the position for Baur, and put forward a compromise plan: Baur was to be appointed to the professorial chair, while to appease the stiff opposition from the conservatives, Harms was to be called to the Trinity Church as First Preacher. Altenstein was also in agreement with this proposal, but Harms could not decide to leave Kiel and the plan fell through. Since Twesten was more acceptable to Schulze than Olshausen, Schulze made every effort to persuade him to come to Berlin. Encouraged also by Neander, Twesten finally agreed and on 29 August 1834 was appointed professor of dogmatics and New Testament exegesis.

2. *The Calling to Halle*

In consequence of the work of August Hermann Franke, Halle on the river Saale by the end of the seventeenth century had become a centre of pietism, but as the eighteenth century progressed the ideas of the Enlightenment began to find a ready acceptance. By the beginning of the nineteenth century the town had become a centre of rationalism in Germany so that the two viewpoints could be summed up in the old saying: 'Whoever goes to Halle returns either as atheist or pietist.'

In 1809 the rationalist Julius Wegscheider had been appointed professor of dogmatics at the University and one year later he received a like-minded colleague in the person of the famous Hebraist, Wilhelm Gesenius, who succeeded to the Old Testament chair. In 1825 Carl Thilo, a friend of Gesenius, became professor of Church history and the following year there was quite a stir in the faculty over the proposal to call the genial pietist August Tholuck[27] from Berlin, where he was then a lecturer. Gesenius and Wegscheider were resolutely opposed to his coming. The Ministry of Education, however, decided that something had to be done to counteract the rationalism in the Halle faculty, which at that time had reached alarming proportions, and after some doubts it finally approved the appointment. Tholuck's geniality and learning made such an impression upon the students that from this time forth the prevailing rationalism began to decline and in little over a decade its power had been broken. Nevertheless, this was not achieved without a long and unpleasant struggle against Wegscheider and Gesenius. From 1829 Tholuck had been heartened by the support of his generous-minded friend Karl Ullmann, although the entrance of C. F. Fritzsche into the faculty one year later brought him his most bitter enemy.

In 1836 Ullmann resigned his chair in order to return to his native Heidelberg and the way was now open for Baur to be called to Halle, at that time the largest theological faculty in Germany. The faculty consisted of six full professors. Wegscheider, Gesenius and Fritzsche were resolute that Baur should be called; Thilo sat on the fence, and Tholuck realized that were Baur appointed, he himself would be isolated in the faculty and have little say in the faculty deliberations. 'I would be in the most difficult position conceivable,' he wrote to Hengstenberg, 'and if in addition to my other opponents Baur too should come, then I couldn't go on.'[28] Thus from Tholuck's point of view it was essential that he should obtain a sympathetic colleague who would support him against the combined opposition of Wegscheider, Gesenius and Fritzsche. For this reason he set out to oppose Baur's calling with all the influence which he could muster in Berlin.

[27] Friedrich August Gottlob Tholuck (1799–1877) came from a very poor family and possessed an extraordinary gift for languages, having studied nineteen before reaching the age of seventeen. He was converted from pantheism and scepticism through pietist influences and became lecturer in the Berlin theological faculty in 1821. He was, without doubt, the leading pietist theologian of the nineteenth century. His successor and most famous pupil, was Martin Kähler. On Tholuck's life see Leopold Witte, *Das Leben F. A. G. Tholucks* (2 vols.: Bielefeld and Leipzig, 1884/6).

[28] Witte, *Das Leben Tholucks*, II, p. 380.

In the May issue of the *Evangelische Kirchenzeitung* for 1836
appeared an article on Strauss and Baur which contained a short
but provocative attack on Baur and his investigation into the
authorship and origin of the Pastoral Epistles. Whether or not this
article was actually motivated by the intention of hindering Baur's
calling to Halle, is unclear, but at any rate, for Baur, it could not
have come at a worse time. The article was all the more harmful
in that it linked Baur with his notorious pupil, Strauss.

As regards Professor Baur, he has already become known as an
exceptionally talented and thorough investigator, but also a very
sceptical one. A new book from him has just appeared: 'The so-called
Pastoral Epistles of the Apostle Paul: A New Critical Investigation'
(Stuttgart, 1835), in which a sceptical capriciousness appears which can
in fact only be compared with that of Strauss. There runs through the
whole work a bitter and irritable spirit against all who oppose the
sceptical criticism in a hostile manner, a spirit which one can hardly
explain except as proceeding from an intimate acquaintance with the
theology of his friend Dr. Strauss.[29]

Baur was in a difficult position and unsure whether or not he
should reply. If he allowed the article to remain unchallenged it
might be taken as a silent admission of guilt; on the other hand a
reply might stir up the hornets' nest even more. Baur thought the
matter over and decided that attack was the best policy, for, as he
wrote to his brother, a better opportunity might not occur again.

Just as I had finished an article on the Epistle to the Romans—which
I had been writing concurrently with the revision of the first edition
of my book on Möhler—for the third issue of the *Zeitschrift*, which is
at present being printed, I received the May issue of the *Evangelische
Kirchenzeitung* with the despicable attack which has been made against
me. As I had previously learnt that the powers in Berlin would gladly
offer me Ullmann's vacant professorial chair in Halle if the party of
the *Evangelische Kirchenzeitung* had not prejudiced the Minister against
me afresh, I immediately perceived this new intrigue and was therefore
all the more resolved to answer this article. I am well aware into what
kind of nest I am thrusting my hand and have therefore considered the
matter thoroughly, but am also convinced that sooner or later I will
still have to break openly with this party, and perhaps later I may not
have such a favourable opportunity to oppose its scurrility as just at

29 *EKZ*, 1836, pp. 290–1.

present. You will see from the article itself how the matter stands. My article was written certainly somewhat quickly as I devoted only eight days to it. I didn't want to concern myself longer with such a matter, but I think that what is most necessary has been said. How it will be accepted near and far is certainly another question.

You can well imagine how vexing for me such matters are, and how loathsome it is to have to skirmish with such a rabble. From day to day the outlook becomes more hopeless in matters of intellect and in life. . . .[30]

Baur began his article, his 'Compelled Explanation', by taking exception to the accusation that he was in some way dependent upon Strauss for his views. He had completed the greater part of his investigations, he claimed, in the autumn of 1834, before the *Life of Jesus* had ever appeared, and had been engaged in his scientific study of the New Testament long previously. With regard to the dating of the various books of the New Testament Baur had nothing more of importance to add to or subtract from what he had already said on the matter and he repudiated indignantly the charge that he had also thrown overboard the Gospel of John. 'What ground does the author of the article have for this assertion? In my book I said nothing about the Gospel of John except what I have just remarked on. Does it follow that simply because I cannot hold the Pastoral Epistles as genuine letters of the apostle Paul, that I must have already thrown overboard the historical authority of the Gospel of John?'[31]

Perhaps the central point in the whole article was Baur's attempt to distance himself from Strauss. 'Is the whole objective basis of Christianity', he asked, 'called into question through my investigation, in the same way as it was through Strauss's?' 'Where in my book—in just one passage—is my criticism based on the mythical view?' And yet Baur could not deny the 'spiteful accusation' that he was friendly with Strauss.

Thus I in no wise deny that I stand in a friendly relationship to Dr. Strauss; at the same time I would also aver that in the long number of years in which I have come to know him more intimately I have been unable to discover in him—just as little as others who have learnt to know him—the demonic nature which the editor of the *Evangelische Kirchenzeitung* with the Argus-eyes of his Christian love wants to see in

---

[30] To F. A. Baur, 29 July 1836.
[31] 'Abgenöthigte Erklärung', *TZT*, 1836: III, p. 201.

him. But what at all is supposed to follow from such a relationship? That I am responsible for principles and assertions which I have not made, for books which I have not written?[32]

Baur's reply was well composed, but no one was really satisfied. Tholuck took the opportunity to write to Baur, expressing his regret that Baur had not repudiated the views of his pupil, and declaring that he felt obliged to oppose Baur's calling to Halle.

I must inform you that my concern about your views regarding the historicity of the New Testament events—which appear to me to agree essentially with the views of Strauss—is very much upon my heart, and I feel compelled to tell you that in the deliberations regarding your calling to the vacant professorial chair here in Halle, just this very concern has forced me actively to oppose your appointment.[33]

In his answer Baur expressed his respect for Tholuck's frankness but regretted that Tholuck's attitude was based on misinformed and erroneous views. Reports from students who had listened to Baur's lectures on the book of Acts and had declared that he had not acknowledged the miracles recorded in the book, could in no wise, Baur asserted, be taken to imply that he rejected the whole miraculous history of Christianity. Nor could the new criticism be called negative and destructive, as Tholuck had described it, instead of constructive. Baur emphatically rejected such a distinction:

How can it escape your notice how one-sided, how subjective, how self-complacent it is to separate all theologians into constructive and destructive categories? . . . Not merely is construction for one what demolition is for another, and vice versa, but objectively considered, what on first, and according to outward, appearance is demolition can also really and truly be construction. If one cannot build without first demolishing and clearing away all the rubble from the ground on which alone one can build, then those who demolish and cart away the rubble also belong to the builders.[34]

---

[32] Ibid., p. 221. I have dealt with the relation between Strauss and Baur extensively in my book *David Friedrich Strauss and his Theology* (Cambridge, 1973).

[33] Tholuck to Baur, 1 Sept. 1836. The letter is printed in Witte, op. cit., II, pp. 380–3.

[34] Baur to Tholuck, undated but probably early in September 1836. The letter is now extant only in Baur's draft (UBT, Md 750, II, 9, 1). Extracts were printed by W. Lang in his article 'Strauss und Baur', *PJ*, CLX (1915), pp. 494–7. The whole letter is printed in my article, 'Die Verhandlungen über die Berufung Ferdinand Christian Baurs nach Berlin und Halle', in *ZKG*, LXXXIV (1973), pp. 233–48.

Tholuck's main criticism of Baur was that he had not repudiated the views of his pupil. If a theologian should arrive at the same conclusions as Strauss, however much in good conscience, he could not be permitted authority or position in the Church; to which Baur replied:

How do you know, let me ask, that such a man is absolutely in error? How do you know that in Strauss's conclusions—if one is led to such conclusions through conscientious investigations—that there is absolutely nothing true or enduring? How do you know with such certainty that the judgement passed on my investigation of the Pastoral Epistles by those two Berlin theologians—in which they also are obviously thinking about Strauss's conclusions—will also be the judgement of posterity? You can only know all this if you have already shut yourself up in your knowledge and believe yourself entitled to ascribe to yourself an absolute consciousness of truth and error. Whoever has so shut himself up, for him truth and error are something long ago decided, long settled, and fixed; there is no need for further investigation into truth and error; one knows already in advance what truth and error are. And yet even you still dare to say: 'Truly, it is not the yardstick of a rigid dogmatic view that I want to see laid on a theological lecturer. I can truly say: on the contrary, I *hate* such a yardstick.' How you conceive such a yardstick of a rigid dogmatic view which alone saves us, is shown by your absolute hate against everything that you love to call the Straussian conclusions. Thus I see the whole content of your letter vanish before my eyes in the vain semblance of the contradiction. But no one ever built up the Church with semblance and contradiction.

Should it ever be that I am called to Halle, should I ever become your colleague—what I peacefully and contentedly commit to the Guide of my life—then you will see from this letter with what principles and convictions I would come; but I would also then come in order to bring you the true picture of my character, my very own self, instead of the false picture which you hold up before me and repulse with all your might. Between the one and the other I will let you choose . . .[35]

By 1836, however, Baur's chances of being called to Halle were greatly diminished by the fact that he now appeared in the bad light cast by his notorious pupil. The whole orthodox party was solidly against him; an academic reference requested from Neander and Twesten was decidedly negative in tone, and even the Crown

[35] Ibid., p. 247.

Prince wrote to Altenstein that he found it impossible to believe that Altenstein intended to call Baur to Halle, 'or you cannot know that Baur has recently adopted the views of Dr. Strauss.'

Against this weight of opposition Altenstein finally had to give way and in 1837 Tholuck's friend Julius Müller was called from Marburg. With his appointment Baur's chances of obtaining a position in a Prussian university faded into the background. From that time on he was apparently never again seriously considered for a theological chair at any other university.

BAUR AND ULLMANN

One of the leading and most influential figures in the Church during the middle years of the nineteenth century was Karl Ullmann. Four years younger than Baur, Ullmann stemmed from the vicinity of Heidelberg, from Epfenbach, where he was born in 1796. His schooling was completed in Heidelberg and there also he attended university. In 1816 he went to Tübingen for his final year of theological study and would almost certainly have met Baur who was then a tutor in the Stift. On his return to Heidelberg Ullmann began lecturing in the theological faculty and on account of his outstanding ability was appointed assistant professor in 1821 and full professor in 1826, the same year in which Baur was called from Blaubeuren to Tübingen. It is probable that they met once again shortly before Ullmann took up his new appointment at Halle in 1829, since we possess a letter dating from 1832 in which Baur addresses Ullmann as 'most respected friend' and expresses the hope he will soon see him once more. Correspondence between them reopened in 1836 when Baur wrote to Ullmann, now co-editor of one of the most important theological journals in Germany, the *Theologische Studien und Kritiken*, asking for information concerning academic personnel and at the same time taking the opportunity to request that his two most recent books 'Christian Gnosticism' and 'The Pastoral Epistles' be reviewed in Ullmann's journal.

In August 1836 Ullmann communicated to Baur the news that he was under consideration for the vacant chair at Halle, a fact which Baur already knew. But by now the article linking Baur with Strauss had appeared in the *Evangelische Kirchenzeitung* and Baur had been forced to reply. 'I must now certainly expect that new offence will be taken at my polemic. But judge for yourself, how could I have answered such an article differently if I should have answered at all?'[36] Baur also expressed dissatisfaction with his salary, which was scarcely adequate for him to live comfortably, and with an inhuman Ministry of Education which was constantly in opposition to him. In September he received the letter from Tholuck and complained to Ullmann about its tone and content.

The whole letter provided me with the clearest proof that in the fundamentals there is no great difference between Tholuck and Hengstenberg. I therefore answered him in a resolute tone, so that he will scarcely have derived any particular joy from my letter. For over against this party, which in no way has its significance in its intellectual capability, I hold resolution and frankness to be the first thing needful for our present-day theology.[37]

Baur's request for his 'Christian Gnosticism' to be reviewed was not forgotten, but instead of the awaited, friendly commendation there appeared a strongly critical article by C. H. Weisse, professor of philosophy at Leipzig. Baur was distinctly annoyed and wrote to Ullmann about it.

In the latest issue of your *Theologische Studien und Kritiken* appears a review of my book on Christian Gnosticism, which in many respects displeased me. As soon as I saw Herr Weisse's name next to the title of my book I knew what I had to expect. It is doubtless the same review which Herr Weisse—as a letter from Berlin informed me—had sent previously to the 'Journal of Scientific Criticism' and which he received back again on account of its superficiality and its injustice to me. Even a cursory inspection of it—as it even now lies printed before us—can tell that it deserves this verdict. Herr Weisse has once again become involved in a subject about which he understands nothing.[38]

Baur decided to compose a reply and intimated this intention to Ullmann, with the thinly veiled threat that if Ullmann refused to publish the article, it would be published elsewhere.

During this eventful year (1836) it must have become more and more clear to Ullmann that Baur had set himself against the traditional orthodox theology. His books on Gnosticism and the Pastoral Epistles revealed only too clearly the way he had chosen to tread, and relations between himself and Ullmann slowly began to cool. In 1838 Baur wrote a fairly pungent criticism of Richard

[36] Baur to Ullmann, 7 Aug. 1836.   [37] Baur to Ullmann, 21 Oct. 1836.
[38] Baur to Ullmann, 15 Dec. 1836.

Rothe's book on the origin of the early Church—'In my opinion Rothe's conclusions are completely erroneous.'[39] Ullmann, who had now returned to Heidelberg where his friend Rothe was also a professor, was offended by the article and told Baur so. Baur in reply sought to defend his views.

I received the book borrowed from the University library here, along with your letter, from which I see with regret that you have taken offence at my article against Herr Dr. Rothe and are of the opinion that the zeal to polemicize has led me too far in many places. As I said, I am sorry about this and, apart from what I have already remarked in the article itself, I can only justify myself by saying that it does not seem to be given me to smooth down my words as often as is necessary. But I can also say that with regard to an opponent, towards whom I stand completely free from personal considerations—as is also the case with Herr Dr. Rothe—I am always motivated solely by the subject under discussion, by the matter itself. Perhaps also in my latest article you disapprove of my repeated polemic against the *Evangelische Kirchenzeitung*; I, however, regard it as good and necessary when such scurrility as the conduct of the *Evangelische Kirchenzeitung*— not at all just in respect to me, but generally—is openly and resolutely opposed from other sides too, especially also by your *Theologische Studien und Kritiken*. Whoever will be a public voice of the Protestant Church must also hold it for his duty not to remain silent in a public scandal of such a kind.[40]

That was Baur's final letter to Ullmann. In his reply Ullmann defended the policy of his journal and also that of the *Evangelische Kirchenzeitung*. 'Along with its shortcomings, also the good and capable qualities of such a journal for maintaining the orthodox point of view may also not be allowed to pass unperceived, and if I can judge correctly, we suffer in the country here far more from the gossip and sickly triviality of the *Allgemeine Kirchenzeitung* than from the intolerance of the *Evangelische Kirchenzeitung*.'[41]

Baur had sent Ullmann his treatise on the Atonement. It was reviewed in the journal, but from this time forward the *Theologische Studien und Kritiken* remained silent and treated Baur as if he had never existed. That was the form in which Protestant books at that time were placed on the Index. The relationship between Baur and Ullmann was at an end.

---

[39] Baur to Ullmann, 19 Mar. 1838.   [40] Baur to Ullmann, 29 Aug. 1838.
[41] Ullmann to Baur, 22 Oct. 1838.

In his book on the history of nineteenth-century theology Baur took his revenge with a sour description of Ullmann, 'the business man of his party', and his writings.

> With such trite phrases, no one knows how to avoid the central issues better than Ullmann; but they are also empty phrases whose emptiness becomes evident as soon as one investigates their meaning. Everything of importance remains completely indeterminate and unanswered. Such representations are basically of no worth, they do more harm than good; they are only concerned with giving a false appearance, as if implying that with these empty forms of speech, yet something real is said.[42]

BAUR AND THE TÜBINGEN THEOLOGICAL FACULTY

The years 1837–43 saw the completion of Baur's long dogmatic treatises 'The Christian Doctrine of the Atonement' and 'The Christian Doctrine of the Trinity and Incarnation'. His Hegelian views were now at their height and in his address, which he as Rector of the University during 1841–2 delivered on the occasion of the silver jubilee of the accession of King Wilhelm I to the throne of Württemberg, Baur did not lose the opportunity to extol the speculative philosophy.

> That the Spirit is the Absolute and, moreover, the Spirit not merely in so far as it is an other-worldly, transcendent Spirit, but also as one directly present and conscious of itself in the reality of the self-consciousness; that just for this reason the finite spirit and the infinite Spirit are not separated from each other by an absolute antithesis which absolutely excludes every mediation; that the finite spirit is also the infinite Spirit which raises itself out of the finitude of its nature to the infinitude of its nature; that the essence of the spirit generally is nothing other than the infinite self-mediation of thinking—this is the standpoint of a philosophy which has won such an important significance for our age. Such a philosophy was able to become a great system of thought, spreading itself through all branches of scientific knowledge and invading all aspects of life, only because it is not—as one thinks—the chance product of a few particular individuals, but rather the necessary and natural result of a long series of aspirations of the human spirit, coherent in themselves and directed to their highest goal, the absolute Idea. To this Idea all earlier systems and standpoints of

---

[42] *Geschichte der christlichen Kirche*, V, p. 406.

philosophy can only be related themselves as the individual stages of the Idea, which possesses movement in itself.[43]

The pietists were greatly annoyed by the speech, but Baur himself was on the whole well pleased with the way everything had gone. He described the occasion and the ensuing audience with the King in a letter to Heyd.

The festivities are now, praise God, all happily over; also in the audience with the King it went very well, although your concern was not completely without foundation ... Among other things he said that the Tübingen theologians had always distinguished themselves through their orthodoxy; metaphysics is a dangerous subject, one deals with matters which are not suited for the people and one must therefore be extremely cautious, for what is already as old as Christianity and possesses such a divine moral content can still only be something divine. He quickly fell into a completely apologetic tone and spoke in such a pious Christian manner about the dear Saviour that I was really touched ... Incidentally, he said all this in a highly friendly and well-meaning way and acquiesced in speaking about metaphysics, but not Hegelianism. I said afterwards to Schleyer, His Majesty seems to have wanted to give me a rebuke, but he was of the opinion I should not take it so. Be that as it may, the address had already been given and in this point will not have tasted sweet to many, but otherwise it was received with interest and I have been urged from various sides to have it printed. I may perhaps still decide to do this if I am previously sure that the censor will not be offended by the political passages.[44]

The years 1837–43 were also marked by deep personal sorrow. It was a great grief to Baur and his family when his wife, after a long illness, finally passed away in 1839. The deaths of his closest friend, Ludwig Heyd, and of his sympathetic colleague Friedrich Kern, in 1842, were also keenly felt by him, even though in later years he and Kern had drifted somewhat apart in their academic and religious views.

Within the theological faculty relations between the professors were not always harmonious and after the publication of Strauss's *Life of Jesus* in 1835, Baur was constantly in conflict with Schmid, who sided more and more with the pietist party.

---

[43] *Rede zur Feier des Gedächtnisses der 25. Regierung seiner Majestät des Königs Wilhelm von Württemberg* ... (ed. F. F. Baur, 1877).
[44] Baur to Heyd, 11 Nov. 1841.

In 1837 Steudal died and the necessity arose of appointing his successor.[45] Baur proposed Eduard Elwert[46] whose views may be broadly described as being influenced by Schleiermacher. However, there were grave doubts about Elwert's health, on account of which he had resigned his position in Zürich and accepted the pastorate of a small village near Tübingen. Kern was not averse to Elwert's appointment, but Schmid supported the candidacy of the lecturer I. A. Dorner,[47] then on the threshold of a brilliant career. The debate in the University senate was described by Baur in a letter to his brother.

So the matter came before the senate last Thursday. Schrader summarized the position and at once it showed itself clearly that the pietists again had their hands in the affair. Schrader, who had been well briefed by Schmid and let himself be guided completely by his pietistic interest, proposed Dorner, and Elwert was to be simply left out of consideration. Since one could not fasten on his bad health any more as an excuse, one fastened on his bad hearing, and since this was not adequate enough, Schrader urged against him that he was not as Christian-minded as Dorner, a view which Schmid expressed: Dorner corresponds better than Elwert to the need of our time for a Biblical-ecclesiastical dogmatics. It was now further debated, especially between Schmid and me; in the vote, Elwert received 12 votes to Dorner's 9. But because the decision regarding the questions, how far Elwert's bad hearing is to be seen as a hindrance to his calling, must be left to the discretion of the Ministry—which will perhaps not take Elwert's certainly doubtful condition so lightly—one cannot know at all how the matter will go. Dorner is, to be sure, not exactly a pietist, although he has some points of contact which will perhaps emerge more in the future; at any rate he is thoroughly on the side of Schmid and in many points just the same. Also I cannot hold the high opinion of his capability for this position which others have of him. Kern also finally voted for Elwert, although he had already supported Dorner too far. In short, here again there were all kinds of remarkable happenings.[48]

The Ministry of Education decided for Dorner and appointed him assistant professor. At the beginning of 1839 however,

[45] Hodgson's account of the professional appointments in the theological faculty (op. cit., pp. 27–9) is in places quite inaccurate.

[46] Eduard Elwert (1805–65) in his final years (1850–64) was *Ephorus* in the lower seminary at Schöntal.

[47] Isaac August Dorner (1809–84), professor of theology in Königsberg (1843–7), Bonn (1847–53), Göttingen (1853–62), and Berlin (1862–84).

[48] To F. A. Baur, 10 Dec. 1837.

Dorner received calls to the position of full professor in Kiel, and also in Rostock. The senate, realizing he was too valuable to lose, asked the Ministry to raise his status to full professor in order that he would remain on in Tübingen. The Ministry declined to do so, Dorner accepted the position in Kiel, and the faculty was forced to seek a replacement.

Baur again hoped that Elwert would be willing to be nominated, but Elwert declared that his health would not allow him to be considered, whereupon Baur then proposed his former Blaubeuren pupil, Christian Märklin. This proposal, however, was doomed from the beginning. For Märklin, now a pastor in the pietist stronghold of Calw, was Strauss's closest friend and had recently written a book on the pietists, in support of Strauss. Thus the pietists, who were under no illusions as to where Märklin's sympathies lay, were up in arms and opposed him to a man. At the beginning Kern had supported Märklin's candidacy, but when the matter was voted on in the senate on 20 June 1839, he changed sides and supported Schmid's candidate—an unimportant lecturer named Stirm. Out of twenty votes Märklin received only seven, Stirm the other thirteen. The Ministry, however, decided to ask Elwert to fill the vacancy and after repeated entreaties from the faculty and certain stipulations on his own side, Elwert accepted. Unfortunately, his bad health made it necessary for him continually to forgo lectures, and in the following year he asked to be relieved for the winter semester 1840/1. This provided Zeller with the opportunity of holding lectures in dogmatics and although he became involved in a number of disputes with the more pietistically inclined students, the lectures were regarded as a success, at least by the more *avant-garde* members of the class.

Early in 1841 a list of suitable candidates was put forward for the still vacant chair and it was hoped to invite someone famous from outside of Württemberg. The names of Lücke, Müller, Ullmann, Nitzsch, and Harless were suggested, but as no one seemed interested in coming to Tübingen it became necessary to choose someone from Württemberg itself. Baur and Kern decided to propose Zeller, but again this plan had little chance of success, since Zeller was now well known for his Hegelian standpoint and Schmid was again resolutely opposed, as Baur related in a letter to his brother.

As Elwert finally declared that he wanted to go back to his pastorate, the replacement for his chair had to be discussed. Here there were new theological disputes, especially in the faculty, for Schmid with his misgivings, obstinacy and hierarchical intolerance declared resolutely to us both (Kern, who in this matter is completely on my side, and me) that there could never be any question of appointing the lecturer Zeller.[49]

The call was finally received by the Swabian M. A. Landerer, who was appointed assistant professor in 1841, but in the following year Kern died and another round of negotiations was once more necessary. Baur again suggested Zeller, although knowing there was little hope of success. The senate was no more inclined to this proposal than it had been in the previous year and the choice finally narrowed down to two candidates—Dorner and J. T. Beck. Baur favoured Beck while Schmid supported Dorner, and Ewald, who had joined the faculty in 1841, came out in opposition to Baur. The senate sat in the spring of 1842 and chose Dorner by thirteen votes to eleven. Dorner, however, desired the opportunity of participating in the academic life of the Stift and was unhappy with the continual struggle between the Baurian and pietist factions in the faculty. Thus before accepting the call he made certain stipulations which the Ministry of Education felt unable to accept, with the result that the appointment fell through. After Karl Hase in Jena had been considered, the Swabian Beck, at that time assistant professor in Basel, was chosen, and Baur enjoyed cordial relations with him throughout the succeeding years.

BAUR AND EWALD

Of all the controversies in which Baur was ever involved, his feud with Ewald[50] was the longest and most bitter. Scarcely ever was a theologian attacked with such venomous invective or so spitefully maligned as Baur.

In 1837 Ewald, along with six other Göttingen professors who had protested against the repeal of the liberal constitution of the Hanover province, was dismissed from his professorship. After spending four months in England Ewald accepted a call to

[49] To F. A. Baur, 18 Mar. 1841.
[50] Georg Heinrich August Ewald (1803–75), the famous Hebraist and Old Testament scholar, was from 1831 professor of Oriental languages at Göttingen.

Tübingen where he lectured first in the philosophical faculty and then from 1841 in the theological faculty. During these first few years he stood in a friendly relationship with Baur, contributing articles and reviews to the *Theologische Jahrbücher* and protesting against the unwillingness of the Ministry of Education to appoint Schwegler tutor in the Stift. A supporter of the *avant-garde* critical approach to the Bible, Ewald was generally regarded as a friend and adherent of the Baurian theological viewpoint. Slowly, however, this attitude of approbation turned to one of avid hostility and hatred.

Ewald had a promising young student in Göttingen, Ernst Meier by name, who followed Ewald to Tübingen and habilitated[51] into the philosophical faculty there under Ewald's patronage. By 1845 Ewald had begun to disagree with Baur and had taken aversion to the School which was forming around him. Moreover, Ewald had also formed a great dislike for Vischer, who in 1844 had been appointed a professor in the philosophical faculty. What brought Ewald's festering animosity towards the Tübingen School to a head was the fact that his pupil, Meier, took sides with Baur, and Baur in turn supported Meier's petition for appointment to the professorial chair of Oriental literature. Ewald was furious and poured out his scorn on Meier's writings, declaring that Meier had no talent for the position and that his writings were full of errors, stupidities of every kind, and saturated with the vainest arrogance.

The feud concerning Meier now turned into a party struggle with Baur and his friends against Ewald. Even the Roman Catholics, who had no love for Baur, took Baur's side, since Ewald was constantly raging against the three enemies of Germany—the Catholics, the orthodox led by Hengstenberg, and the abominable Tübingen School of Baur.

The philosophical faculty decided to support Meier's petition, and Ewald in a fury composed vitriolic pamphlets and wrote to the Minister of Education, who also took the part of the faculty. With such a rebuff Ewald again poured out his gall upon all and sundry—the faculty, senate, Rector, Ministry of Education, and the Government. No one was spared. All were declared incompetent and devoid of any moral character, so that no one in Tübingen

---

[51] Habilitation is the process by which a candidate qualifies for inauguration as a university lecturer.

was sorry when in 1848 Ewald packed his bags and departed for Göttingen.

Baur composed a two-page academic report on the affair, which is notable for its calm, fair, and prudent review of the events. Ewald, however, was not by any means finished, and in the first issue of his new journal, the *Jahrbücher der biblischen Wissenschaft*, he made a long attack on Baur. 'Could one imagine anything worse than this Tübingen School, which has been hatched out during the last fifteen to twenty years, with Dr. Baur at its head, anything more pernicious than the overturning and destruction of all intellectual and moral life? But that is the end to which this School leads; it overpowers even a German university, along with the Chancellor and Minister of Education.'[52]

Baur wasted few words in his short reply—a footnote in his essay on New Testament criticism, which appeared in the following year (1849). Ewald's pathetic exhortation to improvement of his character, Baur declared, left him cold, and if what Ewald practised in his defamatory pamphlets was Christianity, then he would rather stand on the side of the atheists with whom Ewald had numbered him.

But as I have already said, every word that I write about such things is superfluous and I would perhaps even now—as much as I could say from my own experience about the destitute character and unmanliness of such an opponent—have done better to ignore Ewaldian stories of this kind with the deep contempt which they deserve. With a man possessed by the demon of arrogance there is absolutely no chance of any reasonable communication.[53]

Ewald was not to be outdone and in the second issue of his *Jahrbücher* for 1849, he vented his wrath in a long polemic against Strauss, Vischer, and especially Baur.

There is no author too bad whom he does not seek to flatter and lure as long as he can hope to get something from him for his concern and party. But if one holds up the truth to him, he stands immediately ready to shout it down and twist it, or even to ridicule and scorn it. He has not the least modesty and consideration any more, as long as it does not seem dangerous for him. The atheism which he transfers from the theory of his beloved School into practice (and only practical atheism is actually harmful, is more than laughable) bears its fruit a thousandfold. I resigned my chair in Tübingen completely of my

[52] *JBW*, I (1848), p. 20. [53] *TJ*, 1849, pp. 543–5.

own choice, but also in consequence of his character and actions, because it is against my principles to begin a public controversy with a colleague, and what is more in the same faculty and with an older colleague at that. He and his School see themselves compelled to spread lies about this. I now exhort him to Christian betterment—he the first professor of theology and first preacher at Tübingen. He answers this token of earnest Christian love in the way I have already mentioned, and puts out new lies—that I hate philosophy and say one should know that from of old philosophy has been saddled with the charge of atheism. Spoken against me this is a really lying statement because everyone knows that never and nowhere have I rejected all philosophy or even accused it of being atheistic. And the hackneyed reproach of heresy against Herr Baur is ridiculous. Herr Baur, in my opinion, is neither a Christian (and therefore no heretic) nor one of the better heathen. He is one of the literary Jews, this present-day pest of our poor Germany . . . If this Baurian activity and that of his School is not thoroughly extirpated from Germany and the Protestant Church then no Biblical investigation, no certainty of a true religion, and no healthiness of moral life will be any longer possible . . .[54]

Apart from a few remarks in connection with Ewald's latest book, Baur generally ignored Ewald's malicious attack and during the next decade the feud took on a more subdued tone, although Ewald continued to make insulting remarks and spiteful accusations wherever a suitable occasion was offering. There was a longer polemic in 1855 and in 1859 Baur, in his brochure on the Tübingen School, wrote a penetrating criticism of Ewald's views concerning the dating and composition of the Gospels.

In 1861, just after Baur's death in December of the preceding year, Ewald published another long, abusive, and defamatory attack on Baur, in which he related his own experiences at Tübingen. Until 1846, Ewald assured his readers, he had been esteemed a friend of the Tübingen School. Slowly, however, he perceived that Baur's views were other than his own. 'Alas, the experience itself had first to teach me how great was the distance which separated us. Gradually I recognized only too clearly and to my deep mortification that he was merely a man of his own pitiful School, no genuine Protestant theologian, not one who seeks the truth alone and Christ, not one intent on entering the school of Christian living.'[55]

[54] JBW, II (1849), pp. 21–2.   [55] JBW, XI (1860–1), p. 118.

But alas, it is just as unmistakable that Baur, from the time when I began openly to oppose the utter perversity of his method of Biblical investigation, sank in these investigations more and more into the mire. And sad as such a spectacle is to my eyes, it helps just as little when one will not see what is so obvious. And it could not be otherwise. For from the beginning, without exception, all the wisdom with which the man in long books and articles put forward his views on the New Testament writings, their content and worth, and on the earliest Church history, was without foundation and utterly perverse in thought. Alas, weak and inadequate were the objections which were made before 1848 about his views, and so his arrogance and presumption increased. But now as soon as the correct, always more perfect, and undeniable view was persistently held up to him and his School by me, he suddenly became like a door lifted off its hinges; and since the poor and ignoble means which he grasped in such a base cause could never withstand the good weapons of truth and right, it was inevitable that he should sink continually deeper at every point of the controversy which he brought upon himself. Even the learned man who hardens his heart against the truth does not go unpunished; and every perverse means which he employs against the truth in order to protect his beloved and grievous errors which flatter his egoism, turns itself to his own destruction, makes his loudest and most furious words into vain foolishness, and darkens his eyes ever more completely to the radiant light of truth.[56]

In page after page Ewald denounced Baur's deplorable, unscientific, and ignorant writings, his foolishness, his dishonesty, lies, arrogance, and hypocrisy.

Baur was now in his grave, but Zeller took up his pen and wrote a penetrating reply[57] which in turn exposed Ewald's own scurrility. Ewald had maintained that previous to 1846 he had not perceived how pernicious Baur's views actually were. Zeller showed that this could not have been so, that Ewald had been in substantial agreement with Baur, had contributed to the *Theologische Jahrbücher*, and defended Schwegler. It was not the Tübingen School which had changed, declared Zeller, but Ewald, who now fulminated against the same views with which he had previously been in agreement. It was Ewald and not Baur, who was guilty of perverting the truth by now calling black what he had previously called white.

[56] Ibid., p. 121.
[57] 'Ewald's neueste Äusserungen über Baur', *ZWT*, 1861, pp. 319-29.

Zeller's defence of his late father-in-law showed up Ewald in his true light, and no one except Ewald and his friends doubted that Zeller was fully justified in his condemnation of Ewald's character. Ewald's vituperative attacks on Baur brought him nothing but dishonour, while Baur gained respect by his calm and restrained replies. Nevertheless Ewald's polemic did have unfortunate consequences for Baur and his pupils in that it continually drew upon them the attention of the orthodox, and especially the leading figures in the Government. For although everyone realized that much of Ewald's blustering criticism was a mass of bombastic verbiage, yet his attacks must have brought a smile to the faces of Hengstenberg and the pietists who saw the chief enemy of the Christian faith vilified by a man whom they regarded as equally dangerous. When the orthodox saw the Moabites fighting with Ammonites they could only regard it as a God-given victory.

Ewald was a brilliant writer with a ready fund of insulting words and Baur was never able to equal Ewald's rhetorical vivacity. How much harm was caused to Baur's reputation is inestimable. It is true that the great majority had little time for Ewald's verbosity and Baur was widely regarded as an unbeliever, but nevertheless Ewald's rude invective appears to have impeded considerably the influence of the School—especially in England— and perhaps contributed not a little to its demise.

BAUR AND HASE

In marked comparison to the feud with Ewald, Baur's debate with Hase[58] was irenic and courteous. In his article on the Johannine question, in 1854, Baur had described Hase's *Life of Jesus* as possessing 'a decidedly rationalistic tendency in the best sense of the word', and declared that, 'as sparingly and tenderly as Herr Hase is accustomed to deal with particularly the miracles in the Gospels, under his hand they still always lose more or less of their miraculous lustre.' Hase's explanation of the miracles, declared Baur, was weak and had been left deliberately vague.

What then was the raising of Lazarus, was it a miracle or not? One sees easily that Herr Hase does not regard it as a miracle, but he will not say it and also cannot say it without falling into the most palpable

---

[58] Karl August Hase (1800–90) was professor of theology at Jena.

contradiction with his presupposition. .... As often as he speaks of miracles he never takes the miracles seriously, and one finally does not know whether not just the death of Lazarus but the death of Jesus himself was not a mere apparent-death.[59]

Hase protested that he had been absolutely misunderstood, and wrote an 'Open Article to Herr Dr. F. C. Baur'[60] defending himself against Baur's reproaches. He had attempted to interpret the miracles in a rational manner as far as possible, he maintained, but had been forced on account of the unreliability of the historical sources to confess his inability to decide whether or not the miracles had actually taken place. Baur had no intention of allowing Hase to get away with such weak explanations, and in his reply he exposed Hase's futile attempts to tread a middle path.

According to your view of the apostolic origin of John's Gospel you also must hold the miracles related in this Gospel to be those they are held to be according to the Gospel writers. But since the acceptance of miracles does not at all agree with the rationalistic viewpoint of your *Life of Jesus*, herein lies the reason why you avoid putting forward views about miracles more precisely, and therefore one does not know whether you do not hold the death of Lazarus, and even the death of Jesus, for a merely apparent death. 'I have never been able to recognize myself less', you now reply, 'in a picture which is held up before my eyes, than in this contradictory portrayal which certainly intends to understand the "clear meaning" of my words, and yet lays the blame on me for letting the reader suppose the direct opposite of my true conviction.' What then is your true conviction? When you speak of miracles do you accept them as real miracles or merely apparent? 'You know full well', you answer me, 'that I cannot hold miracles in the absolute sense—as an overturning of the laws of nature, the divine will upon earth—to be possible, but that I must acknowledge in Jesus powers still unbeknown to us, especially suddenly-working powers of healing, which also find manifold analogies' (p. 13). The truth of my reproach is therefore this, that you certainly seek out all the features and allusions in the Gospel reports which hint at any kind of a natural course of events, but you do not dare to go further than the historical records allow. Therefore you must certainly so often remain in a state of not-knowing and I viewed this real ignorance of yours as diplomacy (p. 14). Thus you do not really know whether or not Lazarus was actually dead? It is simply a question of whether you must not know

[59] *TJ*, 1854, pp. 253–5.
[60] *Die Tübinger Schule. Ein Sendschreiben an Herrn Dr. Ferdinand Christian von Baur* (Leipzig, 1855).

this, according to the basic axioms which you yourself expressed. As is well known the miracle reports in the Gospels contain no features and allusions which hint at a natural course of events—if one will not somehow return to the miracle interpretation of Dr. Paulus—least of all in the Johannine narrative of the resurrection of Lazarus can anything of this kind be found. If, therefore, you will only go so far as the historical documents allow, then according to the undeniable sense of the narrative you will have to hold the raising of Lazarus to be an actual miracle. But as, on the other hand, you know full well that there are no absolute miracles, then you cannot hold the raising of Lazarus to be an actual miracle. Lazarus can thus not have been actually dead; for if he had been raised from actual death then this would have been an absolute miracle, which cannot be held to be possible. The problem which you express is thus not just that of being really ignorant, but rather of knowing too much, for at the same time you know both that Lazarus was dead, and that he could not have been dead, thus, also, that he was not dead . . .[61]

The discussion of miracles was in fact the central point of the whole debate and Baur showed convincingly that there was no middle way: either one accepted the actuality of the Gospel miracles (in the traditional sense), or rejected them. Three other questions to which Baur and Hase devoted themselves—the historicity of the Gospels, the relation of Jewish and Pauline Christianity, and the conception and method of writing Church history—were too inconclusive to be of any real significance, and Baur simply repeated the views he had long before put forward.

THE FINAL YEARS

The last fifteen years of Baur's life were especially concerned with defending the School which had formed under his name. Baur was the acknowledged head of the School but it was Zeller and Schwegler who were really responsible for its rise. Without the *Theologische Jahrbücher*, which Zeller inspired and organized, it is doubtful whether or not there would ever have been a Tübingen School. Up until 1846 it was the Tübingen School which had been on the attack. From 1847, however, the School was forced to defend the positions which had already been staked out. It was now Baur's turn to be attacked, not by the older theologians such as Hengstenberg, but by a younger generation who hoped to win

[61] *An Herrn Dr. Karl Hase. Beantwortung des Sendschreibens 'Die Tübinger Schule'* (Tübingen, 1855), pp. 19–21.

their spurs. Thiersch in Marburg wrote a strongly critical book which was published in 1846 and had the honour of eliciting a long counter-attack from Baur. The Erlangen theologian Ebrard[62] was a continual thorn in Baur's flesh, with his hostile attacks on Baur's writings. 'This base fellow', wrote Baur to Alexander Schweizer, 'has been so long repugnant to me, that I absolutely cannot read anything more by him; in every statement one doesn't know whether or not he is lying. I trust you will put paid to him once for all so that in future it will suffice to refer to your article against him.'[63] From Baumgarten, Schliemann, Böttcher, Dietlein, and other quarters also—not to forget the blustering Ewald— came a steady stream of vexatious criticism. Baur's break with Ritschl occurred in 1856 and relations with Hilgenfeld during these years were at a low ebb. The continually sinking number of subscriptions to the *Jahrbücher* brought the journal to a complete cessation in 1857, and the final two years of Baur's life were involved in trying to hold the Tübingen School together.

Family problems were also a constant drain on Baur's energy in his later years. Relations with his youngest son Albert were not entirely happy and tragic misfortunes struck the household of his brother Gustav, to whom he was deeply devoted. Nevertheless, Baur's capacity for work was remarkable. 'Summer and winter', wrote Zeller, 'he arose at 4 a.m.[64] and in winter he usually worked for a few hours in the unheated room out of consideration for the servants, even though—as often happened—on especially cold nights the ink froze; and thereafter the regular midday or evening walk was generally the single long interruption in the day's academic work.'[65]

During the final decade of his life Baur was constantly engaged in lecturing on and writing his history of the Christian Church from its inception up until the nineteenth century. *The Church History of the First Three Centuries* appeared in 1853 and was republished in a revised edition in 1860. The second volume dealing with the Church in the fourth to sixth centuries was published in 1859 and volume III, 'The Church in the Middle

---

[62] Joh. Heinrich Ebrard (1818–88), a conservative Lutheran, was professor of theology at Erlangen.

[63] To Alexander Schweizer, 2 Apr. 1851.

[64] One should perhaps mention that Baur suffered from insomnia and preferred rather to work than remain lying in bed.

[65] *VA*, I (1865), p. 363.

Ages', which Baur had prepared for the Press shortly before his death, appeared posthumously in 1861. The fourth volume treating the period from the Reformation to the end of the eighteenth century was edited by Baur's son Ferdinand Friedrich Baur and published in 1863; the fifth and final volume 'The History of the Church in the Nineteenth century' appeared in the previous year and was edited by Zeller from Baur's lecture notes. The whole series represents Baur's attempt to portray the history of the Church from a natural point of view, i.e. from the pre-supposition, that from the beginning the history of the Church contained no supernatural or miraculous element. This pre-supposition was not so explicitly maintained in such a stark form, but rather underlies all that Baur wrote. All the events of Church history are to be explained by a combination of political, social, cultural, and intellectual causes but not, as in the orthodox view, by the ascription of any divine causality. That was the one factor expressly, if not explicitly, excluded from the reckoning. Two other works which F. F. Baur edited after his father's death were the 'Lectures on the History of Christian Doctrine' (3 volumes; 1865–7) and the 'Lectures on New Testament Theology' (1864).

In the theological faculty Baur became more and more isolated. J. T. Beck who had ties with the pietists was called to Tübingen in 1842. M. A. Landerer, who was appointed professor in the same year, belonged to the orthodox party. G. F. Öhler, a pietist, became professor of Old Testament in 1852, and following the death of Schmid in the same year, C. D. F. Palmer, whose sympathies lay with the orthodox, was appointed professor of moral and practical theology. Thus Baur's influence in the faculty was greatly curtailed and in the academic world of his own day he was viewed with distrust and aversion. 'Baur was regarded as the arch-heretic,' wrote Barnikol, 'as the number one heretic, and yet he himself wanted to remain in the Church.'[66]

In his own lifetime Baur was never highly esteemed. Only years later was it possible to evaluate his influence more truly. Otto Pfleiderer writing in 1892 could maintain that 'even today in most ecclesiastical circles Baur's name is more feared than revered.' 'One can well say', he continued, 'that Baur's thirty-four years'

[66] E. Barnikol, *Ferdinand Christian Baur als rationalistisch-kirchlicher Theologe* (Berlin, 1970), p. 18.

activity in Tübingen are the core of the history of theology in our century',[67] and Dilthey even went so far as to declare: 'He was the greatest theologian of our century.'[68]

On 15 July 1860 Baur suffered his first heart attack and although he quickly recovered he was not well enough to hold lectures during the winter semester. It was hoped that his return to health would be lasting, but while participating in a meeting of the University senate on 29 November he suffered his second heart attack from which he never recovered. He died on 2 December 1860 and was buried in the Tübingen cemetery three days later. His tombstone which stands between two trees is now covered over with ivy, but the plaque on which his name is inscribed is easily visible. Almost a century later Albert Schweitzer visited the grave and paid homage to the man who more than any other was responsible for the historical-critical investigation of the Bible.

Most of the tributes paid to Baur after his death were marked by a somewhat artificial tone, and we conclude with the sympathetic words which Hilgenfeld wrote to Zeller a few days after Baur's death. Distinguished by their sincerity and freshness, Hilgenfeld's words provide a most fitting commemoration of Baur's life and work.

As one of the nearest survivors let me express to you my sincerest sympathy on the decease of your revered father-in-law. . . . You may well believe that the death of the venerable man with whom I corresponded for thirteen years has deeply distressed me, all the more since I can no longer carry out my now long-cherished intention of visiting him in Tübingen, which I wanted to do in the next Whitsuntide holidays. And if our relationship was not as friendly and free from troubles as it could well have been under different circumstances, when I now tie up the large number of Baur's letters, then these disturbances recede behind the abiding impression of a grand and noble man of theological science. He had behind him a fine life, rich in activity; in later years he did not taste for long the time of broken powers. He went home as he was about to enter upon the usual goal of the human life, and one can apply to him the Scriptural word in its fullest sense, that he rests from his labours and his works follow him. When his mortal body—which I have never directly seen—is lowered into the grave, there will still remain an immortal part of him active in the

[67] 'Zu Ferdinand Christian Baur's Gedächtnis', PK XXXIX (1892), p. 565.
[68] Wilhelm Dilthey, Gesammelte Schriften, IV, p. 431.

world. And if the nearest friends and relatives mourn for the faithful father and fatherly friend, the theological investigator in Protestant theology will still long be reminded of him by the indestructible memorial of his restless activity.[69]

[69] Hilgenfeld to Zeller, 7 Dec. 1860.

3. Eduard Zeller

OF all the members of the Tübingen School it was Zeller who attained the highest place of honour in the academic world. At the turn of the century he was held in respect in every European university and named along with the greatest scholars in Germany, with Ranke and Mommsen, with Helmholz and Virchow. When in 1894 he returned from Berlin to his native Württemberg, where previously he had been unable to obtain any academic promotion, he returned like a conquering hero, as a Prussian Councillor to whom belonged the title of Excellency and as a member of the Academy of Sciences. Honours were showered upon him, the doctorates of various faculties, the order *pour le mérite*, the Bavarian Order of Maximilian, and many others. On his ninetieth birthday he was greeted by deputations from the universities in which he had formerly taught, by numerous letters and telegrams of congratulation; even the Kaiser himself wrote to him and sent him an autographed photo.

The end of Zeller's life, however, could scarcely have been foreseen from its humble beginning in the little rustic village of Kleinbottwar near Marbach on the Neckar. His father was in charge of the government revenues in the district and in the village he had a not unimportant position which he had attained to by dint of honest and diligent service. In religious matters he was a rationalist, although, as Zeller remarked, he found it better not to say much about his beliefs. To him the important thing was a sound moral training without the one-sidedness and excesses of pietism; he held that the tree was to be measured by its fruit and that honesty of character formed the basis of a successful life. With these religious ideals his wife was in full agreement and apart from meal-time grace there were no family devotions.

The family already consisted of seven children, five girls and two boys, when Eduard was born on 22 January 1814. As the youngest of the family he was treated with great affection, not only by his mother but also by the other children and his childhood was thus extremely happy with much to occupy his interest. The family lived in a modest but spacious house which had once been a small castle and the large lawn surrounded by garden and trees was his favourite playground. Then there were the many household tasks to fulfil, for all meat, fruit, vegetables, milk, and eggs had to come from their own garden and from the animals which were then a necessary part of country life.

The education of the children was undertaken at home by a tutor and under the watchful guidance of the father. In this way the children learnt two and three times as fast as would otherwise have been the case in the village school, and the father supplemented their lessons in history and geography from his own general knowledge with the help of a globe and maps.

Eduard's brother Gustav, two years older than he, was attending a private school in the nearby town of Backnang, and since it was with Gustav that Eduard shared the most intimate companionship, it was thought advisable that Eduard should also be enrolled in the Backnang school. In the autumn of 1821 the headmaster paid a visit to the Zeller house and Eduard was tested to see if he were proficient enough to enter the school where the children were mostly two years older. The result was satisfactory but one obstacle remained in that owing to the fact that Eduard was not yet eight years old and of delicate constitution, his parents wished to postpone his entry into the school until the spring. Since the other pupils in the class would be beginning Greek as soon as the new term commenced, it meant that Eduard would be three or four months behind. The best solution, obviously, was for Eduard to study Greek at home but no teacher was available in the village except the seventy-year-old pastor who was unsuited for the task. This state of affairs led the father to resolve that he himself would learn the language and teach Eduard at the same time. Thus father and son studied together and so well did the scheme succeed that when Eduard began school in the following spring he was in no way behind the other members of the class.

The school in Backnang was divided into two classes, the lower being instructed by the assistant master and the upper by the headmaster. The lower class was in turn divided into an upper and lower group which were together in the same room, so that while the one group received instruction from the master, the other busied itself with exercises. All the other children in Eduard's class were two to three years his senior, but none the less they readily accepted him as one of themselves. The two main subjects were Latin and Greek but in addition there was Hebrew, arithmetic, history, geography, and short essays in German. Both Eduard and his brother were exempted from school singing as 'hopeless'. Zeller related how in the upper class the wrong parsing of Greek verbs used to be punished with a light caning of the hand. The teacher was actually no friend of this educational method and for a time had done away with it, but finding that his pupils became lazy, he reintroduced it, and for the rest of his life Zeller was thankful that he had been forced to learn his verbs with such thoroughness.

During the time in Backnang it became clear that he should enter the Church since this offered the best opportunity of obtaining university education. To this end he prepared for the exam which would provide him with the chance of entering one of the four lower seminaries.

I am scarcely able to say how I ever came to make up my mind to study theology, which the passing of the state exam would make possible. From childhood I knew implicitly that someday I would follow the example of my eldest brother, who since 1820 had been in the Schöntal seminary, then in Tübingen, and had even become the *primus* of his *Promotion*. It would have been almost impossible for my parents to have allowed all their sons to study had not the greater part of the educational expenses been paid for by the state for two of us from our fourteenth year, and this necessary presupposition that we should study for the ministry could cause no concern on the part of my parents who both had the blood of pastors in their veins. And I too would certainly have chosen no other course if the choice had been open to me in my fourteenth or eighteenth year; in this respect my wishes were thoroughly in accord with those of my parents.[1]

His childhood slowly drew to a close; a few months of schooling in Stuttgart during the spring and summer of 1827, the final exam in September, and then in the autumn the doors of the lower seminary in Maulbronn opened once more to receive a new *Promotion*.

THE LOWER SEMINARY IN MAULBRONN

The founding of the Cisterian abbey at Maulbronn is a delightful little story which deserves to be retold. The monks, uncertain as

---

[1] *Erinnerungen eines Neunzigjährigen* (Stuttgart, 1904), p. 41.

to where they should establish their new monastery, loaded their few possessions on to a mule and allowed it—probably accompanied by benedictions and occasional blows—to wander freely. The place where the mule should stop would be the place which God had chosen for the site of the new abbey. At the spring which now lies within the monastery garden and from which fresh water still gushes forth into the fountain, the mule rested and quenched its thirst. There in 1147, the monks began to build their abbey to which they gave the name of 'Maulbrunnen' or 'Mule Spring'. So runs the legend and the fresco in the chapel portraying a mule drinking from the fountain would seem to confirm an underlying historical basis for the story.

Surrounded by wooded hills in the quiet Salzach valley, the site was certainly an excellent one and the old Gothic architecture and wood carvings of the monastery draw the modern visitor back into the Middle Ages, when the cowled monks wended their way with bowed heads silently through the cloisters. In the room under the tower Faust is supposed to have stayed and been visited by the devil, and Zeller relates how one day the students were amazed and shocked when they discovered two small pipes leading to the eyes of the statue of the Virgin Mary on the high altar, by means of which she could be made to weep. 'Our predecessors, the old monks, would on their part perhaps have been surprised at our *naïveté* in taking offence at such an innocent and effective means of promoting religious devotion.'[2]

The teaching staff at the seminary consisted of the *Ephorus*, two professors, and two tutors. *Ephorus* Huber was a well-meaning and understanding man who knew how to preserve discipline without being pedantic, but his lectures were a burden on the students, who derived little profit from them. The elder of the two professors, Hartmann, taught with an enthusiasm and diligence which called forth great respect from his pupils. An excellent preacher in the pulpit, his life hardly measured up to the moral content of his sermons, for he often flew into a rage for the most trivial reason and he lived with his uncultured maidservant. The younger professor, Osiander, a relative of Zeller's, was a gentle, pious, and friendly man who read all his lectures in an extremely boring manner and went through the world as if seeing everything behind a veil. The two tutors were Kraus—honest and

2 *Erinnerungen*, p. 50.

conscientious if not particularly stimulating—and Albert Binder, who had been especially influenced by the agnostic Jean Paul and also by Schleiermacher. Binder was a friend of Zeller's elder brother Wilhelm and therefore showed particular interest in Eduard, offering him his friendship and helping him in his philosophical studies with private lessons. In Eduard's second year they embarked on the study of psychology and studied together Weiss's investigations into the essence and working of the human soul.

For three years Eduard was content and happy in the seminary but by the beginning of his final year he had had enough and wrote to his father that he wanted to leave.

Forgive me if the request which I make of you is not in line with your better understanding, but I must tell you what is on my heart at present. Of the 76 hours which we have during the week for actual studying, classes take 34 and preparation for the classes another 18 at the very least. I know only too well through my own experiences and the experiences of others that by studying on my own without classes I would learn in half the time just as much as or even more than I am learning at present; if I could study on my own I would not merely learn things in order to forget them; my intellect would become more active and more accustomed to reflective thinking than in these classes where we get for the most part nothing more than a pile of scholastic comments which we are supposed to believe on the basis of this or that authority. The simplest way to work this would be if you allowed me to leave the seminary and spend the whole of the next half-year continuing my studies in Kleinbottwar.[3]

However the real reason for his wishing to leave the seminary seems to be that he no longer wanted to continue his theological study and enter the Church. When in the light of later developments we read the letter which he wrote to his father a fortnight later, it would appear that, influenced by the philosophical ideas of Binder, he felt that it would be better to follow another career than to waste his time studying the Christian faith, which he no longer accepted as true.

Although the difficulties of the situation which lie in the way of my leaving the seminary compel me to give up this wish, I still believe I must defend my view, that if the circumstances had permitted it, it would have been better for me to leave; I say this so that you will not

[3] Draft of a letter to his father, 13 Feb. 1831.

believe it was mere flights of phantasy which impelled me to this wish. You warn me about dissipating my mental powers; but this takes place just where one wants to push on us a lot of mere facts, where one wants to educate us with generalities, where every deeper penetration into the details of a subject is reproached—especially by Hartmann—as philosophical casuistry which 'is only a cloak for ignorance but which cannot cover it over'. He complains that Binder has 'sent me crazy with the accursed philosophy', that 'I want mere realities (among which he reckons also philosophy, but probably not history); that I should go to Esslingen and become a pharmacist', and much more of the same rubbish. I therefore believe that there would have been less to fear in Bottwar in respect of a dissipation in the enlarging of my knowledge, against which, here, philosophy serves as a counterbalance. I acknowledge with thankfulness the profit which I formerly had from the seminary and I also believe that my course up until now could not have been better chosen, that a longer period of being left to myself would not have been good. But whether this might not be good for half a year now . . .[4]

In July 1831 an anonymous article on the Maulbronn seminary appeared in a Stuttgart newspaper. The author obviously had inside information about some of Hartmann's former indiscretions and cleverly held him up to ridicule. Hartmann became convinced that the article stemmed from one of his present pupils (it was actually by a former pupil), demanded that the culprit own up, and refused to teach any more until he did so. Every boy swore on oath that he had had nothing to do with the article and Zeller as the class representative had to try and mediate. Hartmann still refused to believe that no one in the class was responsible and the class found themselves in a state of war, which was only resolved when Hartmann's immorality with his maidservant was made known and his resignation from the seminary accepted. Within a matter of hours, to Zeller's great joy, Strauss was temporarily appointed as assistant lecturer in order to fill the position caused by Hartmann's departure.

Strauss's arrival makes our stay here much more pleasant for us all, especially for me. I often talk with him and especially enjoy his lectures in which an extremely philosophical spirit makes itself felt, although he does not despise the traditional. He has the reasonable view that everything has value only in so far as it is related to philosophy (i.e. to the

---

[4] To his father, 2 Mar. 1831.

highest that human knowledge can attain to, the absolute, the idea which brings harmony in all our knowing).[5]

From that time on Zeller's doubts about remaining at the seminary were completely swept away and he found a fresh interest in his study. At the graduation he was named as the *primus* of the *Promotion* and he was in every way well equipped to begin his study at the University in the autumn of 1831.

UNIVERSITY STUDY IN TÜBINGEN

Of the eight semesters which the students at that time had to spend at the University, three were devoted to philosophy (which included Greek, Latin, Hebrew, mathematics, history,' and philosophy in the narrower sense of the word), the remaining five to theology. Zeller set himself especially to master early Greek philosophy and to this end he made a careful study of Plato's *Republic*. With this accomplished he turned to the more recent philosophy of Kant, Jacobi, Fichte, Schelling, and Hegel, making a short summary of each book that he read. In his spare moments he translated English poetry, especially Byron, into German and in 1832 some of his translations were published in an anthology, most of the edition remaining unsold. From the lectures in general he appears to have derived little profit until the summer semester of 1832 when Strauss, who had just returned from Berlin, was called to Tübingen as tutor in the Stift. At last Hegel had an apostle in Württemberg and Zeller found a new interest in the speculative philosophy which Strauss expounded in his lectures on 'Logic' and 'Metaphysics'.

My favourite lectures are those given by Strauss. Never have I found such a clarity and dialectical dexterity combined with such ardour and warm conviction as in this man. His subject also is completely new among the list of current lectures, since he treats it after the manner of Hegel, whose system he has decidedly adopted. A lecture on the topic was certainly due, since the study of Hegel is continually increasing, while Hegel's hitherto-published works are supposed to be difficult to understand (his lectures which are also now being published are supposed to be considerably more comprehensible). Now Strauss possesses the gift of popular lecturing combined with a pleasant appearance to a high degree. This fact and the great reputation

[5] To his brother Gustav, 14 July 1831.

which he had here already explain why his lectures up till now have
been so well attended that he has had to seek a larger auditorium than
the one in which he initially commenced his lectures. I believe that up
till now he has never had fewer than 150 listeners and even if among
these a large number were simply curious to hear him, there would still
be over 90 loyal attenders. In the seminary 60 from all *Promotions* have
already enrolled. Sigwart, from whom he has taken away two-thirds
of his students, is naturally extremely peeved; even Steudel appears to
fear that his innocent herd might be led astray by the wisdom from
Berlin. To be sure, I hold this concern to be not without ground, but
superfluous, for I cannot at all see what is harmful about the Hegelian
philosophy (if philosophy is not already considered to be an evil in
itself) and I also know right pious students who for all their piety are
still Hegelians.[6]

During the following two semesters he heard Strauss's lectures
on the history of philosophy, the history of ethics, and Plato's
Symposium; from the autumn of 1833, however, Strauss ceased
lecturing and devoted his whole time to the writing of his *Life of
Jesus*. Zeller's study during his first semester was in no way
one-sided and while he continued methodically to work his way
through Hegel's *Phenomenology* he also attended a course of lectures
on anatomy and devoted himself to the writing of a prize essay on
the relations between Greece and Egypt up to the time of Herodotus.

In the summer of 1833 Zeller began his theological study
proper. The theological faculty at that time consisted of four
professors, Steudel, Kern, Baur, and Schmid who all stretched
out a friendly hand. Zeller found Steudel's lectures dull and
contented himself with reading the lecture notes of a friend. He
did likewise with the lectures of Kern, who noticing his absence
gave him tacit permission to absent himself, remarking that his
lectures were meant more for the average student than for Zeller.
From Schmid he was able to learn something but it was Baur to
whom he owed most.

Of all the theological professors of that time, the only one whose
pupil in the full sense I could consider myself to be, and have through
my life considered myself to be, was Baur. We encountered in him not
only the model of a scientific mind in exemplary strength and purity,

---

[6] To his father, 21 May 1832.

but while we were still students, we experienced also under his guidance a part of the most important transformations which theology has passed through since Schleiermacher and Hegel.[7]

An even more important influence during these early years was Strauss, whose *Life of Jesus* had appeared in the summer of 1835. Zeller was captivated by it: 'Here was and is still a great sensation over Strauss's *Life of Jesus*. It is really an excellent book, very scholarly, to be sure, but so pleasingly written, like a novel, and deadly hostile to all orthodox Christianity',[8] and later in his 'Reminiscences' he portrayed the situation in greater detail.

One must have lived through this period in order to gain an adequate conception of the impression which this work made upon one's contemporaries among whom it fell like a bomb, shocking them out of the indifference and blind trust with which men of all parties— rationalists as well as supernaturalists and not least the disciples of Schleiermacher and Hegel—almost without exception, interpreted the Gospel narratives. We young people, so far as we stood on the side of scientific advancement, immediately and decidedly took Strauss's part. Not merely the audacity of the youthful critic carried us away with him but also the evidence brought forward seemed to us irrefutable and we were enchanted with the elegance and transparency of his presentation, which in these qualities stood quite alone among all the scientific works written in Germany up until that time.[9]

By the end of his university study in 1835 Zeller stood completely behind Strauss and regarded the Bible merely as a conglomeration of myths and legends in which the Person of the historical Jesus was almost indiscernible behind the later embellishments of the Gospel writers. It was Strauss who introduced him to Hegel and it was through Strauss's influence that he saturated himself in the speculative philosophy. The part which Strauss played at this stage in Zeller's life is extremely important and must not be underestimated.

LECTURER IN THE UNIVERSITY

On graduating from the seminary in 1835 Zeller became curate for a year to his cousin Friedrich Zeller in Nellingen near Esslingen. Here he lived a quiet and peaceful life, studying Aristotle in his spare time and preaching once every Sunday, alternating with his cousin in the two churches under their supervision.

[7] *Erinnerungen*, p. 93.   [8] To Gustav, 1 July 1835.   [9] *Erinnerungen*, p. 100.

After obtaining his doctor's degree in philosophy in the following autumn Zeller set out on a journey to Berlin. He first visited Munich where a cholera epidemic was raging, although this information was kept from the public by the officials on account of the Munich fair. Escaping unscathed to Augsburg, he was joined there by his two companions Bockshammer and Reuschle and after passing through Dresden, Leipzig, and Halle—where they met Wegscheider, Gesenius, Müller, and Tholuck—they arrived in Berlin and found lodgings near the University. Hegel and Schleiermacher were no longer alive, but Zeller met Michelet, Gans, Henning, and Hegel's widow. Vatke especially proved a friend to them all, and Zeller much appreciated his lectures on the Old Testament.

On returning to Tübingen in the summer of 1837 he became curate at the *Stiftskirche* and had the duty of preaching every Sunday afternoon. His sermons, he tells us, were composed in a very short time: during Sunday morning he wrote them out in full and after re-reading the manuscript when lunch was over, it was so impressed on his memory that he required no notes in the pulpit.

In 1838, after five months as curate, Zeller was appointed tutor in the lower seminary in Urach, a position which he found much more congenial; but his time here was short and in May 1839 he was recalled to Tübingen as tutor in the Stift.

During the summer months he prepared for the coming winter semester. Under the innocent-looking title of 'Apologetics' he announced a series of lectures on the Hegelian philosophy, which were intended to deal with the problem of the religious consciousness. About thirty students attended, mostly from his former Urach *Promotion*. In the following summer semester he lectured on the history of Protestant theology before sixty students and his success encouraged him to habilitate in the theological faculty. The *venia legendi* was granted to him, but in taking this step he was unable to retain his position as tutor in the Stift. The way became more thorny and he now came into conflict with the Church authorities, for the first volume of Strauss's Dogmatics had just appeared and Zeller felt he should take a decisive stand on Strauss's side.

The first volume of Strauss's 'Doctrine of the Christian Faith' had just appeared, the second was awaited, and it was a case of taking a stand for or against the devastating criticism which penetrated into every part of the earlier dogmatics. On my part I could not escape from the weight of the doubts which Strauss had raised, most of which had already been put forward in a more moderate form by Schleiermacher, as objections against the faith; just as little, however, could I hide the untenable nature of the Christological theory in which Schleiermacher had taken his final refuge. I declared this openly to my hearers and with a thorough grounding in the individual points. With the help of Hegel and Schleiermacher I took real pains to salvage something of abiding worth with respect to the Person of Christ, but was naturally unable to prevent those who wished the Church tradition to be treated as infallible truth from taking the greatest offence at my lectures. These lectures appeared all the more dangerous the more lively was the interest with which the listeners, about fifty in number, followed them. So it was not surprising when not merely the pietists, and all those who took a similar view, attacked me as an outspoken opponent of the faith . . .[10]

What exactly took place during the semester is not fully clear, but Zeller himself described the lectures as a failure, and probably he fell into great displeasure with the higher Church authorities. 'The young hero,' wrote Diels, 'who realized more than ever that the new teaching would have to be defended by force, forged a terrible weapon for himself in order to accomplish this end.'[11] This 'terrible weapon' was the *Theologische Jahrbücher*, which appeared every quarter and whose purpose was to unite all those wishing to forward the new critical investigation into the Christian faith and the doctrines of the Church. Zeller's new journal became the organ of the Tübingen School and one may say that with its commencement the School in its historical phase first came into being. The acknowledged head of the school was of course Baur, but it was Zeller who was the guiding mind and organizing mainspring of the journal. The bulk of the work fell on his shoulders and he often found himself left in the lurch by his co-workers, who failed to send him contributions. Thus his letters at this time are full of pleas for articles; he complained that Vatke had sent him nothing, that Strauss by his laziness had lost them much influence, and that he himself had to write all the book reviews—a time-consuming task.

In 1843 both Zeller and Baur were attacked in the *Evangelische Kirchenzeitung* and as time progressed it became more and more

---

[10] *Erinnerungen*, pp. 131–2.
[11] H. Diehls, in Zeller's *Kleine Schriften*, III, p. 480.

evident that Zeller's chances of obtaining any further academic promotion were growing ever less. Even the prestige won for him by the first volume of his *The Philosophy of the Greeks* was insufficient to counterbalance the growing prejudice against his heterodox religious ideas. Following Vischer's suspension from lecturing for two years, Zeller's attack on Merz in the *Jahrbücher der Gegenwart*[12] was viewed by the orthodox as a confirmation of the dangerous nature of his views. An attempt was made by the University senate in 1846 to obtain a chair for him in the philosophical faculty, but the King of Württemberg refused his consent. 'As the Minister brought the request of the senate with his own recommendation before the King, his Majesty answered that it would have to be considered, and after two days the resolution came from the Cabinet: "His Majesty cannot decide to honour a man who in his lectures attacks the central doctrines of the Christian faith." '[13]

The chance of obtaining a chair in Prussia was even bleaker, but a new opportunity was now to present itself.

THE CALLING TO BERN

On his way home from Berlin in the summer of 1845, the Bernese philosophy student Friedrich Ries had visited Zeller in Tübingen in the hope of obtaining some private tuition in the Hegelian philosophy. At that time Zeller was extremely busy but he invited Ries to accompany him on his evening walks—an invitation of which Ries made the greatest use. The friendship which Zeller offered was not unappreciated and upon his return to Bern, Ries, who had influential connections, exerted himself on Zeller's behalf in the hope of obtaining a professorial chair for him. The Ministry of Education asked for a reference from the theological faculty and the ensuing report set forth a cautious estimation of Zeller as a man of uncommon natural talent and wide knowledge; his views on the transcendence of God and the immortality of the soul, it continued, were somewhat uncertain, but he did not agree completely with Strauss and he emphatically denied the atheistic ideas of Bruno Bauer and Feuerbach. The Ministry, however, was not at this stage inclined to proceed further and the matter was set to one side.[14]

[12] 'Zur Charakteristik der modernen Bekehrungen', *JG*, 1845, pp. 415–25.
[13] Zeller to Schwegler, 14 May 1846.
[14] Richard Feller, *Die Universität Bern 1834–1934*, chapter III.

However in August 1846 the Bernese, for the first time, elected the Great Council directly and gave the radical party a decisive majority. The radicals were not slow to make use of their mandate and every branch of social, political, and religious life was subjected to the strict criticism of the new emancipated thinking. Economy, education, ethics, and, not least, the Church—all were to be reformed according to the enlightened views of Bruno Bauer, Feuerbach, and the Young Hegelians, who wanted to sweep away all the supernatural superstitions and replace them with those concepts which had been purged by the liberating fire of reason.

The local newspaper in Bern, the *Berner Zeitung*, also came under the control of the radicals, who, being bitterly opposed to the Church, advocated the most extreme anti-traditional and anti-ecclesiastical views; and if all the radical plans were not expressed openly, the anonymous pamphlet circulating in Bern presented a fairly accurate picture of the changes which would take place in the future in the realm of university education: the old professors were to be dismissed and only the younger radicals would be allowed to teach; there would be full freedom for all views (by which was meant all radical views); only free-thinking men would receive promotion, and the judgement of the students would decide those worthy to teach. Attendance at lectures would not be compulsory and all qualifications for attending university would be done away with—the only essential qualification being a free and radical spirit.[15]

In this new situation, Ries, now an important figure in the radical party, once more renewed his attempt to have Zeller appointed to the vacant chair of Biblical exegesis. The radicals were enthusiastic. They wanted someone who would tear down the old obsolete dogmas of the Church, someone who would undermine the Church, educate the laity in the new rational paths of thought, and dispense with the old orthodox superstitions.

Zeller was just the man they required and on 12 January 1847, without even consulting the theological faculty, the new Government appointed him assistant professor of New Testament exegesis, with a salary of 1600 francs. However, before considering the repercussions of this event we turn our eyes to another important milestone in Zeller's life.

[15] Ibid., pp. 133–4.

ENGAGEMENT TO EMILIE BAUR

Zeller's engagement to Baur's daughter Emilie in 1847 was not his first. In 1836 he had become attracted to the sixteen-year-old sister of his friend Gustav Bockshammer, although he had to wait another four years before asking for her hand. The answer was affirmative but early in the following year (1841) Bertha broke off the engagement. Why she did so is not completely clear. In his autobiography Zeller gave the impression that the reason lay in the uncertainty of the new academic career on which he had just embarked, but this cannot have been the whole story, for, he continued: 'She had to act as she did, when she had once come to the conviction that she had deceived herself about me or had deceived herself into believing that I would be able to make her happy.'[16]

Another motive may have been that after the adverse criticism of Zeller's lectures during the stormy winter semester of 1840/1, Bertha discovered that she and Zeller did not share the same views about the Christian faith; but probably it was a combination of all these reasons which brought the engagement to an end.

Zeller's attention was now drawn to Baur's elder daughter Emilie, but since his position as a lecturer was somewhat precarious on account of his religious views, he was in no position to ask her to marry him until he received word of his appointment at Bern.

In my frequent visits to Baur I became better acquainted with his sister, who had kept house for him since the death of his wife in 1839, and also with Emilie, the elder of his two daughters, for whom I conceived a deep affection. This affection, however, had to be suppressed in my heart, so long as I could offer her nothing more than the uncertain position of a lecturer to whom, under the law at that time, teaching could at any moment be forbidden. She was not of great beauty but everything about her had its own particular charm: the dainty and yet not weak figure, her light, flexible walk, the vivacious yet never unbecoming movements, the small oval of her face which looked out into the world with childlike innocence from an abundance of dark curls, her intelligent, perceptive eyes, so searching and at the same time so friendly; but above all the warm heart, the bright, living personality which shone out and which, combined with her great unpretentious-

[16] *Erinnerungen*, pp. 132–3.

ness, won for her at all times in her life so many faithful and devoted friends among both young and old.[17]

The confirmation arrived at last on 16 January 1847 and the way was now open to ask for Emilie's hand.

As soon as I had written to my mother about the turning of my fortune I hastened to Baur, who held his lecture from 8 to 9 a.m., in order to tell him the news, and when I came out of his rooms I went to the ladies in the house with the same intention. There I was in luck. At such an early hour the aunt was not yet dressed to receive visitors, but her niece had no grounds to hide herself from me and so I was with her without anyone else being present in the same hour in which the letter informing me of my call to Bern removed the ban which had hitherto forced me to remain silent. I did not want to miss profiting from this happy wind of fortune and after telling of my news I added the request that she might follow me into the new country where I was going. I could not demand an immediate answer but she promised to give it to me on the following day, and as I once more appeared at the appointed time she stretched out her hand to me and to the covenant which has given me fifty-seven years of wedded-happiness.[18]

THE CONTROVERSY AT BERN

The high-handed manner in which Zeller had been appointed was not something that the orthodox could take sitting down. The indignation aroused was naturally considerable since the majority of the orthodox held Zeller to be a rank unbeliever who denied all the fundamental doctrines of the Christian faith. It was asking too much when they were merely expected to acquiesce in the appointment of such a man as Zeller, who would have the responsibility of instructing the future pastors of the Church in the field of New Testament exegesis. The battle had to be fought as it had been fought in 1839 at Zürich, when Strauss had been prevented from taking up his appointment.

The first pamphlet to appear was a long 106-page brochure by Archdeacon Baggesen, who presented a summary of Zeller's views and showed their incompatibility with the traditional doctrines of the Christian faith.

The result of the previous investigation is that the criticism of Herr Dr. Zeller, as of the School generally to which he belongs, has created

[17] *Erinnerungen*, pp. 146–7.   [18] *Erinnerungen*, p. 147.

an empty space for itself by denying to Holy Scripture not only all divine authority and inspiration but also all veracity and credibility, *in order to get rid of all the central doctrines of the Christian faith*—the doctrine of God, of the creation, of the origin of sin, of Christ, of the redemption through him and of a life after death.

But someone will say, Zeller has, at any rate, left us *Christian ideas*. We will see how much Christianity is left in these ideas and at this point we will just draw attention to what is robbed from faith when the facts upon which faith depends are taken away. How shall the preachers with joyousness *proclaim the mighty works of God*—and this proclamation is still the evangelical gospel, from the first Pentecost until now—when they do not believe in these works, indeed when they know nothing of such works? And how shall the people—and I include here again educated and uneducated together—be edified, strengthened, and consoled with mere ideas which everyone can conceive as he likes; and how shall the people repent and know that they have been reconciled, how shall they be converted and sanctified when they never hear of a living God and a personal Saviour? Or will Herr Zeller commit the monstrous act of hypocrisy which would lie in proclaiming the facts of the gospel without believing in them himself?

That, at any rate, would be the task of the preachers whom he would train, if they should mount the pulpit with his views.[19]

This brochure was followed by two shorter, anonymous pamphlets, 'The Calling of Dr. Zeller' and 'Dr. Zeller and his teaching', the first setting forth the teaching of the Church, with which the views of Dr. Zeller were then compared.

The Christian Church confesses one *God* who exists as spirit independent of the world; he created the world from his own free pleasure and it is created only through him without being mingled with him. Herr Zeller confesses to the doctrine that God and world are at the same moment eternally and inseparably bound together, that God is not a real personality, but only in so far as we human beings imagine him to be.

The Christian Church believes and confesses a personal continuation of each human being after death, and the *immortality* of the soul; the pantheistic school, on the other hand, to which Herr Zeller belongs, denies the continuation of man's rational personality after death.

The Christian Church confesses and believes that Jesus Christ is the Son of God, who according to the Spirit was from eternity one with

[19] C. Baggesen, 'Bedenken gegen die Berufung des Herrn Dr. Eduard Zeller', pp. 48–9.

God and proceeded from God, that he entered into time, becoming incarnate, and as the Son of Man was again exalted to glory. Herr Dr. Zeller, on the other hand, perceives in Jesus of Nazareth only an outstanding man about whose life and deeds one knows little that is certain and which in character are no different from the life and deeds of other men, at most the differences being only a stage in the development of the religious consciousness.

The Church believes and confesses the whole of the New Testament as a part of God's word and as an inerrant source of Christian revelations, because all twenty-seven books of the New Testament have been composed by direct disciples or contemporaries of our Lord under the special guidance of the Holy Spirit; and so these books form one part of *Holy Scripture* upon which we may place our trust as the inerrant word of God; otherwise Herr Zeller. Of the twenty-seven books of the New Testament he allows only five to stand as genuine writings from the apostolic period and he designates all other books of the New Testament (including the four Gospels) as unauthentic, interpolated, and untrustworthy forgeries of a later time or unknown author. Thus, for Herr Zeller the concept of *Holy* Scripture vanishes and with such presuppositions one can well imagine what his interpretation of Scripture will be like.[20]

The Government was incensed and initiated an inquiry into the identity of the author, the prison chaplain, Emanuel von Fellenberg, who was then arrested and sentenced to one year's imprisonment for criticizing the State in matters of religious policy. Such was the freedom of expression under the new regime! The author of the second pamphlet, the pietist Christoph Hoffmann, only escaped a similar fate because he lived in Württemberg. On the other hand, the Bern Government allowed the free circulation of an anonymous pamphlet in which the orthodox were insulted in the strongest language.

But who, then, are those who are raising the hue and cry about the danger confronting religion? Come out into the open and let yourselves be seen! Ugh, so it's you, you Biblicists and pietists! Bankrupt in body and soul you stand there like half-dried-up, leafless trees on a gloomy, raw, misty autumn day. Ugh, we want nothing to do with you, you have already brought so much discord into the land and disturbed so much happiness; you gnaw on the marrow of our Swiss people who are otherwise so healthy. We will not listen to you, we want nothing

[20] Emanuel von Fellenberg, 'Die Berufung des Dr. Zeller', pp. 6–7.

of your religion. Without perhaps knowing it you are doing spade-work for the Jesuits and you belong with them in the same family.

Like a sharp, hot wind, Zeller will scare away the grey mist of piousness and the stinking fumes of the hypocritical Biblicism; a fresh generation of religious teachers, who love freedom and are inwardly bound up with the good of the people, will arise in our midst. So then let the toads and the newts remain croaking and groaning in their muddy swamps.[21]

In his absence Zeller was defended by Ries—now appointed professor of philosophy—who declared that Zeller was no Dr. Strauss and assured that Zeller accepted all the essential doctrines of the Christian faith. 'When, therefore, in "The Calling of Dr. Zeller" it was said at the close: "Herr Zeller denies and disputes all the basic doctrines of Christianity, indeed all the basic beliefs of religion", then we also must conclude with the declaration, that this assertion is a falsehood which reaches up to the heavens.'[22]

In vain, however, did the orthodox protest and write their pamphlets, for the new Government was now firmly in the saddle and any hopes of a conservative *coup* like that in Zürich were not to be entertained. For Zeller's calling to Bern was not merely a theological issue, but also a political one: it was a test of strength between the new radical programme of the Government and the old conservative traditions. If the appointment had not been ratified, then the Government's authority would have been placed in jeopardy, which the Government had no intention of allowing. A vigorous campaign on Zeller's behalf was conducted by the more radical students, who demanded that the University senate support the appointment. The senate, however, had other views on the matter and rejected the proposal by twenty votes to eight, whereupon the enraged editor of the *Berner Zeitung* published the names of all who had opposed Zeller's appointment and held them up to ridicule. 'In opposition to this, the thoroughly worthless senate of the University deemed it good by twenty votes to eight not to fight for the right of freedom to teach, but to open door and gate for the suppression of scientific thinking.'[23]

The Great Council met on 24 March 1847 and Blösch, the

[21] 'Die Zeller'sche Religionsgefahr in Kanton Bern', pp. 8–9; 12.
[22] F. Ries, 'Auch ein Wort über die Anstellung des Dr. Zeller', p. 9.
[23] R. Feller, op. cit., p. 140.

most able speaker in the whole assembly, led the protest against the appointment; but it was of no avail and the radicals emerged victorious by 118 votes to 23. The affair, however, was not yet ended. When Zeller came to Bern in April there were fears for his safety. The coachman who brought him from Basel was instructed to let no one know the identity of his passenger and the house where Zeller spent the first two weeks in Bern was watched every night by members of the radical party.

Nor was the pamphlet war yet over. Ries's assurance of Zeller's orthodoxy somehow did not ring true and Baggesen in reply asked whether Ries was not using the same theological words with a different meaning. Moreover, he questioned whether or not Ries's assurances that Zeller believed the fundamental Christian doctrines were really to be trusted.

When, further, it is confessed in Zeller's name: 'Moreover, we believe in Christ as the Son of God, who according to the Spirit was from eternity one with God and proceeded from God', then we must ask: Where has Zeller made this confession of faith? We have not found it in the twenty-one issues of his *Theologische Jahrbücher* which we have been reading since 1842 and have gone through again for the most part recently. The historical Jesus at least, whom we know and in whom we believe, the Jesus of the four Gospels, has nowhere, according to our knowledge, been acknowledged by Dr. Zeller as the only-begotten Son of God, who from eternity was one with God and proceeded from God. Rather, he teaches about this Jesus that we have no historically attested records concerning his Person and life and that Paul was the originator of the supernatural view about the Person of Christ.[24]

Slowly the excitement died down and Zeller was able to begin his lectures before a small group of students without any disturbances. On 22 June 1847 he and Emilie were married in Tübingen in a ceremony conducted by Dr. Baur and apart from minor incidents their life in Bern together during the next two years was relatively uneventful. Friend and foe alike were surprised, since most of the citizens had expected a fiery revolutionary, whereas Zeller was in fact socially conservative and not enamoured of the radical Government. He led a quiet life, keeping out of politics, and his lectures were no stirring political diatribes but calm,

[24] C. Baggesen, 'Offenes Sendschreiben an Herrn Fr. Ries', p. 5.

thoughtful, and intellectually too difficult for most of his hearers. The radicals became disillusioned with their new professor and turned sourly away.

PROFESSOR IN MARBURG

Zeller remained two years in Bern but found his work on the second volume of his history of Greek philosophy hampered by the inadequacy of the library. The death of Schneckenburger in 1848 was also a sad blow since Schneckenburger had been his closest friend and confidant. Moreover, relations with Ries had chilled owing to a growing animosity between their wives, which slowly poisoned their own personal friendship. In these circumstances, therefore, Bern became more and more unpalatable and it was a welcome post which brought a letter from Professor Gildemeister in Marburg inquiring if Zeller would be willing to accept a call to the theological faculty there. Zeller stated his readiness to go but wondered whether it might not be more advisable for him to be called to the philosophical faculty. In reply to this suggestion, Gildemeister wrote that they already had someone else in mind and Zeller thus consented to accept the theological chair. However, as he wished to give the Bern Government time to find a replacement and as his wife was due to have their first child, he requested the Ministry of Education in Marburg to defer his commencement until the autumn, to which request the Ministry acceded. In the meantime, however, the radical winds of the 1848 Revolution had blown themselves out and were now succeeded by the conservative winds of counter-reaction. For Zeller the situation was extremely delicate as the Crown Prince of Hesse wanted to know nothing of the appointments which the former liberal Minister had made. The orthodox believers, at whose head stood August Vilmar, the influential director of the secondary school, drew up a sharply worded petition protesting that such an appointment was nothing less than an attempt to turn the Christian theology taught in the University into an un-Christian theology, to educate the theological students against the Church, and to undermine the whole Christian religion throughout the land. Such would be the consequences if a man of Zeller's anti-Christian attitude were permitted to hold such an important position in the theological faculty. 'Herr Dr. Zeller has obviously fallen away from the Christian faith, or, to use his own expression, Christianity, according to his view, has become completely antiquated.'[25]

The Crown Prince was in a difficult position and the dilemma was only resolved when Zeller agreed to exchange the theological for the philosophical faculty, a decision 'in which he had no part but which was not in opposition to his own inclinations'.[26]

With this exchange of faculties Zeller's theological career may be said to have come to an end, although theological works still continued to flow from his pen—the commentary on Acts in 1854, the portrayal of the Tübingen School (1860), and his lengthy biographical sketch of Baur in 1861. But apart from a number of smaller essays and theological reviews, Zeller's time was now primarily devoted to philosophical subjects and he was not permitted to lecture in theology.

His anonymous article on the Tübingen School provoked a refutation from Ritschl[27] who described the unknown author as a 'non-theologian' who had misunderstood Baur's views. This led to a debate on the question of miracles, in the course of which Ritschl was cut to pieces by Zeller's penetrating thrusts, the final *coup de grâce* being administered when the identity of the 'non-theologian' was finally revealed.

The years which Zeller spent in Marburg (1849–62) were marked by both happiness and suffering. He found a circle of talented men who shared his interests, and relations in general were cordial; on one occasion, however, he was almost forced to fight a duel with a sensitive and hot-blooded colleague, who was only with great difficulty persuaded that Zeller's ribald, *Quod licet Jovi, non licet bovi*,[28] was not meant to refer to him.

Four children were born during these years, August (1850), Otto (1853), Heinrich (1857), and Richard (1858), but tragedy struck the household in 1854 when both the eldest son Paul and then Otto died of diphtheria within a few days of each other. Perhaps it was as a result of this tragedy that Zeller put into action a plan which had been in his mind for some time. In

[25] Fr. Wiegand, 'Eduard Zeller's Berufung nach Marburg und August Vilmar', *HZ*, CV (3.F.9) (1910), p. 292.
[26] Th. Ziegler, 'Eduard Zeller', *Protestantische Monatshefte*, XII (1908), p. 205.
[27] 'Über geschichtliche Methode in der Erforschung des Urchristenthums', *JDT*, 1861, pp. 429–59.
[28] What befits Jupiter does not befit an ox.

Marburg the beggars were a problem and Zeller proposed public
action which would help the poor and put an end to scroungers.
A survey was made, the town divided into areas, and a society
drawn up to administer contributions to the fund. Such successes
made Zeller an honoured and valued member of the community
and on his departure for Heidelberg in 1862 honorary citizenship
of the town was bestowed upon him.

THE FINAL YEARS

The call to Heidelberg, which Zeller received in 1862, was
especially welcome since he had many friends there and it promised
him a larger sphere of influence. The inaugural address which he
delivered in the same year formally marked the end of his acceptance of the speculative philosophy which he had long previously
discarded. It was Strauss who had introduced the new Hegelian
ideas into Tübingen and Strauss who had been Hegel's foremost
apostle in Württemberg. If Zeller had not been quite as enthusiastic as his friend, he had, nevertheless, been in agreement on the
essentials, and Hegel had been the compass which had guided
him in his early years through the ocean of philosophy.

In the early 1840s he had stood solidly on the speculative basis,
but the new critique of Feuerbach and the retreat of Strauss soon
gave rise to doubt, and the slow process of disengagement from
Hegel was finally completed by the end of the 1840s. And now, in
1862, this abandonment of Hegel was formally signalized in the
declaration that philosophy must return to Kant.

In 1872 Adolf Trendelburg died and Zeller received a call to
Berlin, then second only to Leipzig in importance. At first he was
not enthusiastic but after a week's visit to the Prussian capital his
objections were overcome and he finally accepted. A further call
which came to him from Leipzig was declined.

This year also saw the appearance of Strauss's last book, *The
Old Faith and the New*. Even Zeller remained dissatisfied, as is
shown by his letter to Kuno Fischer.

What do you say about Strauss's latest book, whose third edition is
already being printed? It is a masterpiece of literary art and I am
naturally in agreement with by far the greatest part. But in my opinion
he slips too easily over a few basic problems, especially the question
of materialism, the grounding of ethics, and the concept of the first

cause, which the oneness of the world still forces upon us. He is still far more a critic than a productive philosopher.[29]

This dissatisfaction, however, remained in the family and was never expressed publicly. On Strauss's death two years later Zeller composed a small biography of his friend, edited the twelve volumes of Strauss's 'Collected Works', and in 1895 published selections of Strauss's letters. His friendship with Strauss remained unbroken to the end.

For a further twenty years he remained in Berlin and his students could be numbered by the thousand. With the celebration of his eightieth birthday, however, he felt the necessity of returning to his native Württemberg. His son Albert was now a medical doctor in Stuttgart and here Zeller spent the remaining years of his life. On his ninetieth birthday he received a shower of greetings and congratulations signifying the honour in which he was held. The death of his wife shortly afterward—they had shared fifty-seven years of married life—saddened the remaining four years before his death on 19 March 1908.

Zeller was and remained all his life a pantheist. His God was not a personal, transcendent Creator of the world and the Father of Jesus Christ, but rather the creative basis of all life and existence. As to the historical Jesus, he stood by Strauss and regarded the supernatural Person of Christ as the mythical embellishment of the early Church. A life after death was something in the realm of speculation and all the fundamental beliefs of the Church were scarcely any more to him than scholastic ingenuities and hair-splitting subtleties. Happiness was to be found alone in a circumspect moral character. 'Man's blessedness is found in the moral unity within himself.'[30]

[29] Zeller to Kuno Fischer, 22 Nov. 1872.   [30] *Kleine Schriften*, II, p. 471.

4. Albert Schwegler

THE biographical sketch by Zeller is the fullest account of Schwegler's life that we possess, but Zeller, as Strauss remarked in a letter to the author, knew how to conceal carefully the less attractive features of Schwegler's life and personality.

I have read your sketch of Schwegler's life this very morning so as not to delay its publication, and hasten to send it back to you with my thanks for your letter. I can't think of anything which needs altering; I find it, just as it is, perfectly fitted to its purpose, and when one considers the dry material you had to work on, really excellent. For neither Schwegler's personality nor his life was actually of a biographical nature. That fact you knew how to disguise admirably by weaving the characterization into the narrative, by introducing extracts from his letters and the like. And yet you have indeed portrayed the man just as he was.[1]

Albert Schwegler was born on 10 February 1819, the eldest of nine children, in the Württemberg village of Michelbach (about four miles south of Schwäbisch Hall), where his father was the local minister. Developing early in childhood, both physically and mentally, he soon revealed an alert mind and showed unusual independence of thought. At the age of four he could read well and under the guidance of his father made rapid strides in Latin and Greek. The years from ten to thirteen during which he attended the school at Schwäbisch Hall were among the happiest of his life and it was related that he used to give part of the money he received from school prizes to some of the poorer children in Michelbach.

During the next four years, from 1832 to 1836, the former Cistercian abbey in the quiet and beautiful valley of Schöntal became his home. Founded in 1155 it experienced many misfortunes in its history, being plundered by peasants, occupied by troops and more than once flooded. But the large baroque church with its twin towers and beautifully sculptured marble interior still calls silently to the weary traveller, 'Here you will

---

[1] Strauss to Zeller, 13 Nov. 1857; in Strauss's *Ausgewählte Briefe*, p. 374.

find peace.' And in these peaceful surroundings, Schwegler along with thirty other boys applied himself to Greek, Latin, and Hebrew in preparation for his theological study at the University. In the autumn of 1836 he graduated from Schöntal and took up residence at the Tübingen Stift. Becoming immediately absorbed in the study of Hegel's philosophy, which at that time had reached the peak of its influence in Tübingen, he set out to master the *Phenomenology* and the *Logic*. Such was his zeal that he soon outstripped the rest of his classmates. At first he was convinced of the validity of the Hegelian system, but slowly doubts arose and he had to admit that the speculative metaphysics did not satisfy him, although he continued to occupy himself with the problems involved. Another influence at this time was Schleiermacher, but Schleiermacher as critic and philosopher, and not as theologian; Schleiermacher's concept of theology, in Schwegler's opinion, was too limited.

From the speculative metaphysics Schwegler turned his attention to another field much more suited to his lively imagination, his critical oversight of large masses of historical material and his architectural talent: the historical investigation of the New Testament. In 1836 the seminary was in ferment over Strauss's *Life of Jesus* which had just appeared in the previous year. Schwegler too was gripped by the epoch-making work. He had by this time lost any faith he might ever have had in the traditional beliefs of the Church and was therefore so much the more receptive to the new ideas which Strauss had presented. Either, along with Hengstenberg, one rejected the whole development of Biblical criticism, or drew the logical conclusions as Strauss had done. The former alternative, in Schwegler's view, was obscurantist, and he was both depressed and enraged by Strauss's removal from his position as tutor at the seminary.

To proclaim the truth openly and unreservedly in our days requires self-renunciation and great courage. The world is terrified before the truth. O that I could trample down this cowardly and insidious generation! But what is now whispered in the chambers will be preached on the roof-tops; a time will come when the bronze tongues of this century will be loosened and Strauss will no longer stand isolated.[2]

---

[2] From Schwegler's diary (now lost); quoted Zeller, in the foreword to Schwegler's *Römische Geschichte*, III, pp. xi–xii.

But even as Schwegler wrote these words he reflected as to whether he could really be a follower of Strauss and the more he studied the *Life of Jesus* the more he found to criticize, so that finally he came to the conclusion he could write a work just as well, while standing on a firmer historical basis. Indeed, he even conceived the plan of writing a merciless criticism of Strauss's book, a plan which was soon afterwards abandoned. Schwegler's thoughts during this period were vague and confused. While basically accepting the Hegelian philosophy, he was continually beset by doubts and he attempted to formulate a system of his own. Christianity was to be based on the personality of Christ instead of on an abstract metaphysical and moral principle. Schwegler wanted a practical and not merely a theoretical system; he even wondered whether he might not become a pietist—a concern, wrote Zeller, that had little hope of fulfilment.

A much more lasting and important influence upon him was that of Baur, who had been laying the foundation for his extensive investigation into the early Church. In Baur's studies on the church at Corinth and the Pastoral Epistles, Schwegler found a scholarly command of the material combined with penetrating criticism and an unusual sharpness of perception in detecting hidden historical situations which lay beneath the surface of the Biblical narratives. A new vista of the early Church began to open up before him and from this time onwards he gave himself to historical criticism with a fresh enthusiasm. After the writing of two prize-essays on 'The relationship between the ideal and the historical Jesus' and 'Montanism' he emerged from the University in 1839 as *primus* of the *Promotion*, also gaining the prizes for preaching, and teaching the catechism.

For some months he was busy revising the second essay for publication as a book and in July 1841 he departed from Tübingen via Munich (where he remained a month studying the art treasures), Vienna, and Prague, arriving finally in Berlin at the beginning of October. But Berlin did not please him. He had expected much—perhaps even a position in the University—and was now disappointed. The orthodox ruled in the Church with a firm hand and those who came from the centre of unbelief and apostasy, Tübingen, received a chilly reception. Even from the Hegelians themselves the welcome was not as friendly as he had expected and from the following letter to Zeller it is not difficult to perceive his disillusionment.

What do you say to that, most-honoured friend? It would be of great value for me to hear your opinion of the matter or concerning other literary proposals which you could perhaps suggest. Here I have no one to whom I could go for advice on such questions. Vatke's bearing is far too formal for me to come to him and speak about such matters. The life here is a great burden on me. Silliness, obduracy, hypocrisy, and fawning in all places. Outside of Berlin one has no conception of how much the free course of literature languishes because of the high favour in which the clerics are held. We two— Planck and I—absolutely dare not visit the pious and we have been repelled by the characterless rabble which stand in the middle—e.g. Rheinwald—as those who are diseased. The Hegelian School has finally lost all courage and even its former factious spirit; most of them, Henning in the lead, capitulate; Vatke also, since the time he gained hope that his former ways will be forgiven, Vatke, who in our time generally more and more seems to remain behind, to *want* to remain behind the high opinion which we in Württemberg have of his theo- logical liberalism, although the very latest events, especially the King's refusal to grant him a salary along with the other seven assistant professors who were recommended, shows that he reckons falsely. Only Michelet, who has nothing more to gain, and Marheineke, who has nothing more to lose, fight on with the last courage of despair for the unlucky, God-forsaken Trojans . . . under the present circum- stances there is absolutely nothing for me to gain here.[3]

Although several others from Württemberg—including his school friend Karl Christian Planck—were also studying in Berlin at that time, Schwegler found the Berlin life 'oppressively boring' and was glad to leave at the beginning of May, returning home by way of Holland, Belgium, and the Rhineland to Schwäbisch Hall where his widowed mother (his father had died in 1839) now lived. The problem which now confronted him was that of finding a suitable position which would provide not only a liveli- hood but also the necessary time to continue his literary career. While in Berlin the Prince of Löwenstein-Werthheim had offered him a position as pastor, but acceptable as this would have been to his widowed mother, he decided against its acceptance on the grounds that it would restrict his opportunities for further

[3] Schwegler to Zeller, Jan./Feb. 1842.

study and the possibility of an academic post. In autumn 1842 he resolved to return to Tübingen and for some months he had oversight of the church in nearby Bebenhausen, supplementing his meagre income by giving private tuition and helping with the corrections of Peschier's French dictionary. Soon new avenues for his talents opened up before him. The *Hallische Jahrbücher* edited by Ruge had become more and more dominated by the radical party led by Bruno Bauer, and because of a deprecating attitude to Strauss, the younger members of the Tübingen circle began to consider producing a new scientific journal which would deal with the prominent issues of the day and the newest publications on art and literature. The banning of the *Hallische Jahrbücher* in 1842 accelerated these plans and Schwegler was appointed editor of the new *Jahrbücher der Gegenwart* whose first issue appeared in July 1843.

In the same year he habilitated in the philosophical faculty with a treatise on Plato's *Symposium*. He also had hopes of an appointment as tutor in the Stift, but was passed over, since his views were well known to be completely opposed to the traditional teaching of the Church, and he made little secret of his detestation of the orthodox theologians—that 'clerical rabble which puts a gag in one's mouth'. Nor were his prospects of academic promotion improved by his participation with Vischer and Zeller in the attack on his former friend Heinrich Merz. He had first encountered Merz in Munich in 1841 when Merz was then a zealous Hegelian. In the following year Schwegler enlisted Merz's help in arranging for the *Jahrbücher der Gegenwart* to be published and entreated him to contribute. However, during 1843 Merz was in the process of finding his way back to the orthodox faith and remained cautiously reserved. By 1845 he had completely returned to an acceptance of the traditional beliefs of the Church and on the publication of Vischer's inaugural address in 1845 Merz made a slashing attack on the new professor. Zeller leapt to the defence and in an article in the *Jahrbücher der Gegenwart* severely criticized Merz's former conduct. In his brochure 'The *Jahrbücher der Gegenwart* and its heroes' Merz declared that he had previously been deceived by the speculative philosophy. But God had had mercy upon him; his eyes had been opened to see the error of his ways and the grace of the Lord Jesus Christ in dying for his sins upon the cross. All that had happened before his conversion (Zeller's charge concerned writing articles under a false name) had thus to be explained in the light of this new turning-point in his life. To a large degree the controversy was a personal quarrel between Merz on the one side and Zeller and Schwegler on the other. But as Merz had now returned to the conservative fold the whole dispute only added fuel to the fire and exacerbated the wrath of the orthodox against Zeller and Schwegler.

The five years from 1842 to 1847 were the high-point of the social life of the Tübingen circle and every evening the younger intellectuals—Vischer, Zeller, Schwegler, Planck, and others— would meet at the inn after the day's work was over.

Schwegler, too, soon became part of this circle and maintained his own position in it. One of the more taciturn in the group, he usually only became talkative when the conversation took a literary, theological, or political turning, and especially when a serious debate arose; on many an evening he sat there silent, depressed because of his situation or occupied with his own writings and plans; yet the discussion of others did not escape his attention and often unexpectedly he would interject with an appropriate remark. The others left him to his thoughts; one or two had more personal contact with him and affinity of theological interests; all respected his capability and his rare intellectual qualities. And if he was unable to find among his friends a complete substitute for the unhappy state of his affairs, the social intercourse with them doubtless made his problems substantially lighter.[4]

Another portrait was sketched for us by Vischer.

A dark shadow above the eyes, the strong cheekbones, the tightly closed mouth expressed a hard, proud, and persistent nature; with this agreed the sallow colour of his smoothly shaven face, his thick-set body of more than normal height, the firmly set muscles, and a stiff posture of his left arm which had become one of his peculiarities in walking. Whoever did not know the man who went on his walks alone might well have taken him for an austere and imperious official; in Italy, as he himself jokingly related, he was often looked upon as an Austrian Army officer. But if one looked more closely into his features, if he once became talkative and communicative in society, then in the clear, imposing forehead which arched under his light-brown hair, in the fine contour of the regular nose, in the pleasing and eloquent formation of the lips, the agreeable, almost classical, rounding of the

[4] Zeller in Schwegler's *Römische Geschichte*, III, p. xxiv.

chin, then one immediately perceived his high intelligence, the ideality of his prosaic life, and that he had been called and was accustomed to an artistic training in the intellectual sphere. When the ice of his austerity had melted, the light-blue eyes twinkled good-naturedly and humorously, and a peculiarly soft ring of the bright, somewhat high voice—which one heard especially when he replied with short words of resignation to exhortations to enjoy life—betrayed clearly enough that under the pride and bitterness there was yet hidden a touching softness of heart, love and the need for love, a longing to open his heart, and a deep understanding of the world.[5]

In 1844 Schwegler undertook a new work, the two-volume 'Post-apostolic Age'[6] in which he set himself the task of describing the origin and development of the Church from the time of the apostles to the beginning of the third century. Baur had already sketched out the basic historical framework and Schwegler now contrived to fill in the details, to present a fuller picture of the period and of the origin of the New Testament books. An investigation of the historical Jesus, however, was purposely excluded, since Schwegler believed that on account of the untrustworthy nature of the historical sources such an examination could yield no positive result. The 900-page work occupied him just over a year and the actual writing was completed in six months. It was a brilliantly written book but poorly received, and the almost total lack of acknowledgement embittered him even more against the orthodox theologians. This work marked the end of Schwegler's theological activity and from that time onwards he devoted himself to his historical and philological writings.

In February 1846 he journeyed through Italy by way of Milan, Parma, Bologna, and Florence to Rome, where he spent some weeks studying the ancient monuments and art treasures. From Rome he travelled to Naples where he had the unpleasant experience of being robbed by his landlord. He had carefully locked his money in a chest but the cunning landlord possessed a duplicate key and Schwegler had to be thankful that only a part of the money was taken. At all events the theft did nothing to raise his extremely low opinion of the Italian people in general, and the Catholicism in Italy disgusted him. On returning to Naples after a long journey made on horseback to Sicily, he found

[5] *Schwäbische Lebensbilder*, IV, pp. 328–9.
[6] *Das Nachapostolische Zeitalter in den Hauptmomenten seiner Entwicklung* (Tübingen, 1846).

a letter from Zeller informing him that the King of Württemberg had refused to endorse a recommendation that he (Zeller) be appointed assistant professor of philosophy. In his reply Schwegler expressed his vexation at the news.

Unfortunately I received your last letter—for which my hearty thanks—very late, since it arrived here a few days after my departure for Sicily and has thus been lying here until my return the day before yesterday. Yet that was still time enough to hear the sad news which you sent me from the Württemberg homeland. I won't commiserate with you, since in your affair it is also a case of *mea res agitur*.[7] In the end it is good when the matter is brought to a head and the reaction advances swiftly to its last consequences, because then a recoil and counter-reaction must all the more surely and earlier follow. And to live through and watch the fall of a religion is a spectacle which one does not have every day. This glimpse of the Italian idol-worship has increased my anti-theological trenchancy about a lot of things. I have also resolved to hang on, come what may, and as much as I am able, to make the life of the clerics sour.[8]

Schwegler's trip to Italy was not a happy one but back in Tübingen he was no more contented and with Zeller's departure for Bern the Tübingen circle soon began to break up. 'The usual friends all send their greetings. I cannot tell you enough how much everyone here misses you. The social relationships have all become sick since your departure. I too have lost all desire to go to the inn and mostly remain at home in the evenings. I will bless the day which calls me away from Tübingen.'[9]

The only pleasure which now remained to him was his work. He was a personality, wrote Zeller, who was only content in strenuous activity, who felt lazy and dissatisfied as soon as he had no topic on which to write. In 1847 his translation and commentary on Aristotle's *Metaphysics* was published and in the following year his 'History of Philosophy', which went through three editions and was translated into English and Danish. After the March revolution of 1848 he was at last appointed assistant professor for Roman literature and ancient history; from that time forward he had no further financial problems, but happiness eluded his grasp. He had no close friends and cared little for those around him. Vischer, who at that period probably knew him

---

[7] It's my affair also. [8] Schwegler to Zeller, 19 June 1846.
[9] Schwegler to Zeller, 30 Apr. 1847.

better than anyone else, had little time for him. 'Society: For walks, excursions, discussions Dr. Baur and I. Schwegler also. This man, by the way, has become a consistent, cold egoist. He does nothing for either comrade or cause.'[10]

Marriage and family life might have softened his cold and repulsive nature, but by the time he was in a position to marry it was too late. Strauss suggested that he might be a possible match for the daughter of his friend Ernst Rapp, but Vischer was of a different opinion. 'Schwegler? I don't really know. He is frightfully dry towards women, absolutely indifferent to humanistic literature, discussions, etc. Wouldn't he be too wooden for both girls? Yet he won't bite, you will see.'[11]

And so Schwegler continued to withdraw more and more from society. His judgements grew harsher and more bitter; he became silent, rarely visiting or being visited. When in 1856 Köstlin attempted to revive the evenings at the inn, he invited Schwegler who came once and refused to come again, declaring to Köstlin that these strangers were absolutely repugnant to him. His only joy was found in writing his 'History of the Roman Empire'.

A fortune-teller had once prophesied that he would have a long life; the prophesy was not fulfilled and he died, aged only thirty-seven. His name on the large flat slab which lies above his grave has been almost erased by the weather and a more enduring and fitting tribute, with which we conclude, is found in the letter which Baur wrote to Vischer a few days after Schwegler's death.

Tübingen, 10 January 1857

Dear Vischer,

In the last few days I have often been thinking of you and was actually about to put pen to paper and write to you when I received your letter this morning. The news of our dear friend's sudden death cannot have come to you any more unexpectedly or shatteringly than it did to us here. So, as in a moment, was his life terminated with one stroke. On Monday he held his lecture, from 8 to 9 a.m. without his hearers noticing anything unusual about him; half an hour later his barber found him lying completely unconscious on the floor with foam all over his mouth. Everything that one tried to do in order to bring

---

[10] Vischer to Strauss, 15 Mar. 1850; *Briefwechsel zwischen David Friedrich Strauss und Friedrich Theodor Vischer* (2 vols; Stuttgart, 1952–3), I, p. 248.
[11] Vischer to Strauss, 13 Dec. 1855; ibid., II, p. 99.

him again to consciousness was in vain; there followed from time to time only great convulsions along with heart-rending, whimpering noises. Even on Monday his condition was so bad that no one believed he would live through the night, yet he lasted until 10.30 a.m. on Tuesday. In the dissection there was nothing found which could explain the cause of such an end; everything in him seemed to be healthy, but there can certainly be no doubt that he drew this sad catastrophe upon himself through his excessive, uninterrupted work and his way of life which more and more dispensed with all exercise and relaxation. Yesterday afternoon, in the company of a goodly number, we brought him to the place of his rest. Deacon Pressel gave a really fine and fitting oration, in which he presented a fairly true picture of his life and did not keep silent about the outrages which Schwegler had suffered. Those who spoke to him latterly would have noticed in him a light-hearted mood of a pleasant kind and a tendency which was not usual with him to go from one to the other. Recently I had not spoken with him so frequently, since he withdrew more and more, the last time being a few weeks ago when he brought me the second volume of his 'History of the Roman Empire'. At that time he complained extremely bitterly that along with a 200 fl. increase in salary for his work on the 'History of the Roman Empire', he had been imposed on with the burden of a new lecture, which he had to hold straightway in this winter semester. This was also unjust and certainly contributed to the complete exhaustion of his strength. When one considers how much this must have weakened his powers until his strong constitution finally succumbed, then it is clear that his work in the last few weeks must have exceeded all human measure. Do not believe that Tübingen killed him. I will write no apology for Tübingen and know only too well how little of interest one has here, but one must also not be unjust. Schwegler always had more friends here than I; did he not turn his back on one after the other? Whoever so principally disdains the little which the town offers finally sinks to ruin in the abstractness of his nature. But in addition there is also the hard lot which Schwegler had at home. How sour he had to become in the process of succeeding, how painful it was for him that he was never once made a tutor. Whoever from youth up sees himself compelled to work and to renounce—even when the work still has an intellectual interest for him—falls all too easily into such an excess of work. That the main guilt must finally be borne by his 'History of the Roman Empire' is also my belief, especially since he set his sights still higher because of his rivalry with Mommsen. It became, certainly, his misfortune and yet I believe that only in the writing of it was he in his actual element. He was extraordinarily fitted to deal with a great amount of material, to have a clear oversight of large periods of history, and to work through everything as accurately as possible. Clarity and perspicuity, sharpness of judgement and precision, rounding-off and perfection were thoroughly the characteristics of his brilliant intellect. His 'History of the Roman Empire' is also, as an unfinished work, the most worthy monument to his spirit. One can now contemplate it only with the comforting feeling that he rests from his work. Was he also without consciousness and feeling—as the doctors assure us—in the long period after the death-blow had fallen up to the time of his actual death, then we certainly cannot complain on his account. But for us, unfortunately, he has now gone! and what is more, not merely for us, his friends, but also for the poor sick mother who could not see the worthy son who was her support, even after his death!

I don't need to tell you how painful the fate of this dear friend is to me, he whom I always counted among the best-loved of my little circle. We had such a lot to do with each other in former days; we worked and fought alongside each other, and understood one another so well; even later, too, when he had turned completely away from theology I always felt myself attracted and stimulated anew whenever we again came together. If only this had taken place even more in the latter years, but who would have thought that we would have been separated from him so soon! So I must always see the best depart, one after the other, and stand here ever more lonely and forsaken.[12]

[12] Baur to Vischer, 10 Jan. 1857.

5. Karl Christian Planck

KARL Christian Planck was best known for his extremely complex philosophical system which no one but he himself was ever able to understand. The originality of his system—a mixture of Schelling, Hegel, and other philosophers—was unquestioned, but although a few of his pupils, friends, and family continued to campaign for his enigmatic syncretism, it is doubtful if even they ever managed to understand their master's views. After his death his ideas passed into the dust of obscurity. Planck chose to set himself in opposition to the main stream of philosophy and the main stream of philosophy passed him by. Anyone attempting to read his books today will soon come to the opinion that Planck's ideas are so complex, vague, and ethereal that they will always remain lying in the dust. Here, however, we are not so concerned with the later Planck, but with the earlier, the Planck of the Tübingen School.

Born in Stuttgart, Karl Christian entered the world on 17 January 1819, the first child of the revenue officer Johann Jacob Planck. From 1823 the family lived in Stammheim near Ludwigsburg, but as the schooling in the village was unsuitable, Karl Christian went to live with his grandfather in Grossbottwar where he attended the local school. This early separation from his parents may have contributed to his later shyness and introspection. After seven years in Stammheim his father was transferred to Blaubeuren and as here there was an excellent school where Latin received the highest priority, the family was able to be reunited for a further two years until 1823 when Karl Christian, having passed the necessary exams, entered the lower seminary in Schöntal.

A leisurely flowing stream which meanders through the peaceful valley of Schöntal, the wooded hills lying behind the former Cistercian monastery with its great baroque church—these attractions were part of the charming surroundings in which Planck spent the following four years. He proved to be a versatile student taking second place in the class to Schwegler with whom he was declared to be musically incompetent and incapable of singing in tune. He was often homesick, spent most of his time reading instead of playing with the other boys, and was reticent and reserved. According to one friend he used to wander around as if in a dream and the chief complaint against him was that he spoke too softly.

In the autumn of 1836 Planck entered the Tübingen Stift for five years' philosophical and theological study to which he dedicated himself with heart and soul. He attended a great variety of lectures ranging from history, logic, anthropology, psychology, Greek poetry, and Hebrew to mathematics, as well as lectures by Vischer on Aesthetics and Hegelian philosophy. During his theological semesters he heard lectures from Dorner and Ewald along with Baur's exposition of 1 Corinthians, the history of dogma, and the Gospel of John. As at Schöntal, he was placed second to Schwegler who received the mark of 1a; Planck 1b. Both entered for an essay prize on the subject 'The unity of the ideal and the historical Jesus'. In the judges' report Planck was commended for his 'mastery of the material and his perceptive thinking . . . nevertheless there is something blunt and harsh in the maintenance of the standpoint which he has taken. Schwegler's essay is characterized by spirit, learning, and thoroughness, by critical and perceptive judgement . . .' Schwegler was awarded the prize; Planck received special praise.

At the end of the five years the *Promotion* was generally praised although in the last semester there were many more cases of ill discipline than was usual. In the course of the years a group of students had formed which was a thorn in the flesh of the professors, who viewed the group's activities with great suspicion— especially the constant discussion of Hegelian philosophy and the youthful enthusiasm of the students for the new theological ideas of Strauss and Baur. Planck himself received thirty-six hours' solitary confinement and was warned for drunkenness.

For those students who had passed the final exam with the highest marks the obtaining of the doctorate was almost a formality. As a dissertation Planck composed a twenty-two-page (handwritten) work on the relationship of Islam to the modern world. Ewald, who at that time was Dean of the faculty, found the essay full of Hegelianisms, groundless opinions taken from newspapers, and lacking in a competent investigation of the sources. The other members of the faculty by and large concurred with this judgement and Planck received notice that his dissertation was not acceptable. On returning to Blaubeuren he composed another work dealing with the characteristics of the European people of the present age and this was accepted although without commendation. 'The result of my doctoral thesis', he wrote, 'is certainly not just as I might have expected; yet I have learnt to rise above such things.'

In the spring of 1841 Planck set off on a study trip to Berlin, which was granted to all promising young graduates desiring to follow an academic career. Supplied with letters of introduction from Baur he set off via Heidelberg, by boat down the Rhine to Cologne, and thence to Berlin by way of Göttingen, the Harz, and Magdeburg. He enrolled for two courses of lectures, one of which was by Vatke, but apparently did not attend frequently; his time in the city is perhaps best summed up by his own words: 'What I already previously thought—that there would not be very much for me to learn from the lectures here—has been completely confirmed. The main thing, therefore, is just to get to know the situation at Berlin and not to look for scientific instruction.' In the holidays he visited Dresden and on his return to Berlin he met Schwegler by the Brandenburg Gate just as Schwegler arrived in Berlin for the winter semester. During this semester, in which the number of students from Württemberg grew to nine, he heard Schelling lecture—without being particularly impressed—and was a frequent guest at the home of Marheineke. His main interest at this time was his work on the origin of Judaism but he also composed a review of Bruno Bauer's 'Criticism of the Synoptic Gospels' and a small pamphlet entitled 'Theological Votum', which aroused annoyance in Church circles and called forth a provocative reply from Bruno Bauer's brother, Edgar.

Just a piece of news about the *Deutsche Jahrbücher*. Ruge commissioned Planck to write a review of Bruno Bauer's book on the Synoptics. Planck sent it in but received it back after waiting almost two months (probably Ruge had previously consulted with Bauer himself) because the *Jahrbücher* could not accept anything that was not 'purely and wholly philosophy'. Planck now let his review—since it was already written—be published in the Berlin *Jahrbücher* whereupon Bauer now flew into a great rage and immediately wrote in the *Hallische Jahrbücher* an anti-criticism of such vehemence that it was struck out by the censor, 'because personal attacks may not be tolerated'. In the last few days I have found in the *Hallische Jahrbücher* a review of Planck's 'Theological Votum', a brochure which Planck wrote in the last days of his stay in Berlin. Planck's little work was ripped about quite rudely and arrogantly. And who is the reviewer, the so-called B. Radge? Obviously no one other than Bruno Bauer's brother, Edgar (transposed Radge). It's about time to put an end to the noise which the darling Bauer boobies have been kicking up on the literary market in the last few months.[1]

Even though Marheineke had given his recommendation, Planck had great difficulty finding a publisher for his book on the origin of Christianity.[2] Baur counselled that it should be published anonymously so that Planck's future career might not be harmed; for as a pupil of Baur Planck was already under suspicion, and Baur did not wish him to share the same fate as Schwegler who was passed over for the position of tutor in the Stift. However, an anonymous publication was declined by all publishers and Planck finally decided to allow the book to appear under his own name. A letter to Schwegler just after its publication gives us a glimpse into Planck's life and thought.

With regard to my book, I don't believe that it can do me much more harm than that caused me already by my theological viewpoint in general. Although in one place (namely what concerns the earliest history of Israel) I have been extremely critical, yet in other respects I have also allowed the Biblical representation considerably more validity than Vatke, for example, and really offensive passages are nowhere to be found.

I always still have some hope of a position as tutor in one of the lower seminaries as I still have an influential friend in Mander (please keep that to yourself) with whom my father has special business connections. But if I should exclude myself from this prospect because of my book, then to begin with I wouldn't know what to do, except to work away so that I could establish myself here in Tübingen for a time. At present I'm working with this aim in view on a larger book which strikes into philosophy and history. I think that the smaller book, which will be printed by the middle of April, will at least open up the road for others. What lies beyond this is naturally still mist and darkness; but I have always one last refuge—my pen. For a number of reasons I won't be able to hold out long in my present position, but a formal position as a curate would be abominable.[3]

---

[1] Schwegler to Zeller, 25 July 1842.
[2] *Die Genesis des Judenthums* (Berlin, 1843).
[3] Planck to Schwegler, 15 Mar. 1843.

Planck's desire for a position as tutor was finally fulfilled in the autumn of 1843 when he was called to Maulbronn. Here he was under no obligation to preach; nor was he directly involved in the religious life of the seminary, which was not unwished for on his part since he had now completely rejected the traditional Christian beliefs. The position also allowed him much more leisure time to devote to his philosophical studies and he was able to contribute a number of articles to Zeller's *Theologische Jahrbücher* and Schwegler's *Jahrbücher der Gegenwart*. After a year in Maulbronn Planck was called as tutor to the Tübingen Stift. He announced a series of lectures on the history of recent philosophy but these did not eventuate because no one enrolled. In the following two semesters he did not lecture, but in the summer semester 1847 he read philosophy of religion before twelve students. In order that he might become more independent of the Church he applied to be appointed lecturer in the philosophical faculty; but the faculty had reservations and attempted to hinder the appointment. There were doubts about his capability to lecture and the faculty therefore required him to submit an essay on some philosophical theme which was then to be defended by open disputation. Planck spent the autumn and winter months of 1847/8 working on the essay and also on his first full-length (883-page) book 'The Ages of the World'[4] which finally appeared two years later in 1850-1. With the successful defence of his thesis in March 1848 he was granted the *venia legendi* which gave him the right to hold lectures—always poorly attended—and after obtaining Schwegler's old position as librarian in the Stift he was assured of a small but fixed income which enabled him to give up his position as tutor.

During these years Planck's articles in the Tübingen journals of Zeller and Schwegler made an important contribution to the rise and development of the Tübingen School. Above all it was Planck who first tackled the problem of the historical Jesus and his relationship to Judaism. In his articles 'The Principle of Ebionism'[5] (1843) and 'Judaism and Early Christianity'[6] (1847) he discussed the question which Baur and Schwegler had chosen to ignore. But Planck was dissatisfied with his position in Tübingen.

[4] *Die Weltalter* (2 vols.; Tübingen, 1850-1).
[5] 'Das Princip des Ebionitismus', *TJ*, 1843, pp. 1-34.
[6] 'Judenthum und Urchristenthum', *TJ*, 1847, pp. 258-93; 409-34; 448-506.

The philosophical faculty turned more and more against him and it became clear that he had no further hope of advancement. His 'Catechism of Law' was severely criticized by Robert von Mohl as 'an offspring of Utopian madness' and the greater part of the edition, which had been published at Planck's own cost, remained unsold. For these reasons he applied for a position of senior teacher at a secondary school in Ulm and with his departure from Tübingen in 1854 his active engagement in the ranks of the Tübingen School came to an end.

The later years of his life may be sketched very briefly. After a difficult beginning at Ulm his new position became easier and following his marriage in 1856 there blossomed a happy family life. Twelve years later he resigned his position in order to take up a teaching post at the lower seminary in Blaubeuren where he hoped for more time to devote to his philosophical writings. His books were voluminous treatises covering almost every conceivable aspect of the relationship of man to the world— astronomy, physics, chemistry, botany, zoology, physiology, psychology, anthropology, evolution (Planck opposed Darwin's views), and the laws of nature, metaphysics, Christianity, and much more. However, his writings were scarcely acknowledged or even noticed, not least on account of the great difficulty in understanding the strange ideas expressed within their covers.

The year 1877 brought great disillusionment. He had expected to be appointed to the position of *Ephorus* in the Blaubeuren seminary but was passed over in favour of a younger man. Köstlin was of the opinion that pietist influences had taken offence at Planck's heterodox Christian viewpoint, but it is clear that Planck lacked the necessary practical qualities for the position. Shortly afterwards the chair of philosophy at Tübingen became vacant and Planck applied for the appointment. He was warmly supported by his friend Köstlin, and his former pupils also handed in a petition on his behalf. The faculty, however, was of another mind and decided that he was unacceptable.

Against Planck's appointment is first his age ... but then also the whole character of his activity as a writer. His numerous works—in spite of all the pains taken by the author—are so difficult to understand that the reading of them creates great problems, not only for students but also for those more versed; likewise, with respect to his philosophical lectures, the difficulty in understanding his thought has never been disputed by his pupils. The ideas which he advocates are un-doubtedly original; but they are, at the same time, partly so foreign, partly so opposed to the whole course of philosophical studies in the last decades, as exemplified in the problems growing out of the advance of knowledge generally and especially of the natural sciences, that they have scarcely been able to exercise any influence. We cannot, therefore, expect from Planck a teaching activity corresponding to the needs of his students and which would introduce them to the present stand of philosophical thought.[7]

It was rather as a consolation prize that in 1879 Planck was appointed *Ephorus* in the lower seminary at Maulbronn. But he had not long to live. Soon after Christmas in that same year his strength began to wane; he suffered from great depression and after a nervous breakdown, an inflammation of the lungs precipitated his death on 7 June 1880.

On his tombstone in Stuttgart were inscribed words from his last work, edited by Köstlin and published posthumously in 1881. 'Pure selfless activity is, in its origin, everything; in the selfless translucent willing and working of the eternal total-order of the universe is also thy goal, O man.'[8]

We conclude with the words of Planck's famous nephew, Max Planck.

He stepped on the scene as a Reformer of philosophical thought, as a Reformer of social life and of political thought; he cast his ideas grandly and boldly into the world trusting in the power of the idea . . . But the times had changed since he began his career. At that time philosophical studies were still blossoming; it was still believed that the final and most perfect solution to all the great problems of science and life was only to be found in pure thinking. In this belief our friend both lived and died. But our age no longer shares this belief and so he walked within it as a stranger; he became a solitary figure and stood ever more isolated; even in the last period of his life as the evening shadows had already begun to fall he waited hopefully for a promising sign, a word of acknowledgement, indeed, even of notice: but none was forthcoming.[9]

[7] *Staats-Anzeiger für Württemberg*, Besondere Beilage, 1930, Nr. 6, p. 131.
[8] *Testament eines Deutschen* (Tübingen, 1881).
[9] *Zur Erinnerung an Karl Christian Planck* (Tübingen, 1880), p. 6.

6. Karl Reinhold Köstlin

As a personality Köstlin was the least interesting member of the Tübingen School. No outstanding events mark his life; he wrote no important books; he was never the centre of any theological or ecclesiastical controversy; he lived quietly in Tübingen all his later life, absorbed in his academic pursuits. A letter to Hilgenfeld in 1857 as Köstlin was in the process of stepping over from the theological to the philosophical faculty provides us a glimpse of the current opinion concerning him.

My affairs here now stand somewhat better; a disputation on aesthetics with a Dr. Andresen from Schleswig brought me commendation and turned many—especially those in the non-theological faculties —from the prejudice which easily devolves upon a lecturer who reads (as I did formerly) merely within the seminary walls; for it was considered that I was certainly a well-versed bookworm suited to stimulate aspiring theologians, but not the man for lecturing to classes.[1]

Karl Reinhold Köstlin was descended from a Württemberg family well known on account of its long line of pastors and its interest in culture and the arts. Köstlin's father was the *Ephorus* of the lower seminary in Urach, a charming little town surrounded by steep, wooded hills and nestling on the northern side of the Swabian Alb. Thus, almost from the time of his birth on 28 September 1819, it was foreseen that Karl Reinhold would follow in the footsteps of family tradition and become a pastor. At the age of fourteen he entered the lower seminary at Blaubeuren where he passed four happy years, before proceeding to the Tübingen Stift for the usual five years' philosophical and theological study. Here Baur and Vischer were the important influences in his life, while Strauss's *Life of Jesus* had just appeared and created great excitement in the seminary. Köstlin too fell under the influence of the new Hegelian and Straussian ideas although he was never particularly enthusiastic about the Hegelian philosophy.

[1] To Hilgenfeld, 25 May 1857.

A prize essay in 1840 on the concept of the Gospel in the New Testament provided him with the opportunity to display his talent and after carrying off the prize he passed his exams with distinction and was appointed curate at a village church. In 1843 he journeyed to Berlin in order to further his study and while there he revised his essay for publication. This appeared in the same year, as a moderate-sized book with the title: 'The Teaching of the Gospel and Letters of John and the Related New Testament Teaching'.[2] Of his stay in the Prussian capital we know nothing, but from a letter to his publisher in 1845 we learn that the book had no success.

That my book has had no success in Berlin does not surprise me when I consider the character of the parties there. One cannot fail to perceive that on the liberal side in Berlin and in Germany generally there prevails too much of the old rationalism and Hegelianism, too little tendency to investigate early Christianity scientifically and historically, too much arbitrary interpretation of Biblical doctrine, too much making hypotheses.[3]

From Berlin Köstlin returned to Blaubeuren as tutor in the lower seminary where he spent three years from 1843 to 1846. There followed three further years as tutor in the Tübingen Stift, the last year of which was spent in Stuttgart completing his doctoral dissertation. The question now uppermost in his mind was what he should do when his time as tutor came to an end, for he had no interest in a pastorate. He considered the possibility of accepting a position as assistant to a pastor in Brackenheim near Heilbronn, but the thought of even a limited amount of preaching and catechizing was so objectionable to him that he was continually in doubt.

You have I hope, in good part, so interpreted my long silence as meaning that my situation must be clear, because I haven't written a thing. The probability of actually being a curate at Brackenheim continually depressed me because it now seemed that the bitter apple might actually become a reality. Nor could I free myself from the depression through a trip to Urach in the previous week, and once I burst out so desperately in front of my parents that my father saw clearly I would find no inner peace in a curacy and he himself therefore

---

[2] *Der Lehrbegriff des Evangeliums und der Briefe Johannis und die verwandten neutestamentlichen Lehrbegriffe* (Berlin, 1843).
[3] To G. Bethge, 6 Dec. 1845. Original in the WLS.

urged me to take back my candidature. This, however, I allowed to remain because for other reasons I wanted to hold fast to a certain *terminus ad quem* and in addition I had selected the Brackenheim curacy (which requires only twelve sermons a year) for just that reason. Now, however, instead of me, Paret has been appointed to Brackenheim and—what is really poor—Wächter has been appointed to Blaubeuren instead of Calchreuter, a piece of dirty work which can only be explained by the fact that the Böblingen folk denounced Calchreuter and me as dangerous men, not only openly (which was already known) but also to the King himself; for both Consistory and Ministry seem to have been on Calchreuter's side. I am, praise God, now free from all doubts, have requested my father once more for his permission, and ask you now to send me an application form for habilitation.[4]

The situation was finally resolved with his acceptance as a lecturer in the theological faculty at Tübingen.

Köstlin contributed several articles to Zeller's *Theologische Jahrbücher* the most important of which was that on the history of early Christianity,[5] where he postulated a middle path. According to this view the rise of the early Church was not to be seen as a struggle between two hostile parties (Baur and Schwegler) nor as the immediate triumph of Paulinism (Ritschl) but as the growth of a middle and conciliatory party to which the majority of Christians belonged and from which the Catholic Church finally emerged. In his book on the Gospels[6] (1853) he put forward the hypothesis that while Mark in its canonical form was the youngest of the three Synoptic Gospels, Matthew and Luke had used an earlier version of Mark—a proto-Mark. Köstlin had never been completely in sympathy with the 'barren writings' of Baur and Schwegler and this book marked out his independent position within the School. In the eyes of the orthodox he was always regarded as one of Dr. Baur's protégés, although this would perhaps be too much to say as he strongly sought to maintain his own independence in theological issues. After Zeller's departure for Bern in 1847 Köstlin became Baur's right-hand man at Tübingen, being often called upon to mediate in the disagreements between Baur and Hilgenfeld. His closest and life-long friend was Planck, but he was also on good terms with Zeller, Schwegler,

---

[4] To Planck, 19 July 1849.
[5] 'Zur Geschichte des Urchristenthums', *TJ*, 1850, pp. 1–62; 235–302.
[6] *Der Ursprung und die Komposition der synoptischen Evangelien* (Stuttgart, 1853).

Hilgenfeld, and Volkmar. Ritschl also was highly regarded by him, as is evident from the following letter to Hilgenfeld in 1854.

You ask me in your letter about Ritschl and, if I understand rightly, about the purpose of his visit here. Regarding the latter I have heard nothing, either from him or from Baur, but he seems at any rate to have had the intention of bringing about more friendly relations with Baur; he wanted to do this also with Schwegler who, however, apparently greeted him coldly and brusquely. As regards myself I was very pleased to make his acquaintance and to be able to convince myself that I had earlier judged him too severely and especially in finding his polemic against Schwegler too intentional. I must confess that since I have learnt to know his shrewd, yet open and free character, I have been completely reconciled with him; although he is actively engaged in Church affairs one will have in him a constant defender of the principle of free investigation.[7]

On account of his known 'Tübingen' views, Köstlin was hindered in his attempts to obtain promotion in the theological faculty and not until 1853 following the publication of his book on the Gospels was he appointed assistant professor. But even this advancement was of little significance and it was quite clear that there was no hope of a full professorship. For this reason he decided to resign from the theological faculty and cross over to the philosophical, where his interest in literature, art, and aesthetics promised a better chance of promotion, impossible in the theological faculty. He took up his new position in 1858 and reported the news to Hilgenfeld shortly after:

It is time I let you hear from me once again and at the same time explained why I have only just got around to writing. The decision I made last year to apostatize from the theological faculty and cross over to the philosophical threatened me for a long time with the danger of sitting between two professorial chairs and so long as this possibility hovered over my head I could do nothing except say as little as possible to friends both near and far so as not always to speak and write of uncertain prospects. This long suspense is at last, thank heaven, at an end; I have now been appointed assistant professor of philosophy with a salary of 600 fl. My only regret is that I must say a complete farewell to theology—at least for the next few years. My field is limited to aesthetics and, at most, a few philosophical topics on which I have already lectured. Theology I will have to renounce in order to con-

[7] To Hilgenfeld, 21 Oct. 1854.

centrate on my present lectures and thus justify the trust placed in me that I will worthily represent aesthetics in spite of my relatively short preoccupation with it.[8]

His hopes of promotion were not disappointed and five years later came the desired appointment to the chair of German literature and aesthetics.

Köstlin's life would be summed up best in the word 'uneventful'. He lived simply and quietly, never married, was never in the public eye, and found his greatest pleasure in his writing on art and aesthetics, in his books, and in his thoughts. Apart from a year in Berlin during his student days and a few short journeys to Italy to study the Italian art treasures, he never left his native Württemberg. Neither a gifted nor a compelling speaker, his lectures were generally poorly attended although appreciated by a few who sought to penetrate deeper into the subject. He was apparently friendly, good-natured, and courteous, quiet and retiring. It was said that on his seventieth birthday he slipped away to Italy in order to avoid all festivities in his honour. On 18 December 1893 he suffered an attack of influenza which became complicated by inflammation of the lungs. From this illness he never recovered, and died on 12 April 1894. His name has long been forgotten; even his grave no longer exists.

His obituary concluded with the following words: 'He was a Swabian to the core and only those who knew him intimately realized his qualities. His name belongs to scientific study; personal respect for him as a teacher will never cease among those who have sat at his feet. His life portrayed that which was also the final goal of his scientific study: the harmony of being.'[9]

[8] To Hilgenfeld, 11 Feb. 1858.   [9] *SMSK*, 17 Apr. 1894, p. 762.

7. Albrecht Ritschl

RITSCHL was the apostate of the Tübingen School. He was at first its ardent supporter and enthusiastic member, but slowly distanced himself from Baur, taking up a position of independence while still attempting to maintain at least an outward agreement with the principles Baur had formulated. This was possible only as long at Ritschl did not bring his differences into the open, but since this was sooner or later inevitable, it was only a matter of time until the break between himself and Baur finally eventuated. Ritschl was the first North-German member to attach himself to the School, and after the departure of Zeller and Schwegler from the theological field, it appeared that he would become its new star. The story of Ritschl's relationship with Baur and the other members of the School during the eleven years of Ritschl's membership until his final act of apostasy will form the theme of the following pages.

Ritschl's father was a bishop in the Lutheran Church, General Superintendent of Pomerania, and First Preacher at the castle church of Stettin on the Baltic. The young Ritschl, born 24 March 1822, studied at Bonn where he came under the influence of Karl Immanuel Nitzsch. Three semesters later he went to Halle, where the Hegelian philosophy was then at the height of its influence, and after rejecting the pietism of Tholuck and Julius Muller, he espoused the new speculative ideas with an ardour matched among the other members of the School only by Zeller.

Even before his arrival in Tübingen, Ritschl had shown himself an adherent of the School by his attack on Dietlein's book on the origin of the Christian Church.[1] This anonymous review, signed simply —s—, appeared in the *Theologische Jahrbücher* for 1845 and provided Ritschl with his credentials of acceptance in Tübingen. His father grudgingly gave his consent to the desired semester in Tübingen and Ritschl arrived in his 'promised land' in the summer of 1845. He had long studied the writings of Baur and hoped to gain much from the personal intercourse with the members of the Tübingen circle and especially with Baur himself.

---

[1] W. O. Dietlein, *Das Urchristenthum* (Halle, 1845).

Schwegler, three years older than he and 'in spite of his learning still a very young man', appeared sympathetic. Of Zeller, there is no special mention and Ritschl described his meeting with Baur in a letter to his father. 'I have also visited Baur, the Master of the Tübingen School. He has a typical Swabian gruffness and a rather gauche manner, yet he was most polite and already on the previous day had made inquiries of Schwegler and Wolf after Zeller had told him of my arrival.'[2] In the course of the winter Ritschl and his Prussian compatriot Wolf used to meet regularly with the younger members of the Tübingen circle in the evenings at the inn after the day's work was over, but there were few opportunities for theological discussion and the evenings obviously fell far below his expectation. If we may read between the lines he felt very much out of things in the Swabian society and more and more drawn to his fellow countryman Wolf. It was not surprising that he had no regrets on leaving Tübingen as soon as the semester was over.

During these winter months he had worked hard on his first book, 'The Gospel of Marcion and the Canonical Gospel of Luke', which had Baur's full support and was published in 1846. Zeller reported to Schwegler, who at that time was in Italy, that the book was good, to which Schwegler replied that he was pleased to hear it. This work which dealt with the origin and authorship of the third Gospel was somewhat critical of Schwegler's 'Post-apostolic Age', but only indirectly was there any criticism of Baur. It was in his review of Baur's book on Paul that Ritschl's disagreement with many of Baur's views was first openly expressed, although as early as April 1847 he had declared to his father that he was resolved to oppose both Baur and Schwegler. 'Though I will not deny how much I owe to Baur, I certainly feel obliged to contradict him on many points.'[3]

What strikes one on reading this review is its self-assurance. Ritschl writes not as an admiring disciple still very much under Baur's influence, but rather as an equal, a scholar who at the age of twenty-five now stands on his own two feet and has no inhibitions about criticizing the Master where he believes him to be wrong. Thus he disagreed with Baur's rejection of the authenticity of 1 Thessalonians and the final two chapters of Romans. In fact, right throughout the review there runs a distinctly

[2] OR, p. 112.   [3] OR, p. 126.

negative and critical tone, and such passages as the following were certainly not calculated to please the Tübingen circle.

From p. 167 forward Baur analyses the events in Athens as related in Acts 17:16f. His method will seem to many artificial and unnatural, and even the reviewer has to admit that the objections against the reported speech of the apostle are too subtle for him. . . . Unfortunately the author did not take Kern's essay into consideration at all; this could perhaps have caused him to change his opinion regarding the authenticity of the two letters to the Thessalonians. As interesting as the observations are which the author makes from p. 651 onward, his description of Paul's personal relations with the Jewish Christians is, for the reason given, treated very scantily (p. 668), while the second letter to the Corinthians, so important in this context, has not even been referred to. It would seem that by the time the author came to the main point of the book—the consideration of Paul, not merely as a theologian, but also as a man and apostle—he had become tired out by his work of eliminating all the sources he could not use.[4]

It was not surprising that Ritschl was distinctly out of favour in Tübingen. He therefore decided to write to Zeller, who he hoped would mediate between himself and Baur, implying that the real disagreement in his review had been not so much with Baur as with Schwegler.

I believe that my review of Baur's book has alienated me from the Tübingen School and if you also do not hold me for an apostate, as Vischer is supposed to have called me, then although holding fast to the common principle of the historical view of early Christianity, a radical disagreement in details in which I find myself involved with Schwegler may lead to a disturbance of my relationship to you as regards theological questions. Of course I do not know how far you or Herr Dr. Baur agree with Schwegler, but when I say that in both of Schwegler's books no stone can be left upon another, then I believe I may assume that your confidence in me may be somewhat shaken. . . . But permit me to set out the main points of my disagreement with Schwegler to see if I may gain your approval.[5]

Early in 1847 Ritschl had intimated to Baur and Zeller his willingness to contribute to the *Jahrbücher* an article dealing with the Ignatian letters. This offer was warmly accepted. C. C. J.

---

[4] *Allgemeine Literatur-Zeitung* (Halle and Leipzig, 1847), pp. 124–7.
[5] Ritschl to Zeller, 3 Oct. 1847.

Bunsen, the Prussian ambassador to Britain, had recently supported the authenticity of three Ignatian letters contained in a newly published Syriac manuscript, and Ritschl, too, was convinced by Bunsen's arguments. Baur, however, rejected all of the traditionally accepted seven letters and decided to defend his views against Bunsen's attack. Moreover, in the face of Ritschl's criticism of his book on Paul, Baur was unwilling to allow Ritschl to play the part of advocate for the Tübingen standpoint. Since Ritschl had not indicated in what way he planned to review Bunsen's book, Baur wrote to him asking whether he intended to defend the authenticity of all seven letters or only the three contained in the Syriac recension. 'In the one case or the other,' Baur continued, 'I have doubts about including an article in the *Jahrbücher* which concedes so much to the conservative point of view.'[6] As Ritschl by this time had already written his review, he was naturally highly indignant over the whole matter and viewed it as the end of his association with the Tübingen journal. He expressed his displeasure in a letter to his father.

It did not at all fit in with my theological time-table to put this topic aside, but I realized from what Baur said that further discussion was impossible. In the distinction between conservative and negative criticism lies a total misunderstanding of criticism in general, and he who consciously sets himself on one side or the other is immediately condemned by the very act. You can imagine the abandonment of a principle which is so clear—although I had noticed this long previously—annoyed me very much; but this was especially so because in this particular case I had made absolutely no concession to the conservative point of view since there was nothing to concede, but through the new discovery a development in the earliest history of the Church emerged, which was not at all welcome to the conservatives. In my reply I emphasized this difference quite clearly, and formally declined the invitation to write further essays in the *Jahrbücher*, as the reproach of conservative criticism must certainly also apply to my disagreement with Baur with regard to the Pauline epistles, and I could not allow myself to be governed according to Baur's own opinions. I was fully aware that such a reply would evoke no sympathy from Baur, as he takes any disagreement badly, above all anything that hits at his weaker side. But I owed it to the subject as well as myself not to conceal my opinion and I hope, too, that the manner in which I wrote in no way offended him.[7]

In 1850 Ritschl's book on the origin and development of the Church[8] was published and on the express wish of his father, Ritschl sent a copy to Baur. In his reply Baur expressed his disagreement on numerous points, regretted the frequent and not always fair polemic against Schwegler, but wished Ritschl well in his future work.[9] From this time onwards relations appear to have been formally polite, with both suspicious of each other. In the autumn of 1853 Baur sent Ritschl a copy of his *Church History of the First Three Centuries* and Ritschl expressed his opinions to his father.

I recently received, with a very friendly covering letter, Baur's latest book . . . which contains a fair bit of polemic against me—partly justified, and partly unjustified because of his misunderstanding. The dubious side of Baur's view of history, incidentally, emerges in this book with an unprecedented openness, namely in the opinion that one can only be a scientific theologian when one at least leaves the fundamental doctrines of Christianity on one side, his real view being that they are to be rejected.[10]

In 1854 Ritschl decided on a policy of better relations and made plans to visit Tübingen. 'I would like to see old Baur again and assure him that my personal disposition towards him has not been harmed by my theological course of development.'[11] Baur on his part was also pleased that Ritschl intended to come. 'It would give me real pleasure if after your arrival you would come straight to my house and be my guest. You shall in no way be incommoded and that way we could spend time with each other most conveniently.'[12]

Ritschl journeyed south to the Swabian land in August and gave an account of his visit to Tübingen in a letter to his father.

This letter comes to you from Hell, in whose lowest part I am staying though I am writing to you now from its uppermost region. This Hell is actually the name for Baur's official residence which is built into the terraced slope of the hillside above the Neckar and into which one enters through the top storey which opens on to the street. In this Hell I feel very comfortable having been most kindly and cordially received

---

[8] *Die Entstehung der altkatholischen Kirche* (Bonn, 1850).

[9] OR, pp. 167–8. Cf. Baur's letter to Zeller, p. 220, which gives a truer picture of Baur's opinion.

[10] To his father, 18 Oct. 1853; OR, p. 247–8.

[11] To his mother, 20 July 1854; OR, p. 258.

[12] Baur to Ritschl, 23 July 1854; OR, p. 259.

by its occupant. When I arrived here by mail-coach midday on Monday, after a direct journey from Bonn to Stuttgart, Baur was waiting for me at the coach-station, and after lunch we were straightway involved in a lively theological discussion on Lutheranism and Calvinism and on my dogmatic principle. He told me at once and has often repeated it that he greatly delights in this theological exchange of views, as he has nobody else. I have therefore arranged my other visits so that each morning and afternoon I can devote a certain time to conversation with him. We have certainly not been without differences of opinion, but even in such points where I differ from his cherished presuppositions, I think I have convinced him that I do so methodically and not because of a lack of method. We have discussed all possible topics and not once did I detect in the old gentleman any displeasure at the fact that I had concerned myself with other problems than he. Only in the debate on the concept of God did he become somewhat animated when he forced me to make clear the differences between the logical method which the one and the other uses—a fact which in this case I was very interested to note in order to ascertain how much philosophical obscurity is connected with Hegelianism. His mind was also somewhat set at ease that I introduced more concrete concepts, while he still finds it necessary to think in more abstract terms. But precisely this is the injustice against the real world. Between times we indulge in our best humour.[13]

Schwegler, whose works Ritschl had so cuttingly criticized, avoided him.

Baur very soon said that he was in suspense as to how Schwegler, who is very badly disposed towards me, would receive me. He has become an increasingly isolated, egoistic bookworm, and in his systematic mistrust has so interpreted my polemic against him, that I wanted thereby to put myself on the credit side. When I came to him he was just getting dressed to go out to dinner and he used this as a pretext for ushering me to the door. He promised to visit me and also to appear the next day at an inn where he was in the habit of meeting with the others; but he did not turn up, neither here, nor there, and Baur is quite angry about the matter and has repeatedly referred to it. I gradually inquired after the reason for Schwegler's displeasure towards me, and noticed that Baur, too, shared the same suspicion. I then explained that Schwegler's work had impressed me very much, but after I had convinced myself of its superficiality through my own study of the subject, maybe an annoyance at this disappointment had caused my pen to become too sharp. That is what really happened and Baur

[13] To his father, 18 Aug. 1854; OR, pp. 259-60.

believed me. If he had any further doubts at all about my 'apostasy' then they will certainly have been removed through this visit. He must convince himself that I have not deserted to the opposite camp, but that I have gained my theological independence, which I owe to the inspiration received from him.[14]

Ritschl felt that the visit had been a great success and summed up his over-all impression in a letter to his mother.

Baur has obviously fully reconciled himself to the fact that I am pursuing a different theological course from his, and as he is able to speak his mind to me completely freely, he finds it an attractive proposition to encounter a free and methodical disagreement with his views. He is otherwise very sensitive about this, but as I have repeatedly told him that I am not, he has therefore gained confidence in his conversations with me . . . As concerns my relationship to Baur I think I have overcome any remaining ill feeling he may have had towards me. It was characteristic that as Baur's sister on one occasion asked whether such and such a theologian was a friend of mine, he said: 'Oh, he has no one but friends!' For it had obviously impressed him that I am on good terms with men of different parties without thereby being dependent on them, while he obviously regrets his own complete isolation at the present time. I was allowed to leave only with the warmest invitations to come again.[15]

The new cordiality, however, did not last. A few months later Baur published in the Tübingen journal an article on the Essenes which Ritschl had submitted. In this article Ritschl had defended the authenticity of the second and third Pastoral epistles, maintaining that the heretics attacked by Paul in the epistle to Titus were the Essenes, and that Titus should not be interpreted according to the exegetical results of 1 Timothy—in Ritschl's opinion a completely false procedure. Baur, understandably, was not pleased with this criticism, since for twenty years he had denied the authenticity of all three Pastoral epistles.

When at the end of your essay you hold out the prospect of a new solution to the problems of early Christian history, then the first thing which will come to stand alongside the Essenes in the letter to Titus will doubtless be the authenticity of the Pastoral Epistles. If I may say frankly what I think then it seems to me that it is time for everyone who is not of the opinion that criticism up to the present day has been

---

[14] To his father, 18 Aug. 1854; OR, pp. 261–2.
[15] To his mother, 28 Aug. 1854; OR, p. 262.

beating the air, to cease from continually wanting to lay a foundation upon which one can only build with wood, hay, and stubble. As long as there is nothing more compelling than the hypothesis of the Essenes in the Epistle to Titus, I at least cannot give up my whole theological view, which does not hang on such slender threads. We will find it extremely difficult ever to reach agreement on this point.[16]

These objections, however, made no impression on Ritschl. 'I must fear', he wrote to his father, 'that Baur is considering writing against me, whereby he could harm not me, but our relationship. He has a strange conception of criticism; he does not mean the methods in historical investigation, but the dogmatized result of his negative opinions, and he is always ready to see apostasy from criticism where one differs from him, even where one does not mention his name.'[17]

During 1855 the gap seems to have widened and in a letter to his father at the beginning of 1856 Ritschl expressed his disappointment at Baur's attitude towards him.

Old Baur has recently written to me in a strange way. He makes fairly caustic remarks about my taste for certain books and my uncritical tendency to rescue the authenticity of New Testament writings, which he would never think of doing 'since he understands the writings as they purport to be and then sets them in the place where they belong'. What a superstition this old Hegelian has in the objective nature of his views. He adds, by the way, that this is no wise touches his cordial relations with me; once he has conceived a respect and attachment for someone he maintains it, provided the other allows him to do so. And one can really allow him to do so, although it is a pity that he has become so obstinate.[18]

The immediate cause of the final break between the two men was Ritschl's review of a recent book by Karl Schwarz on the history of the most recent theology.[19] In the midst of this review, which appeared in the *Literarisches Centralblatt*, was found the following passage: 'The Tübingen School has fallen to pieces and its initiative will only deserve recognition in the measure that it leads to opposition against the system of early Church history as presented by Baur and Schwegler, and as it furthers the

[16] Baur to Ritschl, 26 Dec. 1854; OR, p. 265.
[17] To his father, 30 Dec. 1854; OR, p. 266.
[18] To his father, 7 Jan. 1856; OR, p. 271.
[19] *Zur Geschichte der neuesten Theologie* (Leipzig, 1856).

cultivation of Biblical theology more than has been the case up to now.'[20]

As was customary in the *Centralblatt* the review appeared anonymously and Baur, who at that time was at loggerheads with Hilgenfeld, immediately jumped to the conclusion that Hilgenfeld was the author. Hilgenfeld, on learning through Köstlin that Baur suspected him of being responsible for the article, wrote to Zarnke, the editor of the journal, who informed him that Ritschl had contributed it. Armed with this evidence Hilgenfeld then wrote to Baur protesting his innocence and communicating Zarnke's disclosure.

On 15 June Baur wrote to Ritschl asking whether he was the author of the review, and the following letter to Zeller a few days later reveals Baur's feelings on the matter.

I have made a fine discovery in the last few days concerning our friend Ritschl. I wrote to you last time that the author of the review in the *Centralblatt* on Schwarz's book was without doubt Hilgenfeld. When Köstlin informed Hilgenfeld of my assumption, the latter wrote to me himself in a very annoyed manner and included a letter written to him by Zarnke saying that he was unable to accept his offer of a review of the work, since Ritschl had already submitted one which he could not refuse. This was perfidious enough—to criticize me in such a disdainful manner, while at the same time, as I can show, he had written the most appreciative letters, full of his respect. I wrote to him briefly a few days ago asking him to answer the question as to whether he was the author of this review, telling him he could be assured that I understand perfectly well what was said in two places referring to me, and that he could well believe how interested I was to know whether or not he was the author. I have still received no answer but whatever it may be I will let him know what I think of such conduct. Hilgenfeld, too, in his letter made so many petty and personal remarks that I have told him quite bluntly my opinion about them. With this man who is plagued by ambition and vanity I shall have as little to do as possible.[21]

Ritschl replied to Baur on 21 June, confirming he was the author of the review and hastening to justify what he had written.

I made that statement in opposition to Schwarz according to my conviction and out of an interest purely in the subject-matter, and for my part I believe myself justified in so doing since this author reckons

[20] *Literarisches Centralblatt*, 26 Apr. 1856, pp. 261–2.
[21] Baur to Zeller; the letter is undated but must have been written about 20 June.

me also as belonging to the Tübingen School. I would ask you to note that the judgement I made concerns my writings no less than those of the others who are reckoned to be in this theological group. And if anyone attaches significance to this review he will have been able to turn that judgement against me just as much as against you. I would earnestly request you through these considerations to suppress the attitude which seems to ring through your letter. I am not in the least conscious of detracting, through my statement, from the respect in which you are held, any more than through differences over details in your theology concerning which I have expressed myself both publicly and to you in private and which have not hindered you from continually favouring me with your personal kindness.[22]

Baur wrote to Zeller on 26 June enclosing Ritschl's letter and the draft of his own to Ritschl.

I wrote to you recently that Ritschl was the author of the article and that I had questioned him about it. Included is the reply which I have received in the meantime, from which you will see in what a sophisticated manner he seeks to twist and disguise the whole affair. At the same time Hilgenfeld wrote to me that Ritschl was furious with him and had accused him of inciting me against him; also Zarnke (to whom Ritschl must have written before he replied to me) was very angry that Hilgenfeld had misused his confidential letter . . . Hilgenfeld, too, is now extremely angry with Ritschl. When I consider how my relationship with Ritschl has always been up till now, and how he has continually expressed himself to me in his letters, this malicious attack on me seems doubly despicable. I therefore have it in mind to rebuke his behaviour openly and break with him completely. This perfidious man deserves nothing else. But I would be very pleased if you would let me know your opinion on the matter. I cannot leave his letter unanswered for he will think everything is all clear. Now I could certainly tell him bluntly that I have broken off relations with him, but I do not know whether it is not better to tell such a person plainly what one thinks about him. What do you think?[23]

Zeller replied on 3 July.

Dear Father,
I return to you herewith Ritschl's letter. His perfidy is certainly very badly disguised in it. However much he may deviate from us in this matter, that is something quite different from telling us—and especially in an anonymous article—that our achievements deserve recognition

---

[22] OR, pp. 274–5.   [23] Baur to Zeller, 26 June 1856.

only in so far as they lead to opposition to our views. Whoever says this has no right to affirm his respect for you. I am therefore in complete agreement with you that you must break with him. It is perfidious and at the same time an impertinence. It is as if to say, 'from the material you have collected I alone know how to make something of it.' Such self-praise under the mask of anonymity would under any circumstances be repugnant, but towards you it is a shameful attitude, equally revolting in its arrogance and dishonesty. I think you should let him know that in the most appropriate way, and that in so doing you should not simply confine yourself to expressing your indigation at his conduct, but also give your reasons in a short analysis.[24]

In a long letter to Ritschl on 6 July Baur declared that Ritschl's explanations had not made the slightest impression upon him. It was not, he held, a question of the rightness or wrongness of Ritschl's views about the School, but rather concerned the fact that Ritschl had chosen to express his opinions anonymously. At bottom Baur considered that Ritschl was playing a double game— on the one hand trying to maintain his relationship with the School while on the other hand trying to purify himself from any suspicion of belonging to it.

The whole affair was formally concluded on 22 July when Ritschl wrote to Baur the following reply.

Sir,

You have written me a letter, the injustice of which I on my part have no need to discuss. Only for your sake do I feel obliged to explain to you herewith that I neither do nor did entertain any of the intentions and designs which you falsely attribute to me. My disposition is a sphere on which I alone can give information and which is not discovered by means of the criticism which you employ. You would do truth a service if you would also communicate this statement to those who share your judgement of me.[25]

We have chosen to concentrate on this break in relations between Baur and Ritschl for two main reasons: (1) because of the number of erroneous statements about it—it has been ascribed to varying causes and even been dated as occurring in 1857; (2) because the letters between Baur and Zeller have never been printed, and thus the account of the affair in Otto Ritschl's biography tends to be a little one-sided.

[24] Zeller to Baur, 3 July 1856.   [25] OR, p. 275.

When we look back over the events which formed the milestones of the unstable relationship between these two great theological figures of the past it is clear that the break between them was ultimately occasioned by Ritschl's rejection of the historical premises which formed the basis of the Tübingen perspective evolved by Baur and Schwegler. For Ritschl found himself more and more unable to acquiesce in the Tübingen hypothesis of a continuing struggle in the early Church between Pauline and Jewish Christian parties. As a consequence of this he perceived that the results of Baur's investigations into the authenticity of the New Testament writings were for the greatest part invalid. Thus Ritschl slowly abandoned the original Tübingen perspective and turned back to a more conservative evaluation of the authenticity of the earliest Christian documents.

For almost ten years Ritschl did his best to minimize the differences separating himself from Baur until finally they became so acute that they could no longer be repressed for the sake of preserving the peace. There is no doubt that Ritschl always had a great respect for Baur's achievements, but he also saw these achievements subverted and vitiated by Baur's false historical premises. Baur on his part could not but see in Ritschl a younger rival who threatened the whole of his life's work. On the other hand he desired to hold Ritschl as one of his followers. But a follower Ritschl could never be. He intended to be his own master and not stand under another's shadow, so that the break with Baur was sooner or later inevitable.

After the appearance of the second (revised) edition of his 'Origin and Rise of the Early Catholic Church' in 1857 Ritschl departed the field of Church history in order to concentrate upon his dogmatics. In 1864 he was appointed professor of theology at Göttingen and his subsequent rise to fame in the 1870s made him the most important and influential theologian in Germany up until, and after, his death in 1889.[26]

[26] A more comprehensive account of Ritschl's life and theology will appear in my forthcoming book, *Albrecht Ritschl and the Ritschlian School*.

8. Adolf Hilgenfeld

'I SEE Hilgenfeld has gone', wrote Marcus Dods, the great Scottish New Testament expositor, '—flying his flag to the last; an able warrior.'[1] Of all the members of the Tübingen School no one had greater claim than Hilgenfeld to be reckoned as the hero of the School. If Baur was its head, if Zeller gained the most coveted honours, if the apostate Ritschl succeeded in becoming the most influential theologian in Germany, it was Hilgenfeld who flew the critical flag most valiantly and battled to the end against all foes—the Jena theological faculty, the governing powers, critics from every side, and even—if need be—against his friends. Of him pre-eminently can it be said that he looked neither to the right nor to the left, but pressed on straight ahead in his crusade for the truth—the truth, at any rate, as he himself saw it. Here was no respecter of persons: friend and foe alike were all measured against his own personal theological yardstick and whoever should fail to meet the test ran the risk of receiving one of Hilgenfeld's theological broadsides. For forty years he waged an unceasing struggle to obtain a professorial chair and only after the death of Hase in 1890 did he finally achieve his life-long cherished ambition.

STUDENT YEARS IN BERLIN AND HALLE

Hilgenfeld's father was a pastor; he had studied theology at Halle and then at Berlin, where he sat at Neander's feet; in Wittenberg he was friendly with Richard Rothe. His first appointment was to the little village of Stappenbeck near Salzwedel in the Altmark land north of Magdeburg, and here on 2 June 1823 Adolf Bernhard Christoph Christian Hilgenfeld was born. The father was a firm adherent of the traditional Christian faith and warmly inclined toward pietism; on Adolf's mother's side flowed a more rationalistic spirit through his grandfather, the learned theologian and schoolmaster Christian Woltersdorff, who had studied in

---

[1] To the Revd. H. S. Coffin, 16 Feb. 1907. *From the Later Letters of Marcus Dods* (London, 1911), p. 241.

Königsberg under the famous philosopher Immanuel Kant and was now rector of the secondary school in Salzwedel which Adolf attended. More liberal influences were also imbibed from his uncle and later father-in-law Dr. Gottfried Woltersdorff, First Preacher in the church at Osterburg. Woltersdorff was an enthusiastic supporter of the rationalistic 'Friends of Light' movement, a movement which caused much misgiving and opposition among the orthodox clergy. Adolf as a boy was certainly attracted to his uncle's views, but since his father was much opposed to the new movement, Adolf found it best to adopt a mediating attitude.

In line with the family tradition it was foreseen that Adolf should study theology, and after completing his secondary schooling in Salzwedel he made ready to begin university in the spring of 1841. The two universities nearest to the Altmark were Berlin and Halle, but since Halle was notorious for its rationalism and rowdy student life while the faculty in Berlin pursued a conservative direction, the father required no long deliberation as to where his son should go, and in April Adolf was duly enrolled at Berlin. Nevertheless things did not turn out as his father had desired, for instead of being influenced by Hengstenberg, Neander, and Twesten, Adolf was attracted by the lectures of the conservative Hegelian Marheineke—and worse, by Strauss's friend Vatke. Hengstenberg he apparently never bothered to hear; Twesten he counted among the 'theological rabble', and although at the beginning he praised Neander's lectures on Church history, he soon became dissatisfied with his exegetical lectures on Romans and John.

'With great enthusiasm' he heard Marheineke's lectures on dogmatics in the winter semester of 1841/2 and in the following semester those on symbolics, Christian morality, and the famous lectures directed against Schelling in which Marheineke gave an outline of the most important philosophical systems formulated since Jacob Böhme. The greatest influence upon him, however, were the lectures of Vatke. He profited greatly from listening to Vatke's Introduction to the Old Testament, Introduction to the New Testament, and Philosophy of Religion, declaring himself completely satisfied with what he heard. From the autumn of 1841 he reckoned himself among Vatke's grateful pupils: 'I have now fully accepted the standpoint of the speculative theology under Marheineke's, and still more, Vatke's guidance. I hold the last-named to be the most sterling theologian in Berlin.'[2] It is clear that Hilgenfeld was not in agreement with all Marheineke's views and we find in his letters a number of negative statements about him; however, these should be seen rather as attempts to set his father's conservative conscience at rest. He would never, he assured him, be a rationalist of the Bretschneider–Wegscheider variety and he found it most convenient to describe himself as being influenced by Schleiermacher, in whose theological method he perceived the combination of personal piety and scientific investigation. Schleiermacher, at any rate, was less odious to his father than the pantheist Hegelians, whose teaching had been taken to its logical conclusion by Strauss, Feuerbach, and Bruno Bauer.

From day to day I adopt Schleiermacher's viewpoint more and more, and stand essentially on the standpoint of the 'Speeches on Religion'. This point of view unites the great truth of rationalism, namely the principle of the unconditional free conviction, with the truth of pietism, namely the respect for the depth of the inward pious spirit. Schleiermacher seems to me, generally, to have perceived the essence of religion in a far deeper way than Hegel and his whole school; that can be pardoned in a man who was merely a philosopher. Hegel's view of religion when taken to its logical conclusion seems to me to lead to Feuerbachianism . . .[3]

The new organ of the Tübingen School, Zeller's *Theologische Jahrbücher*, made its first appearance during the winter of 1841/2 and Vatke drew Hilgenfeld's attention to the new venture. From that time on Hilgenfeld became an enthusiastic reader of the journal and a convinced adherent of the Tübingen principles, so that by the end of the winter he had finally abandoned the traditional theistic viewpoint. Not that he completely accepted the Hegelian philosophy; Hilgenfeld was never as philosophically inclined as Strauss or Zeller, and, moreover, he stood in the shadow of Feuerbach's attack on Hegel, so that although he recognized Hegel's great genius he was never completely convinced of the Hegelian viewpoint. Rather is God equated with truth in general, and when Hilgenfeld uses the word 'God', the word 'truth' may usually be substituted.

By 1843 Hilgenfeld was tired of Berlin and desired a change. He had hoped to go to Griefswald where the student life was more

[2] To his father, 29 Jan. 1842.   [3] To his father, 6 Feb. 1843.

merry and unrestrained, but his father refused his permission. In Halle, however, student behaviour was now more disciplined than formerly, although still freer than at Berlin. Gesenius was now dead; Wegscheider's influence had dwindled and Tholuck and Müller were now the leading lights in the faculty, so that Hilgenfeld's father grudgingly acceded to his son's request for a change of university.

In the early 1840s Halle was a centre of the speculative philosophy and Hilgenfeld enthusiastically praised the two Hegelian philosophers J. E. Erdmann and J. Schaller: 'The actual philosophical faculty is considerably better than that in Berlin, for in the whole Berlin philosophical faculty there is neither an Erdmann nor a Schaller.'[4] At the beginning of his study he also heard Tholuck and was able to soothe his father's mind with the report that Tholuck pleased him very much, although later he found only 'thick darkness' in Tholuck's views. However, it was more the philological side to which Hilgenfeld was attracted and at the end of his study he was fairly proficient in Persian and Arabic with a good foundation in Syriac and Ethiopian. His main teacher was the Church historian Carl Thilo, who guided him into the world of the apocryphal books, the patristic Fathers, and especially the Clementine *Homilies* and *Recensions*. However, probably the greatest influence upon him during these years in Halle were the writings of Baur and his pupils in Tübingen. He read Baur's works avidly, declaring to his father that he saw in the Tübingen writings 'no hostile tendency', and finding Baur's three-volume treatise on the Trinity 'fabulous'. 'The old Gnosis in the classic portrayal of Baur, who at present is regarded as a heretic, is exceedingly instructive and interesting. It is a shame how this man is now slandered, especially in Halle.'[5]

The faculty exam was passed in November 1845. Hilgenfeld reported that the old Wegscheider examined him so laxly that it was a shame for the whole Protestant theology, that Müller was shocked by his theological views without being able to deny him the mark of good–very good, and that Hupfeld and Tholuck, to his great joy, did not examine him. His sermon, however, was adjudged poor and lacking in Biblical emphasis; moreover, he was described as being 'completely unsuited' for the practical life of a pastor. Thilo therefore counselled him to give up any

---

[4] To his father, 14 Aug. 1843.   [5] To his father, 21 Aug. 1845.

thought of a preaching position and to concentrate on an academic career, although he also warned him of the difficulties he would encounter here.

In May 1846 Hilgenfeld completed his doctorate with a dissertation on Spinoza and at the end of the year he wrote to Zeller offering his investigation of the Clementine *Homilies* and *Recognitions* for publication in the *Jahrbücher*. Zeller handed the work over to Baur who returned it to Hilgenfeld with the recommendation that it should be published separately as a book. In 1847 Hilgenfeld began his long list of book reviews in the Halle *Literaturzeitung* and in the new Jena *Literaturzeitung*; these reviews soon made him known as a friend of the Tübingen School. In July of that same year he received a letter from Baur inviting him to contribute to the *Jahrbücher*: 'I think our views run in the same direction and we would certainly welcome other co-workers from outside of Württemberg.'[6]

Since there was no opportunity of habilitating in the faculty at Halle—nor at any other theological faculty in Prussia—the only possibility appeared to lie in the liberal and free-thinking faculty at Jena in the duchy of Saxe-Weimar. The faculty was one of the poorest in Germany and the Weimar Government declared that it could offer him no smiling prospects for the future. Hilgenfeld's father also expressed his disapproval of the plan on account of the liberal theological climate in which his son should have to work and Adolf attempted to allay his father's doubts with the assurance: 'It is free-thinking and genuinely Protestant here, but no more rationalistic than Clement of Alexandria, Origen, and Schleiermacher.'[7] In the summer of 1847 he habilitated into the faculty and prepared for his first lectures in the autumn.

THE YEARS AT JENA

Jena on the river Saale was a small town of 6,000 people when Hilgenfeld arrived in the autumn of 1847. The theological faculty at that time consisted of four full professors: A. G. Hoffmann, Karl Hase, Eduard Schwarz, and Leopold Rückert, the average salary which each received being in the region of 700 taler—about one half that paid to professors at other universities. The number of students was not large and the majority attended classes held only by the professors, especially Hase. Hilgenfeld, moreover,

[6] Baur to Hilgenfeld, 4 July 1847.   [7] To his father, 5 Dec. 1847.

was an extremely poor lecturer; his voice was monotonous, his lectures were dry, and he read straight out of his notebook. Small wonder that so few of the students felt inclined to pay out their precious money for his courses. Often he had no students at all; once he reported that he could not begin lecturing because half his class—namely, Herr Groth from Holstein—had not turned up; another time he had to postpone his Hebrew class because 'my student is at present sitting in the university lock-up'. Only after 1850 did numbers in his most popular lecture on the history of theology begin to climb to two figures.

In 1848 his investigation into the Clementine writings was published and in the following year his book on John. This latter work brought down upon him the odium of the orthodox for it was only too plain that Hilgenfeld denied all the traditional beliefs of the Church—the virgin birth of Christ, his divinity, miracles, and the work of redemption. Certainly he declared himself ready to accept all these doctrines when interpreted in a different manner from that of the traditional orthodoxy, but that was of little consolation to his critics and the outlook for the future with regard to a professorial post at any university appeared bleak. He considered applying for a vacant position in Bern but was advised against it by Zeller. In 1850 he was made an assistant professor, but without salary, and only on the express condition that no claim for further promotion or salary could be raised on account of it. He was thus in a miserable financial position, living almost from hand to mouth and helped by grants from his father and the honoraria from book reviews. Zeller's description of his situation summed the matter up succinctly: 'The man is almost just too productive; certainly he has to write in order to live and so it is not surprising that he seems almost to live just in order to write.'[8]

In this same year (1850) his book on the Gospel and letters of John was sharply attacked by the Göttingen theologian Gerhard Uhlhorn and the Hanover Rector, Düsterdieck. Hilgenfeld, indignant and angry, was not one to take criticism sitting down and hit back with a 72-page brochure against the 'defamations and damnatory statements' which had been levelled against him. 'God will judge between me and my persecutors!' Baur and others advised against publication of the reply but Hilgenfeld

[8] Zeller to Baur, 20 Feb. 1850.

refused to listen and the exaggerated polemic only did further damage to his already bad reputation.

The years 1851–3 brought a deep dissension between Hilgenfeld and Baur which began after Baur had described Hilgenfeld's views on the Gospel of Mark as 'completely weak, untenable, and without principle'.[9] Moreover, Baur was annoyed at Hilgenfeld's attempt to defend the authenticity of 1 Thessalonians: 'It is impossible for me to believe that the apostle wrote such insignificant and unmotivated letters, devoid of all thought.'[10] What was here at stake was not simply the authenticity of one letter, but Baur's whole historical method. For having worked out his total-view of the apostolic and post-apostolic age, Baur now determined the dating of the letters from this historical framework. Hilgenfeld on the other hand, renounced this method as far as possible (although he could not do so completely) and devoted himself to special investigations of the New Testament and extra-canonical writings, without concerning himself about any such total-view of the early Church.

I renounce any claim to have a self-contained total-view of the course of development in the early Christian Church, into which the individual details need merely to be fitted, and I limit myself to delivering contributions to that general conception of the development of the early Church, through special investigations, even when the trouble I have taken and the results obtained do not find acknowledgement everywhere; such a general conception still seems to me to be only an approximate solution to the problem.[11]

The bad feeling between the two almost caused a break in relations on a number of occasions and Zeller and Köstlin were often called upon to mediate. At the end of 1854 Hilgenfeld composed a defence of the authenticity of 1 Thessalonians and sent it to Baur for publication in the *Jahrbücher*. Hilgenfeld waited four weeks and since he received no answer he assumed that the article had been accepted. To his surprise Baur returned the article after a month with the reply that at the time of reception he himself had been composing an article on the same subject and that Hilgenfeld should revise his article taking his (Baur's) into consideration. Hilgenfeld was furious and wrote to Zeller

[9] Hilgenfeld, *Die apostolischen Väter* (Halle, 1853), p. vi.
[10] Baur to Hilgenfeld, 1 Dec. 1850.
[11] *Die apostolischen Väter*, p. 8.

complaining bitterly and threatening to send no more articles to the *Jahrbücher*. 'For if I should send, for example, an article on the letters of John, I could never know whether or not Baur was just in the process of writing on the same topic and could compel me to take my article back.'[12] Indignant letters on both sides continued to be written during 1855 and it was therefore not surprising that Baur immediately attributed the anonymous review of Schwarz's book to Hilgenfeld. Köstlin was pressed to write to Hilgenfeld and inquire as to whether he was the author of the review. Hilgenfeld, thoroughly indignant, wrote to Zarnke, the editor of the *Centralblatt*, who unsuspecting that anything was amiss informed Hilgenfeld that Ritschl was the author. Armed with this piece of evidence Hilgenfeld protested his innocence in the whole matter and Baur was forced to apologize.

> I hold it now for my duty earnestly to request you not to be offended, that in the first supposition which thrust itself into my mind about the author of the article, I thought of you. I can only excuse myself for so thinking, in that the ill feeling which some time ago unfortunately crept in between us, set me thinking in this direction. I now see plainly how much I was wrong about you; I must reiterate, however, that even if it had been you who had written the article, it would not have had half the moral significance for me which it had in Ritschl's case.[13]

After seven years lecturing at the University Hilgenfeld still received no salary and had little chance of obtaining a theological post outside of Jena. His book on John had made him *persona non grata* in the theological world and in order that he might finally be able to marry (he had been engaged for six years) he accepted a position as assistant librarian in the University library with a salary of 200 talers (about one third of a professor's salary). Advantages were direct access to all books in the library, the influence upon new acquisitions, and connections with all the great libraries in Europe. But although he had a certain amount of free time for the continuation of his lectures, the position took up much of the time which would otherwise have been devoted to his theological investigations. However, it was a secure position and he was not unhappy to remain there for fifteen years.

In June 1854 he married his cousin Louise, the eldest daughter of his uncle Dr. Gottfried Woltersdorff. When Dr. Woltersdorff

---

[12] Hilgenfeld to Zeller, 7 Dec. 1854. [13] Baur to Hilgenfeld, 26 June 1856.

died two years later he left a large family behind to be cared for. The position of Hilgenfeld's deceased father-in-law was a highly remunerative one carrying a salary of over 2,000 talers and in order that the family might all remain at Osterburg, Hilgenfeld himself decided to apply for it, to which end he requested ordination as an assistant preacher. His friends Lipsius and Krause were amazed at his resolve and that he should be prepared to sign all the necessary confessions of faith; for they both knew that his views were quite contrary to the traditional teaching of the Church. Hilgenfeld, however, felt that he could sign the articles with a good conscience *in so far* as these confessions were in agreement with the Bible, the Bible—which he did not add—as he himself interpreted it.

He was selected as a candidate for the vacant position by the magistrate in Osterburg (a friend of the family) and then had to apply to the Higher Consistory in Magdeburg for confirmation of the nomination. He summarized his theological convictions in the following short declaration which was laid before the Consistory.

After I had enjoyed the benefit of a truly pious and Christian upbringing in the houses of my parents and grandparents, I heard with great enthusiasm in the winter 1841/2 Marheineke lecturing on dogmatics; at the same time I was especially stimulated by Schleiermacher whose 'Christian Faith' made a deep impression upon me. But I can honestly assure that from the beginning Strauss's Dogmatics, which appeared during my university years (not to speak of Feuerbach), did not satisfy me since I am of the opinion that this speculative pantheism must be overcome with scientifically reasoned arguments. I have constantly held fast to the belief in the oneness of truth with what is genuinely Christian—a oneness (which must open itself up more and more to the deeper scientific investigations; and this faith of mine rests on the certainty that what is essentially grounded in human nature— such as the interest in religion and in truth—cannot stand in any irreconcilable contradiction. From 1848 to 1851 I attempted to carry through this conviction in lectures on Christian apologetics, whose outline, however, no longer satisfies me, and also, as the opportunity provides, in my writings. My conviction has also been continually strengthened through so many events in my life. And as I believe in the living God before whom everything past and future is eternally present, so that he does not first require the human spirit for the realization of his own consciousness, so also I acknowledge in the historical Christ as the pioneer and perfecter of our faith (Hebrews

12:2) his highest archetypal revelation. I believe in the Holy Spirit of God who reigns in the Christian Church, and in knowledge of life first communicates the true peace of God; I believe in the Spirit through which man must be born anew in order to partake of the eternal blessedness which exists beyond this earthly life. With these statements I do not intend to imply that I have expressed a full dogmatic point of view, but certainly the basic tenets of a confession which may be further amplified, but which can never perish, and which enriches me through science and life.[14]

The Magdeburg Consistory was not at all convinced of the candidate's orthodoxy in the face of reports from the Consistorial Councillor K. H. Sack and the General Superintendent Lehnert, who found Hilgenfeld's writing riddled with heresies:

Herr Dr. Hilgenfeld knows of no trustworthy records relating the *history* of Christ and of the apostles. What is contained in the Gospels is, in his opinion, a mixture of historical truth and the arbitrary embodiment of dogmatic ideas. The Christ of the Gospels originated gradually. His varied forms in the different Gospels are the product of a process of thinking in which the Gnostic systems also belong. The Acts of the Apostles is a completely untrustworthy book, more a kind of novel than a historical work. A greater part of the apostolic letters, which are acknowledged by the Church as authentic, are, according to Hilgenfeld, unauthentic.

He rejects the truth of the most important Christian *doctrines*. Christ is a mere man. The narrative of his supernatural birth is not historical. The teaching about his second coming is a Jewish conception. Prophecies and miracles are not acknowledged.[15]

and Lehnert's report concludes:

With such an attitude to Holy Scripture and the teaching of Scripture Professor Hilgenfeld is in no position to place himself with good conscience under the obligation of holding fast to the word of God, as it is contained in the prophetic and apologetic writings of the Old and New Testaments and repeated in the confessional writings of the Protestant Church. He can administer a spiritual office only, either according to his own views—which deviate from the word of God and the doctrines of the Church—or in continual contradiction to his own views, in both cases, therefore, without blessing for the Church.

Even less can one promise blessing from his administration of a pastorate, since the way in which he treats the New Testament writings

[14] Heinrich Hilgenfeld, 'Der Fall Hilgenfeld in Osterburg', *ZWT*, 1907–8, pp. 302–3.
[15] Ibid., p. 307.

and especially the way in which he interprets the Gospel of John allows us to conclude a lack in his moral character, a lack in his feeling for the truth.

In my opinion, therefore, his presentation for the first preaching position in Osterburg is to be most emphatically rejected.[16]

Tholuck, who was called in to give his opinion, was also of the same mind and the Consistory in due course communicated to Hilgenfeld its resolve not to confirm the nomination of the magistrate. From 1856, however, Hilgenfeld's financial position continued to improve and when Karl Schwarz was called from Halle to fill the position of Court preacher in Gotha, he was able to exercise his influence on the sympathetic Duke with the result that Hilgenfeld received welcome additions to his income.

Since Zeller's departure for Bern in 1847 the *Theologische Jahrbücher* had been edited by Baur, and as far back as 1849 Ritschl had declared in a letter to Hilgenfeld that 'in consequence of Baur's exclusiveness and contentiousness the *Jahrbücher* are in agony and it will be difficult for the situation to change.'[17] Hilgenfeld had often expressed the wish to found his own journal but there were so many obstacles in the way and he could not set up in direct opposition to Baur. However, by 1855 the *Jahrbücher* were in financial difficulty and Baur approached Hilgenfeld about taking over the editorship or, alternatively, founding a new journal which should be a continuation of the old. Hilgenfeld declined and Baur carried on, but two years later the number of subscribers had sunk so low that the publisher informed Baur it would have to cease. Baur still had hopes that Hilgenfeld might be persuaded to take over the editorship and was suddenly surprised by the news that Hilgenfeld had resolved to undertake an entirely new journal whose title *Zeitschrift für wissenschaftliche Theologie* was carefully chosen to avoid all association with the old *Jahrbücher*. Unfortunately Hilgenfeld's attempt to win a large number of contributors was unsuccessful. The Jena faculty, after initially agreeing to help, left him in the lurch; his nearest friends Lipsius, Schwarz, Zeller, and Köstlin were busy with their own programmes and lacked the time to contribute; Baur initially refused but later relented and Lipsius, who also decided to help, was diligent in supplying articles; but other possible contributors

---

[16] Ibid., pp. 307–8.   [17] Ritschl to Hilgenfeld, 13 Dec. 1849.

such as Dillmann, Reuss, and Credner saw in the new journal simply a continuation of the old Tübingen *Jahrbücher* and distanced themselves from it. Others contributed only mediocre articles or were soon disillusioned with Hilgenfeld's narrow-minded editorship; and the more that Hilgenfeld, through lack of articles from others, was forced to fill the gaps with his own writings (which was fully in accord with his own desires), the more limited in scope the *Zeitschrift* became. Nevertheless, new contributors were won and it continued right down through the remaining years of the century finding readers in all parts of Europe—especially Holland, Switzerland, England, France, Scandinavia, and even Budapest, Moscow, St. Petersburg, and Kiev—as well as in America. Only in 1914, seven years after Hilgenfeld's death, did the *Zeitschrift* finally come to an end.

Hilgenfeld's relationship to the Jena theological faculty is one long unhappy story. For forty years he was prevented from becoming a full professor in order that he should have no voice in the faculty deliberations. In 1864 Hoffmann, professor for Old Testament and the senior member of the faculty, died, and Hilgenfeld who had been giving lectures in Old Testament subjects for the preceding five years hoped at last to gain the coveted position. Instead of proposing him, however, the three other professors in the faculty put forward the names of two other candidates—August Köhler, the young orthodox Old Testament lecturer from Erlangen, and the mediating theologian Eduard Riehm from Halle. Hilgenfeld, bitter and angry, requested the Zürich pastor Carl Egli to write a review of the most recent writings of the two candidates, which was published in the next issue of the *Zeitschrift*. Egli's review was designed to demolish their reputations and written in biting, sarcastic language. Riehm was criticized for his 'intellectual muddle-headedness and orthodox narrow-mindedness', Köhler for his 'musty, antiquated interpretation of the Bible, which is pervaded with rabbinical–Talmudic sophistry'. Preceding this review was a declaration from Hilgenfeld in which he attacked the other three members of the faculty, 'the three pillars reputed to be something' (Gal. 2:9). But all that helped not in the slightest and Köhler was finally appointed. He had little success for Hilgenfeld and his friends 'read him dead' through regular lectures in the Old Testament held in opposition. Hilgenfeld lectured each winter semester on Introduction to the Old Testament; Gustav Frank read Old Testament exegesis; Merx and the Orientalist Stickel also held lectures on Old Testament subjects, with the result that Köhler's lectures were poorly attended and sometimes had to be abandoned for lack of hearers. It was a happy event for all concerned when two years later Köhler received a call to Bonn and departed from Jena for good. In his place came Ritschl's friend Ludwig Diestel; Hilgenfeld was again passed over.

As compensation, however, Hilgenfeld received an extra 250 talers from the Duke of Gotha so that by the end of the 1860s he was receiving almost the equivalent of a professor's salary. In 1869 he was appointed honorary professor; thus while he now drew a professor's salary—in consequence of which he was able to resign his position in the library—he was still excluded from the faculty deliberations. His first wife had for many years been in bad health and after her death in 1868 he married Eugenie Zenker. In 1876 she received a portion of her uncle's large estate and from that time onwards Hilgenfeld was relieved of all further financial worry. The family moved into the lavish Fromann house, and there was money enough to make frequent holidays.

One last wish remained to be fulfilled—that of becoming a full professor. In 1867/8 he was proposed for a vacant chair at Heidelberg but was not appointed; attempts to gain chairs at other universities all came to nothing. In 1870 following the death of Eduard Schwarz, Otto Pfleiderer was appointed; after Rückert's death in 1871 Hilgenfeld's friend Lipsius was called from Kiel; in 1872 Diestel left for Tübingen and was succeeded by the Assyriologist Schrader. And so it continued: the Jena faculty under the domination of Hase continually passed him by until the death of Hase in 1890. At last the way was open and Lipsius proposed the establishing of a fifth chair to which Hilgenfeld, now sixty-seven years old, was unanimously elected.

Why was it, asked Friedrich Nippold in his commemoration address, that Hilgenfeld was excluded from the faculty for so many years, for without doubt, he was the most knowledgeable Biblical scholar of the whole of the nineteenth century. His energy was amazing. Scarcely anyone could have read and written as much as he. There were in fact three main reasons.

(i) Hilgenfeld rejected all the traditional beliefs of the Christian faith and this certainly prevented any appointment in the conservative Prussian faculties. But this fact cannot account for his exclusion from the Jena faculty, for Lipsius's views were just as radical and the faculty was renowned for its liberal views.

(ii) An important factor in the faculty's judgement was that Hilgenfeld was a poor lecturer who had little drawing power; the faculty naturally desired professors who would attract students and it did not want a liability like Hilgenfeld on its hands.

(iii) But the main reason for Hilgenfeld's exclusion was undoubtedly his tactless, contentious, and often self-opinionated behaviour, The other professors had no desire for such an obnoxious and quarrelsome colleague, who had once even designated himself as a *Dictator perpetuus*. For this reason Hase, in particular, was adamant that Hilgenfeld should have no say in the faculty.

In 1906 Hilgenfeld celebrated the diamond jubilee of the attainment of his doctorate, was made a Knight of the Weimar Order, and received an honorary D.D. from St. Andrews University. However, he did not live to see the diamond anniversary of his habilitation as a lecturer, but passed away peacefully on 12 January 1907 in his eighty-fourth year.

9. Gustav Volkmar

'ONE more request', wrote Lipsius to Hilgenfeld in 1857 as Hilgenfeld was preparing the first issue of his new theological journal; 'for heaven's sake leave Volkmar at least out of the prospectus; the man will ruin everything for you otherwise.'[1] And if on the other hand Köstlin's opinion was somewhat more favourable: 'While I was on a holiday-trip in Switzerland I got to know Volkmar and found him to be a very friendly, energetic man who puts up with his situation with a cheerful courage and the most rigorous application to his work',[2] it would still be true to say that Volkmar's ideas often appeared to be so far-fetched that even the most liberal of the liberals (to say nothing of the orthodox) threw up their hands in horror. Even for Strauss he was too radical: 'A foolish fellow, who, however, is not without some flashes of insight . . . what he brings forth is madness, yet it is not without method (and unfortunately this method is partly Baur's: i.e. I sometimes find it difficult to draw the line which cuts the logical sequence between Baur's premisses and Volkmar's conclusions).'[3] Like it or not Volkmar belonged to the Tübingen School. He was the most radical and revolutionary of the School and perhaps its greatest embarrassment.

Volkmar stemmed from Hesse (the region north of Frankfurt) and with Ritschl and Hilgenfeld was one of the three North Germans in the School. Neither the spelling of his family name nor his date of birth is known precisely. In the church register Volkmar and Volckmar alternate and only after 1853 did he consistently write the former; the baptismal register records his Christian names as Gustav Hermann Joseph and his date of birth as 1 a.m. on 12 January 1809; he added to these names a Philip and maintained he was born on 11 January.

His father Adam Valentine Volkmar was musician and organist at the court of Rotenburg on the Fulda and from 1804 town organist in Bad Hersfeld, where three children were born—a

[1] Lipsius to Hilgenfeld, 20 Aug. 1857.
[2] Köstlin to Hilgenfeld, 6 Oct. 1855.
[3] Strauss to W. Vatke, 7 Feb. 1861; quoted H. Benecke, *Wilhelm Vatke* (Bonn, 1883), p. 503.

daughter in 1806, Gustav in 1809, and Wilhelm in 1811. In 1817 the family shifted to Rinteln where the father had been appointed music master in the secondary school and organist at the church of St. Nicholas. Here Gustav completed his schooling and in 1829 began his study of theology and philosophy at the University in Marburg. After completing his studies in 1832 he went to Frankfurt for a year as tutor in a wealthy family, but the Frankfurt climate was not congenial to his health and he returned to Rinteln as a teacher in the local secondary school. He remained here two years and after two further years' teaching in Kassel, where he married Elise Köhler, the daughter of a Government official in Kassel, he was appointed to the secondary school in Bad Hersfeld. The following years brought a period of peace and quietness in which he devoted himself to teaching and his philological pursuits. His first son was born in 1838, a second born in 1840 died four years later, and to this family was added a daughter. In 1838 he was granted his doctor of philosophy degree from Marburg and from 1844 he belonged to the teaching staff of the Marburg secondary school, whose director at that time was the ultra-conservative August Vilmar.

Volkmar had long been in agreement with the mythical viewpoint put forward by Strauss and he stood solidly behind the programme of the *Theologische Jahrbücher* to which he first contributed in 1846. In his article[4] which dealt with a historical error in the Gospels, Volkmar asserted that Herodias was not the wife of Philip (as in the Gospels) but of a Herod, and from this certainty he proceeded to generalize 'that the Gospels generally build merely on the vaguest data from the common sayings of a later time, and that the details of the stories are invented'. His scepticism regarding the Gospel sources rivalled that of Bruno Bauer and he made such a strong attack on Ebrard, that 'charlatan' and 'liar', that the editors of the *Jahrbücher* felt compelled to add a footnote of apology, announcing that they allowed such sharp criticism to stand simply 'to make clear to that learned man [Ebrard] the consequences of his own polemical tone'. More important was the article written four years later[5] in which Volkmar so convincingly shattered Ritschl's hypothesis that the

---

[4] 'Über einen historischen Irrthum in den Evangelien', *TJ*, 1846, pp. 363–83.
[5] 'Über das Lucasevangelium nach seinem Verhältnis zu Marcion . . .', *TJ*, 1850, pp. 110–38; 185–235.

Gospel of Luke was a working-over of Marcion's version, that Ritschl acknowledged his mistake and retracted his former view. This article provided the groundwork for Volkmar's first book on the Gospel of Marcion, which appeared in 1852. 'Finally, finally,' he wrote to Hilgenfeld, 'this child has been born, and I hasten now, honoured Professor, all the more to recommend it to you, since it has been conceived from you and with your help. It is entitled: "The Gospel of Marcion, Text and commentary . . . Leipzig, 1852".'[6]

Volkmar's contributions to the *Jahrbücher* showed only too clearly where his religious sympathies lay and he also made no secret of his political views. In 1846 he wrote a small political pamphlet supporting the liberal Catholic demands for reform in Hesse. Since its publication was banned in Marburg, Volkmar arranged for it to be printed at Siegen. Vilmar's anger was aroused and Volkmar was transferred to the secondary school at Fulda. Following the 1848 revolution, which found in Volkmar an enthusiastic supporter, came the counter-reaction in which the conservative right clamped down upon the liberals and radicals with a heavy hand. In 1850 Volkmar expressed himself again even more strongly in an anonymous pamphlet published at Fulda, a fiery protest against the ultra-conservative policies of Hassenpflug, the Minister in charge of education. It was astonishing that the Government was so long in taking action against him; not until two years later was he arrested and taken to the prison in the military barracks at Kassel. By an order of the Government in February 1853 he was dismissed from his position and deprived of his Hessian citizenship.

Now he was in a sorry plight and forced almost to beggary. He was helped by friends, especially Eduard Zeller who was now at Marburg and who advised him to try his fortune at Zürich. There, in the city which had so often provided asylum for persecuted theologians, Volkmar too found a welcome. He applied for appointment as lecturer in the theological faculty and on 28 April he held his trial lecture; his application was accepted and on 9 June he was granted the *venia legendi* which permitted him to hold lectures. He related his good fortune in a letter to Hilgenfeld shortly afterwards.

The poison, the book on Marcion, which ate through my previous

[6] To Hilgenfeld, 29 June 1852.

position has now at the same time become the most healing antidote: this piece of investigation awakened so much sympathy here with Hitzig, Schweizer, and others, that I have been able to begin my new career at the University here in Zürich right from the beginning of the semester, and I hope that nothing will separate me from it. I now rejoice in being able to dedicate myself completely to my beloved studies, and to the true interests of Protestant theology, so as to benefit the Church also. God grant that I may find in this, really liberal support.[7]

Zürich proved to be a haven for him and apart from short visits back to his native Germany, he remained there for the rest of his life. His forty years' activity in Zürich were not always easy and especially during the early years when he was forced to live extremely frugally. However, he was never destitute. The position of assistant preacher in a Zürich church provided him with a small income and this, supplemented by other small amounts from his University position, enabled him to weather these first few years. And slowly his position improved. In the winter semester of 1857/8 he was appointed assistant professor and exactly five years later his status was raised to full professor 'of criticism and exegesis of the New Testament'. Among the orthodox he was regarded as one of the more obnoxious unbelievers and on this account he often had much trouble in finding a publisher for his books—the publisher naturally being unwilling to lose money, as invariably happened. Even the librarians in the University library regarded him with great suspicion, as we learn from a letter which he wrote to Hilgenfeld requesting books which the library lacked.

I tried this Easter to arrange to get books from Leipzig through Herr Dr. Tischendorff, especially in order to obtain from there a number of periodicals which I cannot order here just for myself (for even our Protestant clergy are indifferent to everything connected with scientific criticism). Tischendorff promised to do this but so far I haven't received anything. Moreover, I still lack good texts from the Fathers, and newer, more expensive works. Only a few days ago, against the priest-like narrow-mindedness of the library staff who see the devil incarnate hidden in every work which I recommend, did I manage—almost with force and with the threat of bringing a complaint —to acquire the Septuagint, and the New Testament edited by Tischendorff.[8]

---

[7] To Hilgenfeld, 19 July 1853.   [8] To Hilgenfeld, 19 July 1853.

His relations with other professors were never happy. With Alexander Schweizer and A. E. Biedermann he had little personal contact. Between himself and Theodor Keim there was mutual dislike and ill feeling. With Hilgenfeld he was in continual disagreement. Relations between them were at first cordial, but with Hilgenfeld's sensitiveness it was only a short time before their theological differences grew more intense and annoying. Hilgenfeld, on his part, had little respect for Volkmar's investigations into the New Testament and Volkmar's blunt rejoinders such as: 'I have read your reply with great interest, but permit me to say here straight away: you will never succeed in this fashion?'[9] were not calculated to help matters. Although both, on Volkmar's proposal, had originally agreed to 'dispute but not to fight', things slowly developed into a vexatious controversy between them in which Hilgenfeld, as editor of the *Zeitschrift für wissenschaftliche Theologie*, held the upper hand. The most disputed point concerned the dating of the apocalyptic books in the Old Testament—4 Ezra, Judith, and Enoch, which Hilgenfeld placed in the first century B.C. Volkmar, however, dated them at the end of the first century A.D. in order to make them harmonize with his theory that they were dependent upon the apocalyptic and eschatological Christian ideas, a theory which Hilgenfeld attacked with ever increasing obstinacy and scorn.

Volkmar was a revolutionary. Undaunted after his political experiences in Hesse he took up the political fight once more as soon as he had arrived in Switzerland. And not half-heartedly: Volkmar was only interested in a truly radical programme. Thus, it was a triumph for him when after the radical party had emerged victorious in the 1869 Zürich elections, he was elected president of the governing committee of the Church. But once in this position he became such a dictator that all his friends were pleased to see him resign in 1872, because he had not ruled democratically enough. His home became ever quieter as his daughter married and his son took up a position in Germany. After the death of his wife he lived alone and devoted his time to reading, writing, and to his lectures, which he never failed to deliver right up until he was taken ill in October 1892. His death followed on 9 January 1893.

Volkmar's writings represent a complete and utter denial

---

[9] To Hilgenfeld, 5 Aug. 1857.

of the traditional Christian faith and yet one has the impression that Volkmar considers himself to be an orthodox believer, indeed, the *only* orthodox believer. Volkmar is a man convinced that his view of Jesus and of Christianity is the true view and that what is true is also the true orthodoxy. We may sketch very briefly his view of Jesus.

Jesus, according to Volkmar, was born not in Bethlehem, but in Nazareth. He also confessed his sins like other great men and started out on a public ministry of teaching. Some of the people saw in him a prophet, although Volkmar recognizes him only as a great teacher. Nor did Volkmar deny all of Jesus' healing miracles; some he admitted might have taken place, but these are left unexplained and Volkmar simply bows before them as before a great mystery.

Volkmar will portray Jesus as a religious reformer—at most, a prophet (with prophecy being divested of any supernatural character). It is particularly interesting here to note what pains Volkmar takes to exclude all possibility of Jesus' claiming to be the Son of God. Even the charge of the high priest at Jesus' trial is whittled away, so that Jesus may claim only a divine sending, the right of a prophet. Instead of allowing Caiaphas' question: 'Are you the Christ, the Son of the Blessed?' to stand, Volkmar softens it down to: 'Will *you* be the *Prophet*, whom Moses proclaimed? *You*—are you the anointed of the Blessed?'[10]

According to Volkmar, Jesus never claimed to be the Son of God; this title was ascribed to him after his death; it was a product of the resurrection, which Volkmar denies as being a resurrection of Jesus' earthly body. 'Jesus is raised for the disciples', i.e. in the minds of the disciples. Volkmar knows that Jesus's body was never buried in a tomb, but either thrown on a rubbish heap or covered over with earth. How the disciples came to believe in Jesus' resurrection was to be explained by visions, seen first by the women (who are more excitable than men) and then by the disciples. Nor did Jesus ever think of himself as returning to earth after his death. All apocalyptic sayings and prophecies originated within the early Church. Jesus was in no sense an eschatological or divine figure, although Volkmar made every effort to do justice to Jesus' greatness.

Here the greatest, purest, and most liberating of all teachers of

[10] *Jesus Nazarenus* (Zürich, 1882), p. 150.

humanity; here the fulfilment of the highest, what the people of God in the Old Testament strove after; here in truth the King of the kingdom of God, the one and only king who for Israel could have been and will be; here also the personally enduring ground of the universal redemption, raised in truth above the whole human world or to the right hand of power over all peoples and ages. From this height he comes and has come at all times for the salvation of all who seek him, for judgement upon all who reject him.[11]

Volkmar was a somewhat eccentric theologian and for this reason his writings are perhaps the most interesting of the whole Tübingen School. The ideas he put forward never lack interest and above all else he possessed the gift of originality—two traits undeniably lacking in most modern theological treatises. His investigations usually produced the most astonishing results and were invariably greeted with scorn and derision; but he went his way, unperturbed by the criticisms of friend or foe, and took no notice of his more famous contemporaries, Weizsäcker, Holsten, or Holtzmann. Yet his investigations were not as absurd as was often thought and, as Strauss remarked, there was method in his madness. Thus when Volkmar discovers everywhere in the New Testament Pauline and Jewish Christians, Gnostics and anti-Gnostics; when Paul entreats Euodia and Syntyche to agree in the Lord (Philippians 4:1) and Volkmar argues that the names refer not to two individuals but to the Pauline and Jewish parties; when he expresses the view that the stories about Jesus in the Gospels are actually descriptions of Paul, then he is only carrying Baur's principles to their logical conclusion.

Volkmar must be understood in order to be appreciated and when he has been truly understood then one can even enjoy reading him—if only to chuckle at his preposterous conclusions. His works have now been completely forgotten, perhaps because he was a hundred years ahead of his time.

[11] Ibid., p. 401.

PART II

THE TÜBINGEN THEOLOGICAL AND
HISTORICAL PERSPECTIVE

10. Baur's Theological Development

BAUR's life can be divided into three formative periods of theological development—first, his university years in Tübingen when he came under the influence of the Old Tübingen School; secondly, the 1820s when he occupied himself with Schelling and was attracted by the methodology of Schleiermacher; and thirdly, the period during which he adopted the speculative philosophy of Hegel. Finally, as we shall see, Baur turned back to a rationalistic view of Christianity.

THE INFLUENCE OF THE OLD TÜBINGEN SCHOOL

The three years which Baur spent in the theological faculty at Tübingen from 1811 to 1814 were extremely important in emancipating him—or, at least, beginning the process of emancipation—from the traditional orthodox theology in which he had been reared. If we are to understand this process of emancipation it will be necessary to examine carefully the influences which surrounded him during these years. This will mean investigating the character of the Old Tübingen School, which reached the height of its influence at Tübingen during the first two decades of the nineteenth century.

Theologically, the members of this School[1] are invariably all considered under the ambiguous description of rational supernaturalism, the reader being left to work out the meaning of this enigmatic designation for himself. The beginning of the School may be dated from 1777 when Gottlob Christian Storr (1746–1805) was appointed to the theological faculty in Tübingen. Storr was a man of great perception and unusual talent who combined a profound learning with upright piety and moral earnestness. His main concern was to provide a scientific undergirding for the authority of the Bible and to demonstrate that divine revelation was neither absurd nor contrary to reason. The old orthodox theory of verbal inspiration was now abandoned and authority

---

[1] On the Old Tübingen School see: Baur's chapter in K. Klüpfel, *Geschichte und Beschreibung der Universität Tübingen*, pp. 216–47; Herzog's *Realencyclopedie*, XX, pp. 148–59; *Württembergische Kirchengeschichte* (Calw and Stuttgart, 1893), pp. 566–9.

centred in Jesus and the apostles rather than in the Bible itself. Storr in fact wished to prove the authenticity and integrity of the New Testament writings from external and historical evidences, rather than tacitly accepting its divine authority without question. From this point he set out to show that Christ has the authority of a 'divine ambassador', this being substantiated by his perfect ethical thought and conduct, not least by his miracles. The truth of Christ's doctrine, the authority of the apostles, the truth of their teaching, and the recognition of the divine inspiration of the Scriptures all follow on logically from this initial authoritative starting-point. There is no doubt that Storr remained solidly supernaturalist and had no intention of denying or even deprecating the revelation contained in the Scriptures; he wished only to make the Scriptures more intelligible. However, in this process an emphasis appeared which we find to a much greater degree in his successors—an emphasis on the teaching of Christ as the mediation of the divine truths of revelation.

While Storr stood fundamentally on a truly supernatural basis his successors did not, and with the brothers J. F. and K. C. Flatt a Kantian rationalism begins to make itself felt. The elder brother Johann Friedrich Flatt (1759–1821) was an enthusiastic follower of Kant and the first member of the philosophical faculty to lecture on the Kantian philosophy. Transferred to the theological faculty in 1792, he became responsible for Christian ethics and New Testament exegesis. In the writings of the younger brother Karl Christian Flatt (1772–1843) the influence of Kant is again to the fore and rationalistic tendencies are easily observable. In his book on the Atonement[2] he endeavoured to show that not only is the forgiveness of sins determined by the moral improvement of the individual, but in his opinion such a view was the only reasonable interpretation which could be derived from the New Testament itself.

Storr's direct successor was Friedrich Gottlieb Süskind (1769–1829), an acute thinker and able lecturer who was generally esteemed as the first theologian in Württemberg. Süskind remained only seven years as professor in the theological faculty (1798–1805) but in this short time he exerted great influence. In his writings he stressed that above all it is the teaching of Jesus

[2] *Philosophisch-exegetische Untersuchungen über die Lehre von der Versöhnung der Menschen mit Gott* (Göttingen, 1797).

which is to be regarded as divine; Jesus' divinity was somewhat glossed over and Süskind tended to the view that Jesus' divine nature was evidenced by the divine moral and ethical truths which he taught.[3] It was only one step further to the ethical supernaturalism which characterizes the teaching of Bengel.

The fifth member of the School[4] was Ernst Gottlieb Bengel (1769–1826), grandson of the famous prelate Johann Albrecht Bengel. The younger Bengel, as he was commonly known, was appointed professor of theology in 1806, and through his strength of personality he exercised a commanding influence on the whole of Württemberg theology for the next twenty years, and especially upon Baur. With Bengel the word supernatural has a double meaning and he uses the word in a moral and ethical rather than in its traditional sense. His writings possess the appearance of orthodoxy but one does not have to read very far before noticing that the emphasis is entirely on the moral and ethical side of Christianity. Revelation, to be sure, is still necessary, but it is a revelation of moral truths rather than that of a Person, and Jesus is described as 'the divine teacher', 'the teacher of truth', 'the highest educator of humanity',[5] phrases which once more remind us of Lessing and Kant. Certainly Bengel never denied the miracles which Jesus performed, but neither did he explicitly affirm them as actual historical events. Moreover, while he treated the resurrection of Christ as the best-attested fact of history, he also left open the possibility that it might be explained by a more natural and rational explanation than had so far been discovered. Thus with Bengel the supernatural is simply an ethical supernaturalism, which may be understood either in the sense of Kant's moral law, or as 'truth', and revelation is only necessary in order to communicate the divine truths to human reason.

If Christianity is really what it purports to be and what we confess it to be—a revelation of the infinite reason, which we through our own reason are obliged to believe implicitly—what new heights of *assurance* does Christianity then grant us out of the most precious truths taught in natural religion and morality? In Christianity we find the same

[3] *In welchem Sinne hat Jesus die Göttlichkeit seiner Religions- und Sittenlehre behauptet?* (Tübingen, 1802).
[4] Others who may be included in the School were J. F. Wurm (d. 1847), C. B. Klaiber (1795–1836), and J. C. F. Steudel (1779–1837), professor of theology in Tübingen from 1815 to 1837.
[5] *Reden über Religion und Christenthum* (Tübingen, 1831).

things which we learn from a thoughtful attentiveness to our own rational nature and the voice of our own moral feeling concerning the Author and Ruler of all things. . . . In Christianity we again find pure and unadulterated this same content of natural religion and morality.[6]

Baur's Review of Kaiser's Biblical Theology

It is against this broadly deist background that we must evaluate the review of G. P. C. Kaiser's book, 'Biblical Theology, or Judaism and Christianity according to the Grammatical-historical Method of Interpretation', which Baur probably composed during his time as tutor in the Tübingen Stift (1816–17). This review, which appeared in Bengel's theological journal,[7] was signed simply with —r and is the only long piece of writing which Baur composed before his 'Symbolics and Metaphysics' which appeared in 1824/5. Its importance in determining the development of Baur's theological views during this early period is therefore crucial.

The generally accepted view is that Baur at this time was still a supernaturalist who stood under the influence of Bengel and the theology of the Old Tübingen School. Confirmation for this opinion was found in the fact that Baur had defended the resurrection of Christ as an actual historical event. But this estimate of Baur rested on an inadequate understanding of the theology of the Old Tübingen School and failed to see Baur's statement concerning the resurrection in the context of the whole review.

Kaiser, a convinced rationalist, had examined the historical religions in order to extract the universal element common to each and thus synthesize the true universal religion.

He wants, as he himself says, 'to set forth not just the path which all religions in the world have taken, but rather to provide a very general sketch of world history by means of a philosophical and critical comparison of the world religions, or better, to provide a description of the main points of religion, obtained by comparing the different religions of the world, in order to solve the theological riddle of Judaism and Christianity by setting both in this comparison of religions'. He wants 'to remove the veil which hung over ancient Palestine in order to ascertain truly the eternal, ideal religion'.[8]

With this plan Baur was in substantial agreement.

[6] Ibid., pp. 143–4.
[7] *Archiv für die Theologie und ihre neueste Literatur*, II: 3 (1818), pp. 656–717.
[8] Ibid., p. 657.

We share with the author the high respect which this study of religions deserves and are completely convinced that it is above all the comparison of the history of religions which can preserve us from those one-sided and narrow-minded views quite incompatible with the spirit of true religion, and can make a true assessment of the service which Christianity has rendered, even though we are not able to agree completely with the results which the author believed he could attain through these investigations.[9]

What displeased Baur about Kaiser's book was not the aim of Kaiser's programme, but the fact that Kaiser had made such a poor job of carrying the programme out. Thus when Kaiser presented a picture of the development of man, which could be roughly described as a forerunner of the Darwinian, Baur expressed his agreement with the general direction of thought and criticized only some individual aspects, regretting that Kaiser had not dealt more thoroughly with the question. 'We believe that the execution of the whole would have gained much if the author had gone more deeply into these psychological ideas and had separated the different stages in the development of mankind in a more precise manner instead of merely holding on to that distorted analogy, all the more since he himself (p. 52) draws attention to a more correct view.'[10]

An important issue was the universality of revelation, and here Baur sided with Kaiser in accepting a general revelation which manifested itself in various forms and degrees of reality.

We do not deny that the source of revelation must be a universal source accessible to every man, and that a historical, and for just this reason, particular revelation could not possibly be acknowledged as the source of the true religion, if with this declaration was bound up the assertion that the true knowledge of religion can only take place exclusively in connection with this particular revelation, because it would be blasphemous to maintain that God had ever withdrawn himself from a section of mankind.[11]

Kaiser's acceptance of mythical elements in the New Testament, especially the stories of the birth of Jesus, also found a sympathetic hearing, although Baur stressed that the probability of mythical elements was proportional to the time elapsing before the oral tradition had been written down.

---

[9] Ibid., p. 658.   [10] Ibid., p. 670.   [11] Ibid., p. 663.

It certainly appears to us that it can scarcely be doubted that the possibility of myths also being present in the Gospel history must in general be conceded. Just where a history is passed down from generation to generation only by word of mouth, where the content of this history itself claims a high degree of feeling and fantasy and must be set in relation to conceptions which had already formed themselves into a certain system, just there the origin of myths with respect to psychology and according to the analogy of similar experiences, is certainly not unthinkable or improbable . . . Yet even here the probability has its varying degrees according to the character of the individual narratives. The greater the period of time between the oral tradition and the writing down of the narratives, the less chance there would be of an attested observation either of the event itself or of the special circumstances in which it was written down, and the probability of myths being accepted into the Gospels would then be even greater. In this respect—if the presence of myths in the New Testament is at all to be accepted—one would have to reckon the narratives relating the history of the birth and childhood of Jesus among those in which this mythical element would be present with a higher degree of probability.[12]

But Baur denied Kaiser's assertion that the resurrection of Jesus was not a real historical event. 'Accordingly, we may rightly maintain that as certainly as the origin of the Christian Church was only possible through the firm faith in the Resurrected One, just as certainly this faith could rest on no other ground than on the historical truth of the resurrection of Jesus.'[13]

What strikes one in reading through the whole review is the mixture of orthodoxy and rationalism, which reveals the transition through which Baur's views were at that time passing. Kaiser's book had set almost everything in the New Testament in doubt and it is interesting to observe how much Baur actually conceded to Kaiser's arguments. Baur did not attempt to answer all the objections which Kaiser had raised, but contented himself mainly with a general criticism of Kaiser's procedure. The noteworthy thing is not so much what Baur said, but rather what he did not say; for in fact he could hardly have conceded more to Kaiser without stepping outside the boundaries of the orthodoxy of his time.

In this setting we must also view Baur's statement about the resurrection. At this period Baur did not categorically deny the

---

[12] Ibid., pp. 711–12.   [13] Ibid., p. 715.

historicity of the narratives of Jesus' birth and childhood (as was later the case); but he affirmed only that all narratives possessed a certain degree of probability. With regard to the resurrection Baur considered this degree to be so high as to be almost certain, for he could find no other explanation as feasible as the traditional one. The problems involved in explaining the resurrection away by visions or an 'apparent death' were far greater than those involved in an acceptance of the traditional view. Baur simply saw no reason to deny the traditional explanation.

But if at this time Baur accepted the resurrection, one cannot maintain that he still stood on a completely orthodox and supernatural basis. Revelation for Baur was not a particular revelation in history, but a general and universal revelation of truth. In this view Baur stood far more within the rationalistic orthodoxy of Bengel than in the traditional supernaturalism from which he was just in the process of shaking himself free. Whether or not he still accepted the concept of a transcendent personal God is uncertain; perhaps he thought of God as the upholder of the moral law, but probably he left the question open without deciding either way.

It is difficult to be more explicit about Baur's standpoint at this time for his review is essentially a criticism of Kaiser and not a statement of his own personal belief. Nevertheless, we may say that in this review the gradual emancipation away from orthodoxy towards a more rationalistic point of view is certainly observable.

THE INFLUENCE OF SCHELLING

Baur made very few statements in his early years about Schelling's philosophy and it is therefore not easy to reach a clear and incontrovertible conclusion as to precisely how far and in what way Baur was influenced by the new transcendental Idealism. We may recall that while Baur was attending the higher seminary in Maulbronn, Schelling's father was the prelate for the district and Baur's attention would doubtless have been drawn to the prelate's famous son. In 1812 the Tübingen professor K. A. Eschenmayer,[14] who was well acquainted with Schelling's works, gave a course of lectures which surveyed the history of theology and especially

---

[14] Karl August Eschenmayer (1768–1852) was both a medical doctor and a philosopher, from 1811 professor of medicine and philosophy at Tübingen. In the early 1800s he was an enthusiastic admirer of Schelling's philosophy and in his later years a resolute antagonist of Strauss.

the more recent theology.[15] These lectures may have stimulated
Baur to delve into Schelling's writings, but at the same time he
may have also read Süskind's book 'Examination of Schelling's
Teaching concerning God, the Creation, Freedom, Moral Good
and Evil' which appeared in 1812 and was penetratingly critical
of Schelling's ideas. In all probability Baur would have read the
book during his university years, and since Süskind's analysis was
so competent in exposing the errors of Schelling's system, it may
be accepted that Baur too, from that time onward, was somewhat
reserved in his attitude to Schelling's philosophy.

However, we must also take account of the letter which Baur's
brother Friedrich August Baur wrote to Zeller in 1861 describing
the development of Baur's theological viewpoint.

I know that he diligently studied philosophy at the University and
was regarded in the *Promotion* as the one who had accomplished most in
this subject; I also know that in accordance with the idealist character
of his spirit it was Fichte and Schelling with whom he especially
busied himself, and with the latter also in Blaubeuren from where he
urged me to study Schelling's 'Transcendental Idealism'.[16] And his
'Symbolics and Mythology' attests him the friend of Schelling's
philosophy of identity not less than the man of classical literature.[17]

Baur's interest in Schelling is also attested in a letter written to
Ludwig Bauer, a former pupil of Baur's in Blaubeuren.

Without doubt Schelling's philosophy, which is far more living and
rich in phantasy [than Fichte's], will already have attracted you more
and I would advise you to read through carefully especially his 'System
of Transcendental Idealism', a work which has pleased me immensely.
You will find that this work is also a compensation for Fichte and that
through it one can form generally for oneself the true concept of the
strict scientific construction of a [philosophical] system. I know of no
other work after Fichte's *Wissenschaftslehre*[18] which one can read with
greater profit for especially the formal philosophical training.[19]

[15] Carl Hester, 'Gedanken zu Ferdinand Christian Baurs Entwicklung als Historiker anhand zweier unbekannter Briefe', ZKG, LXXXIV (1973), pp. 249–69; p. 254.
[16] F. W. J. Schelling, *Das System des transcendentalen Idealismus* (Tübingen, 1800).
[17] F. A. Baur to Zeller, 12 Jan. 1861. The letter was printed by Barnikol in 'Das
ideengeschichtliche Erbe Hegels . . .', p. 282.
[18] Fichte's *Wissenschaftslehre* is expounded in many of his works and especially in
his *Grundlage der gesammten Wissenschaftslehre* (1794); *Über den Begriff der Wissenschaftslehre* (1794); *Grundriss des Eigenthümlichen der Wissenschaftslehre* (1795); *Die Wissenschaftslehre in ihrem allgemeinen Umrisse dargestellt* (1810).
[19] Baur to Ludwig Bauer, 2 Nov. 1822. The letter is printed by Carl Hester, op.
cit., pp. 264–7.

The question which arises out of these letters is how far Baur's philosophical and theological views were influenced by Schelling and in what way. In his review of Kaiser's book there is little really discernible evidence that Baur in 1818 had adopted Schelling's ideas, although in the preface to his 'Symbolics and Mythology' (1824/5) this influence is much more evident. Yet in this preface, for some unaccountable reason,[20] Baur made no mention of Schelling's name among those to whom he regarded himself indebted.

In his later writings Baur was always highly critical of Schelling's speculative system, and when Schelling was called to Berlin in 1841 Baur wrote to Heyd in rather scathing terms.

It would be fine if, while Schelling once more steps on to the Berlin stage as *restituens rem*,[21] the old butting goat could appear in the same character and exert his authority. You will have also read the article in the *Allgemeine Zeitung* about Schelling. It is indeed an unprecedented arrogance with which this man steps forth. It is as if he had come to Berlin just to pour scorn on Hegel's grave. Even his former silence is supposed to be viewed as magnanimity. I hope this pride comes before the fall and say in the name of Hegel: *exoriare aliquis*.[22]

It is true that one cannot place too much emphasis on this passage, for first, Baur was now at the height of his enthusiasm for Hegel and viewed Schelling as a pale usurper of his Master's mantle. Secondly, he saw Schelling's appointment as having been engineered by Neander, who seven years earlier had been primarily responsible for preventing his own call to Berlin. Even so, when all this is conceded, it still remains true that Baur nowhere acknowledged the validity of Schelling's philosophy. He did not deny the ingenuity of Schelling's system or the interest his ideas had aroused, but he could not accept that these ideas were true and he criticized Schelling for construing Christianity too one-sidedly out of elements derived from Spinoza. Thus it is extremely difficult to determine precisely to what degree and in what regard Baur was influenced by Schelling. The ideas which Fichte and Schelling propounded were at that time quite familiar in academic

[20] Possibly this was due to his new occupation with Schleiermacher and his unwillingness to identify himself in any way with Schelling, about whose ideas he was now somewhat sceptical?
[21] Restorer of true philosophy.
[22] May some avenger arise. Baur to Heyd, 30 Nov. 1841.

circles and we need not suppose that Baur's theological development in this period was indebted to Schelling alone. Baur would
have noted the positive virtues of Schelling's thought, but he
must also have perceived its weaknesses.[23] Any influence which
Schelling may have exerted upon him, however, was soon
superseded by a stronger and more lasting one.

THE INFLUENCE OF SCHLEIERMACHER

It was probably during the spring and summer of 1823 that Baur
first read through Schleiermacher's *Christian Faith* and reported
to his brother:

> No theological work has yet attracted me in so many respects as
> this, and apart from each peculiarity of view, it contains in each individ-
> ual section so many rich ideas and so much for correcting the tradi-
> tional dogmatic views that in fact it should be noticed more than seems
> to be the case at present. . . . The most admirable feature of all is the
> so completely integrated arrangement and execution of the system,
> and then along with this dialectical art a genuine religious spirit, which
> is otherwise so foreign to the customary dogmatics, permeates and
> animates the whole.[24]

Following his calling to Tübingen in 1826 Baur presented his
inaugural dissertation to the students and staff of the University.[25]
The dissertation was divided into two parts, the first part being an
analysis of Gnosticism, the second consisting of a comparison of
the central principles contained in Schleiermacher's *Christian
Faith* with the Gnostic views which Baur had adduced and
summarized in the first part. In this second part Baur numbered
Schleiermacher among the Gnostics, not, however, intending
this appellation in any unfriendly way. But since Schleiermacher
in the introduction to his Dogmatics had expressly excluded the
Gnostic heresy from the Christian faith, it was entirely understandable that the great man did not feel flattered by Baur's
description of his theological standpoint. In his reply Schleiermacher indignantly rejected Baur's criticism, and being under the

[23] Cf. *Dogmengeschichte*, III, pp. 338, 349, 445. 524f.; *Geschichte der Christlichen
Kirche*, V, pp. 79–85.
[24] To F. A. Baur, 16 July 1823. The letter, preserved only in Zeller's copy of the
original, was printed by Barnikol in 'Das ideengeschichtliche Erbe Hegels . . .',
pp. 316–18, and by H. Liebing in *ZTK*, LIV (1957), pp. 238–43.
[25] *Primae Rationalismi et Supranaturalismi historiae capita potiora*. Baur provided a
German rendering of the first two parts in his 'Anzeige der beiden academischen
Schriften von Dr. F. C. Baur', *TZT*, 1828: I, pp. 220–64.

impression that it had proceeded from a conservative point of view, he numbered Baur among the members of the Old Tübingen School.[26] Not until Schleiermacher's visit to Tübingen in 1830 did the two men meet personally and have the chance to exchange views face to face.

Baur's opinion of Schleiermacher's theology never essentially changed throughout the years. From his first reading of Schleiermacher's *Christian Faith* in 1823 Baur perceived astutely the central principles of Schleiermacher's system. A letter written to his brother in July of this same year reveals Baur's first impressions of the work.

Blaubeuren, 26 July 1823

Dear brother,

I have just finished reading Schleiermacher's *Christian Faith* and in accordance with your wishes will pass on a few remarks to you about it. I found the work so original and deep that, because of the shortness of time that I was able to spend on it, I was not capable of mastering its whole content in one reading, and therefore I do not know whether or not I shall be able to satisfy you completely. Nevertheless, I will draw your attention to a few points.

One can consider the work from its philosophical and theological side. With regard to its philosophical side the basic view is certainly pantheistic, but one can just as well say, idealistic. The philosophical system in the work never appears in a definite form and for this reason one must beware of immediately describing it by some well-known label. But this is certain, that both viewpoints are held so over against each other that in their end-points they want to pass over into each other. Idealistic is above all the constant development of all the principal doctrines from the self-consciousness; pantheistic is especially the treatment of the doctrine of God which, certainly, sets God as the Absolute in the purest sense, but at the same time in such an abstract way that not just the essence of God but even the most general attributes (approximately the same ones as Spinoza, according to the distinction of being and thinking or knowing, leads all the remaining concepts back to) are taken into consideration; and in order to exclude every finite antithesis in the divine essence there can be no more talk of God as an actual personality. Even the concept of God's rationality is accepted only in a more negative sense (cf. § 68) and the only positive concept ascribed to God is that of causality in the most general sense.

---

[26] 'Second open Letter to Lücke', *TSK*, 1829, pp. 505f. Baur's reply was contained in his 'Christian Gnosticism', pp. 647–52.

Thereby the question immediately arises how the idea of freedom harmonizes with this view. On this point also one seeks in vain in the work for a clear explanation, as it is generally Schleiermacher's way in the work to let one simply surmise the importance of certain philosophical main-ideas on which his whole system nevertheless rests, rather than to discuss these ideas explicitly, since he always wants to move only within the theological sphere. . . .

It is impossible for me to view his system, as it is here set forth, as a purely self-contained one; indeed, he himself always points out that his representation appears in this form only with reference to the feeling of dependence. As regards the theological side of the work in which the historical and the Christian element comes into consideration, his originality shows itself here completely. I know of no representation of Christianity in which the peculiar essence of Christianity is so acutely comprehended and made so thoroughly the middle point of the whole system, none which could be held as being more Christian and ortho-dox. And yet, in the last resort everything is conceived entirely otherwise, from a completely different viewpoint as in the previous dogmatics. The distinction between this new viewpoint and the old customary one consists, to put it briefly, in the fact that while the old view accepts the external revelation or the writings of the New Testa-ment as the sole source of knowledge of Christianity, according to Schleiermacher, the primary source of Christianity lies in the religious self-consciousness, out of whose development the principal doctrines of Christianity are to be obtained. . . .

Finally, with regard to the question as to how far this system acknowledges the character of a supernatural revelation in Christianity, the Christian element is, to be sure, invariably called supernatural in contrast to man's natural incapability to redeem himself, but this supernatural is still only a natural one, since it is expressly stated (§ 61) that in the whole sphere of piety and revelation there is absolutely nothing supernatural. In no way, however, is the miraculous element in the inception of Christianity disputed or explained in the common natural manner; but it is only a relative supernaturalism. This question is most important with respect to the Person of Christ. In Schleier-macher's dogmatics too, Christ receives all the predicates of divine worth which the traditional dogmatics ascribes to him, the divine and human natures were united in him in so far as his consciousness of God was a true being of God. On the other hand archetypal and historical in him are distinguished, and he himself is called the per-fected creation of human nature. I must admit that I find this part of the system the most difficult to comprehend and grasp in its whole deep connectedness. When the principal doctrines concerning the Person of the Redeemer are themselves deduced from the religious self-consciousness, with the result that the external history of Jesus is viewed as a history of the inner developments of the religious self-consciousness, then I can think of the Person of Christ as the Redeemer only as a certain form and capacity of the self-consciousness which appeared in an external history merely because the natural development of the self-consciousness in its highest perfection must necessarily at some time take this form. Christ is thus in every man and the external appearance of Jesus is here also not the original form of Christ; but in the historical form only the archetypal, ideal form is supposed to be demonstrated and the inner consciousness brought to clear view. It is abundantly clear how precisely this view hangs together with the pantheistic–idealistic basic view of the whole system . . .[27]

Three points may be noted in passing.

1. From the beginning Baur recognized clearly the non-super-natural character of Schleiermacher's Dogmatics. Schleiermacher simply changed the meaning of the word 'supernatural' by enlarging the boundaries of the natural realm to include all that was formerly understood as an other-worldly supernatural; or, conversely, he brought the supernatural into the realm of the natural so that there was no longer any absolute supernatural but only a relative one (i.e. within the natural realm). Baur perceived the situation plainly and astutely. Granted the existence of a transcendent personal God, then miracles are possible and the rationalists had no sufficient reason for trying to explain them away. But if there were no such God, then there could obviously be no miracles. Baur expressed this point succinctly in his lectures on the history of the Church in the nineteenth century.

To be sure, Schleiermacher also maintains that Christianity has a supernatural character, but when he at the same time associates with this statement the assertion that the supernatural is not absolutely supernatural, but that everything supernatural is also natural, then one can soon see how it stands with Schleiermacher's supernaturalism. Schleiermacher excludes the supernatural far more strictly and resolutely than rationalism. Rationalism certainly denies miracles, but with its theistic basis it was not capable of cutting the roots of the miracle concept. The miracle is the direct consequence of the traditional theism. If God is once thought of as an other-worldly absolute Will,

[27] To F. A. Baur, 16 July 1823.

then one must concede an activity of this Will in the world; but this activity as the intervention of a transcendent principle into the course of the world can only be supernatural, a miracle. From its supernatural presupposition concerning the relationship of God to the world, rationalism has, therefore, no right to dispute the consequence of theism.[28]

2. Baur also recognized the pantheistic character of Schleiermacher's Dogmatics. The word 'pantheistic' was not used by Baur in any rigidly defined sense, nor in the traditional sense as used by Spinoza, where God was equated with the world; it was employed, rather, to denote a concept of God which can be described neither as theism, nor as outright and open atheism, but as something in between. The pantheistic concept of God may thus be understood in a Kantian sense, where God is equated with the moral law, or as a grandiose idealistic system in which God is viewed as a metaphysical process. That Baur never changed his views on this point is shown in his later lectures.

Schleiermacher was the first to abolish absolutely the concept of the miracle in that he conceived the relation of God to the world not theistically but pantheistically. Schleiermacher's pantheism is certainly a very disputed question and Schleiermacher himself always protested exceedingly earnestly against the reproach of pantheism which was continually brought against him. But if each viewpoint which defines the relation of God to the world as an immanent relation can rightly be called pantheistic, then Schleiermacher's *Christian Faith* must also put up with this designation.[29]

3. In logical consequence of Schleiermacher's denial of the supernatural element in Christianity it was only too clear that Schleiermacher's attempted identification of the ideal Christ with the historical Jesus could not be maintained. For Schleiermacher, Christ was not the divine Son of God in the traditional sense, but rather an Idea—the most perfect Idea of the highest God—which represented a particular stage in the development of the religious consciousness. Schleiermacher thus transposed the traditional concept of the God-man into a concept expressing the essential unity of the divine and the human, by which Schleiermacher meant the inner harmony of the religious consciousness. This inner harmony, which Schleiermacher refers to as God-consciousness, received its highest human expression in the Person

---

[28] *Geschichte der christlichen Kirche*, V, p. 184.   [29] Ibid., V, p. 184.

of Jesus as the perfect archetype of what every man should be and become. Christ is thus the Redeemer by virtue of the archetypal religious consciousness which he possesses.

Christ is Redeemer in that he absolutely abolishes the subjection caused by the feeling of absolute dependence, the subjection which in every man makes a satisfying path for the consciousness of God impossible; or he is Redeemer through the archetypal nature which essentially differentiates him from all other men, i.e. through the constancy of the consciousness of God which expresses itself through inerrancy and sinlessness. This constancy as the absolute power of his God-consciousness was the being of God in him.[30]

Schleiermacher was never able to bridge the gulf between the Christ of speculation and the Jesus of history. His Christ always remained a product of his own analysis of the religious consciousness, a product which in Baur's opinion had no connection with historical reality.

Whether or not the Person of Jesus of Nazareth really possesses the attributes ascribed to him by Schleiermacher in the concept of the Redeemer, which he here sets forth, is in fact a purely historical question which can be answered only through a historical investigation of the literary documents of the Gospel history, documents which in the introduction to this *Christian Faith* are certainly nowhere brought forward as actual sources of knowledge for Christianity.[31]

When we take into consideration all Baur's utterances concerning Schleiermacher's *Christian Faith*, then it becomes quite evident that along with a deep respect for Schleiermacher's Dogmatics, Baur also recognized the faults and failings of the work. Baur's judgement never essentially changed throughout the years and in his later lectures on the history of the Christian Church, he was just as perceptive, laudatory, and critical of Schleiermacher as he had been in 1823.

But if Baur saw so many defects in Schleiermacher's system, why then was he so impressed with it? The reason is that Baur recognized the brilliance of the system which Schleiermacher had evolved—a system which interpreted the whole of the Christian faith from non-supernatural premisses. The rationalists had interpreted the Bible piecemeal and in a wholly negative fashion; Fichte and Schelling had formulated metaphysical

---

[30] *TZT*, 1828: I, p. 235.   [31] Ibid., p. 242.

systems which had little connection with Biblical history. But in Schleiermacher's non-supernatural construction every doctrine of the traditional Christian faith was allotted its own rightful place. Baur perceived the defects which Schleiermacher had been unable to correct, but the attempt had at least been made and the problem was to create something better. Thus we may say that Schleiermacher's influence upon Baur was certainly not as important as has sometimes been assumed. Baur was always critical of the content of Schleiermacher's theological system, although admiring the intention which lay behind it.

The lectures on the history of the Church in the nineteenth century provide probably the most penetrating and lucid analysis of Schleiermacher's theology which has ever been penned by any theologian, either in the nineteenth or in the twentieth century. It may be maintained that few people ever understood Schleiermacher as well as Baur, and for this reason we conclude with a longer passage from Baur's masterly critique.

Schleiermacher refuses to discuss the concept of miracles; he does not consider this to be the task of his *Christian Faith* which is based only on the standpoint of the religious consciousness. But when from this point of view he sets up the basic proposition, that from the interest of piety a necessity could never arise of conceiving a fact so that its conditionedness by the laws of nature could be absolutely abolished through its dependence on God, or in other words, that no religious requirement could ever establish the necessity of miracles, then the concept of miracles is thereby dogmatically abolished. Without this necessity the concept of miracles has no philosophical interest; if it also has no religious interest then the question can only be whether the facts of the Gospel history do not compel us to acknowledge miracles, and whether or not our concept of the Person of the Redeemer —no matter how high it may be set—is formed in accordance with Scripture, if we do not also consider his supernatural conception and birth, his resurrection and ascension—as maintained by the traditional Church doctrines—to be essential features of his personality. Schleiermacher was unable to avoid this question in his *Christian Faith*, but it is only too clear from his answer how little significance the miracle can have for him. Concerning the supernatural conception of Jesus he says (*Christian Faith*, pp. 405–6): 'The general idea of a supernatural conception remains essential and necessary if the peculiar pre-eminence of the Redeemer is not to be diminished. But the more precise definition of this supernatural conception as one in which there was no male participation, has no connection of any kind with the essential elements which constitute the peculiar worth of the Redeemer, and thus in and by itself is absolutely no constituent part of Christian doctrine. Whoever accepts such a supernatural conception accepts it only on the ground of the narratives referring to it contained in the New Testament writings. And so belief in it, like belief in many matters of fact which have little necessary connection with the worth and work of the Redeemer, belongs only to the teaching of Scripture, and each one has himself to decide about it by the proper application of those principles of criticism and interpretation which he has verified for himself.'

Schleiermacher maintains that the facts of Christ's resurrection and ascension, as well as the prophesying of his return to judge the world, cannot be set forth as actual constituents of the teaching concerning his Person. Since the redeeming activity of Christ rests on the being of God in him, a direct connection between those facts and this teaching cannot be demonstrated. The disciples recognized in Jesus the Son of God without having any presentiment of his resurrection and ascension and we can say the same about ourselves. Here already the whole duplicity and sophistically reasoned artifice of Schleiermacher's *Christian Faith* show themselves to us. Schleiermacher cannot hold all those events in Jesus' life to be actual miracles, because for him, from his standpoint, there are no miracles at all. But why does he not say this openly? Why does he try to give the impression that he does not set in doubt the actual reality of these miraculous events, as if it were not a question of the events, but only of their significance? And with what right can Schleiermacher maintain that all those miracles, which even he speaks of as though they were actual events, in no wise have the significance for the Person of the Redeemer which is usually ascribed to them? We can form our concept of the Redeemer, certainly, only from the Gospel history; but why then should it be so immaterial whether or not precisely the most extraordinary features which are supposed to have belonged to the life of the Redeemer shall be considered as an essential part of his personality? It is abundantly clear that if the birth, resurrection, and ascension of Jesus actually happened as the Gospel history relates, then just these miraculous events must serve as the main proof that Jesus' whole appearance generally possessed the supernatural character which belongs to the concept of the Redeemer. But if one will not cast doubt on the factual reality of those miracles while continuing to allow them no essential significance for the Person of the Redeemer, then this is quite inconsequential and it is impossible to remain standing half-way. And if these attributes are supposed to have been something incidental and unessential for the Redeemer, so that he can be thought of just as well without these miracles as with them, then the most natural conclusion which can be

drawn is certainly that these attributes were no particularly extraordinary features, and thus not miracles. This is also Schleiermacher's
actual opinion; for whoever accepts no miracles at all can also not
accept the birth, resurrection, and ascension of Jesus as miracles.

But why then does Schleiermacher not say this openly and frankly?
Why does he speak as if he had absolutely no interest in admitting the
factual reality of these miracles, as if the whole matter was merely a
question of their significance for the Person of the Redeemer? Indeed,
how can he say with respect to the birth of Jesus that whoever accepts
a natural conception, in his meaning, can scarcely find any reason to
deny the historical character or depart from the literal explanation of the
supernatural conception contained in the New Testament narratives?
This is absolutely false, for whoever accepts a supernatural conception
of Jesus in Schleiermacher's sense must deny it in the sense in which
the Gospel history lets him be supernaturally conceived. How can
Schleiermacher, therefore, still hold the content of the Gospel narratives to be historical truth? According to the principles of Schleiermacher's *Christian Faith* the history of Jesus can contain nothing
miraculous and truly supernatural; the whole life of Jesus can only
have run a natural course.

But now when Schleiermacher, notwithstanding, never clearly
and openly expresses this difference between his *Christian Faith* and
the traditional Church teaching, and always wants to have that which
constitutes such an essential distinction in his whole standpoint
considered only as a secondary matter, then this can have its ground
only in the fact that he wants his *Christian Faith* to appear more orthodox than it really is. No other Dogmatics has—partly through its
general principles, partly through its critical analyses of the individual
doctrines—so methodically loosened and undermined the basis of the
orthodox view as Schleiermacher's, and none will so little admit it and
allow it to come to an open break with the traditional doctrines of the
Church. Whoever does not let himself be deceived by this orthodox
exterior and the artful play with traditional-sounding statements and
phrases, which are always used in another sense, sees clearly enough
that everything here is quite different from what it seems to be. One
must recognize this peculiar character of the Schleiermacherian
Dogmatics, this artful endeavour to conceal the modern philosophical
view under the cover of the old orthodox faith, in order to comprehend it as the product of a time which made it its highest task to unite
the antitheses which were once there and which could not be mediated
in any other way than in this outwardly plausible manner.[32]

[32] *Geschichte der christlichen Kirche*, V, pp. 185–8. The fact that during the 1820s
Baur shared Schelling's understanding of history (Hester, op. cit., p. 259) does not
necessarily prove that Baur read Schleiermacher's *Christian Faith* through the eyes of

THE INFLUENCE OF HEGEL

We have already seen how Baur adopted the Hegelian philosophy as his own personal viewpoint. Three other questions must now be considered, as interpreters of Baur are not in agreement concerning Baur's relationship to the speculative philosophy. These questions may be formulated as follows: 1. How convinced an adherent of the new Hegelian philosophy did Baur become? 2. How far are we to interpret Baur's exposition of Hegel's views as representing Baur's own personal viewpoint? 3. How long did this Hegelian period last?

1. To what extent did Baur actually become a follower of Hegel? Zeller, followed by Hodgson, maintained that Baur never 'unconditionally surrendered' himself to Hegel's views, that Hegel was for Baur never an 'infallible authority', that in later years Baur made himself more and more independent of Hegel's influence, and that Schleiermacher was in fact the one predecessor after whom Baur could be named.[33] Friedrich and Geiger, on the other hand, asserted that during this Hegelian period Baur set himself completely under the banner of Hegel. Certainly Baur never regarded Hegel as an *infallible* authority or surrendered *unconditionally* to Hegel's views. These are simply exaggerations by Zeller, designed to make it easier to underplay Hegel's influence. That in later years Baur made himself more and more independent of Hegel is also not in dispute. What has to be decided is whether Baur fully adopted the essential Hegelian tenets, or whether his acceptance was more an acknowledgement of Hegel's greatness without a convinced and decided appropriation of his thought.

It must first be said that Zeller cannot be accepted as a completely impartial witness; it must be remembered that he was writing shortly after the death of his father-in-law, when it was important to defend Baur's name and reputation. From 1835 until

---

Schelling or that he misunderstood essential features of it. Certainly Baur himself admitted that his critique of Schleiermacher in 1827/8 should have been more accurately formulated, but he saw in the vexed tone of Schleiermacher's reply the proof of the fact that he had rightly touched the most sensitive point of Schleiermacher's *Christian Faith* (K. Klüpfel, op. cit., p. 406). I find no evidence that Baur ever changed his views about Schleiermacher as regards the fundamental axioms of Schleiermacher's *Christian Faith*. The main criticisms brought forward by Baur in his lectures on the history of the Church in the nineteenth century are all contained in embryo in the letter of 1823.

[33] *HZ*, VI, pp. 371–2; Hodgson, p. 65, n. 102.

the time of his death Baur had been forced to put up with continual accusations that he was a Hegelian, and in 1861 Ritschl also mounted an attack on Baur from that quarter. Thus Zeller found himself in a difficult position, for it was highly embarrassing to be forced to admit that Baur had taken a blind alley, a blind alley which he had followed for roughly fifteen years; to have laboured for so long under so great an error of judgement—indeed under a delusion—was no flattering compliment to Baur. It was, then, only natural that Zeller should desire to play down Hegel's influence by elevating that of Schleiermacher. For these reasons, therefore, Zeller's explanations are not to be uncritically accepted as representing the true state of affairs.[34]

The main reason which leads us to the conclusion that during the years 1833–47 Baur stood unreservedly under the Hegelian flag is his defence of the speculative philosophy. In 'The Christian Doctrine of the Atonement' (1838) and 'The Christian Doctrine of the Trinity and Incarnation' (3 vols.: 1841–3) Baur defended Hegel against all attacks, and when one reads carefully Baur's 'Christian Gnosticism' (1835) then one finds that whereas the views of other theologians, e.g. Schelling and Schleiermacher, were trenchantly criticized, Hegel's views, on the other hand, were constantly commended. Only on one essential point did Baur disagree with Hegel: in the Christological question Baur sided with Strauss, who had declared that the unity of God and man is expressed not in a single individual but in humanity as a whole. This is certainly a deviation, but it is a deviation within the whole Hegelian system and the fundamental Hegelian tenets are still unreservedly held.

It is true that in 1836 Baur attempted to distance himself from Hegel in his 'Compelled Explanation': 'I am no adherent of any philosophical system because I know well how easy it is to be deceived by making oneself dependent on human authority, but nevertheless I have the conviction that from Hegel, too, there is a great deal for theology to learn . . .'[35] But this statement must be viewed in the light of the fact that in 1836 Baur was forced to defend himself against the charge of Hegelianism. When seen against this background the second part of the statement takes on a much more positive tone. It is an irresponsible procedure when

---

[34] Carl Hester (op. cit., p. 264) is of the same opinion.
[35] *TZT*, 1836: III, p. 225.

one attempts to argue from statements not seen in their true context. Baur did not deny that he was a Hegelian; he merely asserted that he refused to be labelled as an adherent of any philosophical system. Against the whole tenor of Baur's utterances during these years, no isolated statements of Baur himself or opinions of his later interpreters can overthrow the Hegelian testimony which breathes through so many passages where the dogmatic content of the Christian faith is under discussion.

Just as we cannot agree with Zeller that Baur must be named as a follower of Schleiermacher, if he is to be named as a follower of any system or man at all, so we must also judge that Zeller's evaluation of Hegel's influence upon Baur is too low. The influence of the Schleiermacherian system upon him was perhaps more significant, but as only a transition-point, and not as something lasting. Certainly he would not have adopted Hegel's system had it not lain right in the path of his development; but still, it was in Hegel's system that Baur first found the keystone of his world of thought and the end of his searching, and in so far he can only be designated as a disciple of Hegel.[36]

2. Related to the preceding question is the problem of how far Baur's exposition of the Hegelian views contained in 'Christian Gnosticism' represents Baur's own personal views. This problem raised its head in the year after Baur's death when Ritschl wrote his criticism of Zeller's anonymous article on the Tübingen School.[37] Ritschl maintained that Baur's historical investigations into the New Testament were not 'purely historical' but determined in advance by Baur's Hegelian viewpoint. In support of this assertion, Ritschl quoted Baur's statement in 'Christian Gnosticism': 'What the Spirit is and does is no history'.[38] A second cardinal point of criticism which Ritschl made was that, for Baur, faith in the God-man has as its presupposition not Jesus as the divine personage represented in the Gospels, but Jesus as a mere man.[39]

In his reply Zeller pointed out that Ritschl had quoted Baur's words as if they were Baur's own opinions and not his exposition of Hegel's views. Moreover, argued Zeller, Baur himself had criticized Hegel's failure to provide a clear connection between

[36] G. Fraedrich, *Ferdinand Christian Baur* (Gotha, 1909), p. 108.
[37] 'On the historical method of investigating early Christianity', *JDT*, VI (1861), pp. 429–59.
[38] Ibid., p. 437; Baur, *Die christliche Gnosis*, p. 696.
[39] Ibid., p. 448; Baur, *Die christliche Gnosis*, p. 713.

the Jesus of history and the Christ of speculative philosophy. Baur's criticism of Hegel, however, was not a fundamental criticism of Hegel's viewpoint, but rather of a deficiency within the Hegelian system. Happily this deficiency was not of a serious nature and Baur knew how to correct it. In 'Christian Gnosticism' there was essentially no criticism of Hegel and in the light of the fact that Baur's exposition of Hegel's views was substantially a defence, there remains no valid reason for not concluding that Baur's exposition of the Hegelian philosophy was fully in accord with his own personal viewpoint.[40]

3. For roughly fifteen years Baur held fast to his Hegelian views. Only late in the 1840s did he finally abandon the speculative philosophy and return to the rationalism of the Enlightenment and the ethical emphasis common from that time onwards. Exactly when this abandonment of Hegelianism took place cannot be determined with certainty; by 1853 in *The Church History of the First Three Centuries* all trace of his former Hegelianism has vanished and what remains to Christianity is of purely ethical worth: but Zeller is undoubtedly right in dating the change in the late 1840s.[41] From this time forth Baur's emphasis falls on the ethical side of Christianity. Not the Person of Christ as the God-man, not his death or resurrection, not the unity of the divine and the human is now important; it is the ethical alone that has value.

The absolute content of the Christian principle expresses itself in the moral consciousness. What confers on man his highest moral value is alone the purity of a truly moral disposition which rises above all that is finite, particular, or merely subjective. But this moral content in the disposition is also the determining standard of man's relation to God. That which gives man his highest moral value also sets him in the new relationship to God which corresponds to the idea of God.[42]

What makes Christianity the absolute religion in comparison with all other religions is, in the last analysis, nothing other than the purely ethical character of its facts, teachings, and claims.[43]

[40] Here also Hodgson uncritically accepts Zeller's explanation and makes no attempt to evaluate its correctness (op. cit., p. 62, n. 92). In Hodgson's opinion Ritschl simply confuses Baur's own theology with his exposition of Hegel's. But Ritschl was no amateur theologian; he understood Baur's views too well to make such a simple mistake.

[41] *HZ*, 1862, p. 105.

[42] *Das Christenthum*, p. 31.

[43] *Die Tübinger Schule* (Tübingen, 1860), p. 30.

11. Baur's Theological Viewpoint

BAUR perceived well that all historical criticism of the Bible is, in the last resort, dependent upon the theological presuppositions of the critic.

Criticism is not possible unless the critic who intends to make some historical event the object of his criticism proceeds from a definite standpoint. Whatever this standpoint may be, the critic can only derive the basic axioms, according to which he must comprehend and evaluate the object of his criticism, from the standpoint which he adopts within the general culture of his time. . . . It is, therefore, all a question of the presuppositions from which one proceeds, which standpoint, which stage of intelligence and culture in general one adopts, what kind of basic axioms one makes the guiding norm of one's critical methodology.[1]

Thus, before we begin our consideration of the historical perspectives developed by the Tübingen School, it will be necessary to turn our attention to Baur's own theological views, since these views ultimately determined the critical path which Baur and his pupils pursued. Where Baur's theological viewpoint is not clearly understood or lucidly presented[2] then the historical

[1] *Die Ignatianischen Briefe* (Tübingen, 1848), pp. 119–20.
[2] Hodgson's evaluation of Baur's theological viewpoint is often ambiguous and misleading, mainly because he strives to present Baur as a pious Christian believer who nevertheless rejected the supernatural element in Christianity, the concept of a personal God, and the divinity of Christ. This dichotomy runs through Hodgson's entire presentation. Perhaps the greatest difficulty which confronts the reader is Hodgson's (and Baur's) use of the word 'God'. Both Hodgson and Baur use the word in its traditional sense, and Hodgson too often neglects to emphasize the fact that for Baur the word 'God' has a completely different meaning, in that Baur rejected the theistic concept of a transcendent personal God. Nor does Hodgson differentiate clearly between Baur's Hegelian and ethical periods. In addition, his whole interpretation of Baur is made even more difficult in that he quotes Baur's orthodox phraseology as if such statements (especially those contained in Baur's sermons) were Baur's own personal views. Herein lies the *real* difference between the evaluations of Geiger and Hodgson. Geiger treats Baur as a Hegelian who turned back to the rationalism which always underlay his Hegelianism. He emphasizes the fact that Baur rejected the supernatural and miraculous element in Christianity, from which Baur's denial of the fundamental doctrines of the traditional Christian faith logically followed. Hodgson, on the other hand, who also knows full well that Baur abandoned all the traditional Christian doctrines concerning the

criticism of the School cannot be accurately assessed. To present a full account of Baur's theology is neither possible nor necessary. Baur never gave a systematic account of his views, but from his writings it is possible to derive a clear understanding of his beliefs about the two fundamental Christian doctrines upon which all other doctrines are dependent—the concept of God and the Persson of Christ.

THE CONCEPT OF GOD

The concept of God determines every theology and theological system. Baur perceived this well and Ritschl saw it even more clearly. But before we examine Baur's concept of God we must pay some attention to the often ill-defined and ambiguous terminology employed in any discussion of the existence of a divine being.

The traditional concept of God hinges upon two attributes—transcendence and personality. Transcendence as traditionally understood indicates that God is not immanent, not part of the world-process, but that as the Creator who has made the world out of nothing he is entirely independent of the world. It signifies that God is other-worldly, that he is 'above and beyond' the world, although this 'beyondness' is not to be thought of merely in spatial or temporal terms. The so often caricatured concept of a God 'out there' is neither meaningless nor nonsensical, but expresses the other-worldly nature of God and delimits an undefined boundary beyond which man may not pass; it demarcates a distinction between God and the world, which pantheism and immanence blur and confuse.

Hand in hand with transcendence goes the concept of personality which marks the great distinction between the living God

existence of a personal God and the divinity of Christ, nevertheless wants to play down this fact and present Baur in as orthodox a guise as possible. It is therefore not surprising that there appears to be a quite irreconcilable difference between the interpretations of Hodgson and Geiger. Even in his later reply to Geiger's views, Hodgson confined himself to discussing the secondary differences while seemingly avoiding *the one fundamental point of disagreement*—whether or not Baur was an atheist in the traditional sense of the word. Thus Hodgson's statement: "Baur's rejection of supernaturalism does not mean that he denied the existence of God as an other than finite, transcendent being, but it does mean that God's revelation and action in nature and history must not be understood as occurring 'supernaturally'" (op. cit., p. 5, n. 13) is simply one example of the way in which Hodgson desperately strives to portray Baur as more orthodox than he really was. What Hodgson means by a 'finite, transcendent being' requires further clarification.

and an impersonal, abstract deity or principle. To speak of God as personal implies that God is a rational Agent possessing both consciousness and rationality, mind and will. But God's personality is not simply human personality, for it is the creative source of all personal and rational being, whereas man's personality as created by God is derived. God is *persona personans*, whereas man is only *persona personata*, contingent and dependent personality. Nor is God held to be personal merely because man is personal, i.e. God is not personal because he is a God whose existence is believed in by persons, i.e. he is not a God who is personal merely *for us*, but is inherently and independently personal in his own nature, apart from us altogether.

This concept of a transcendent personal God is substantially that to which the Church and traditional theology through the centuries have held. With this description of God's transcendence and personality by no means everything has been said or was intended to have been said about the nature of God. But apart from the attributes of transcendence and personality the other divine attributes have no reality. An abstract, impersonal God can never be known or make itself known. Revelation implies a personality which is capable of revealing its nature. Whether or not such a transcendent personal God actually exists is another question, but quite apart from its ontic reality the concept itself is certainly not incomprehensible.

We now come to the question of defining the terms 'theism', 'atheism', and 'pantheism'. Atheism may be broadly defined as the denial of the existence of God. In that a more exact definition is determined by the meaning of the word 'God', two main definitions of atheism are thus possible.

(i) The denial of all and every kind of divine being, however such a being may be thought of—as transcendent or immanent, personal or impersonal.

(ii) The denial of the transcendent personal God of the traditional Christian faith.

The first definition naturally includes the second, but it is generally too broad for practical discussions within the framework of Christianity, and most philosophers and theologians who have denied the existence of God, e.g. Feuerbach and Strauss, rejected the transcendent personal God of traditional Christianity, the Creator of the world. This is the usual sense in which the term has been used within Christian circles and we shall here retain this definition. Theism, then, will be correspondingly defined as the affirmation of the existence of a transcendent personal God.

In the nineteenth century the word 'pantheistic' became a convenient label to describe all concepts of God—both well-defined and ill-defined—which could not be designated as theistic. Thus when Baur, for example, described Schleiermacher's *Christian Faith* as pantheistic, he did not mean this in a strict Spinozian sense, but simply desired to imply that Schleiermacher's concept of God was not that of traditional theism. We may briefly distinguish the three most important forms of pantheism.

(i) Originally pantheism possessed the meaning that God and the universe are identical (*deus sive natura*) or at least the obverse of one another, and this is still the 'classical' meaning of the word. The material world is understood as possessing an etherial divine character, although the nature of God is always vaguely defined.

(ii) More usual is a second form of pantheism, where the material world is simply the external manifestation of an under-lying invisible and spiritual foundation—the world-soul of Schelling, Schopenhauer's primal Will, or Tillich's ground of one's being, for example. This pantheism is also immanent; it possesses in itself no personality, although it may be defined as the ground of all personality.

(iii) Another common form of pantheism is known as panen-theism. This is an inconseqent conception which attempts to harmonize the transcendent personal God of theism with the immanent impersonal God of pantheism. Panentheism has been described by a number of varying definitions, which when carefully analysed will generally be found to be contradictory or nonsensical; or else they may be reduced to the resulting combination of a transcendent personal God and an immanent impersonal being which permeates the world. How the two concepts are to be harmonized is rarely discussed, because this distinction is usually not clearly drawn. Panentheism is so often allowed to remain as a vague and ill-defined concept. God is simply transcendent and immanent, personal and impersonal at the same moment, and the panentheist tries to hold both ideas together and be both a theist and a pantheist at the same time.

We have previously seen how Baur's theological views may be divided into three periods—a period in which he did not substantially depart from the orthodoxy of the times, a Hegelian period, and finally a period in which the stress falls on the ethical character of Christianity. We shall now trace Baur's concept of God through these three periods.

1. The Orthodox Period

During the 1820s there was a move by Baur away from an uncritical acceptance of the traditional concept of a transcendent personal[3] God. We are unable to date this move precisely and can only surmise that it was probably through the study of Schleiermacher's *Christian Faith* that Baur gradually became conscious of the fact that he was no longer satisfied with the traditional representations of a personal God, with which he had been brought up and educated. Thus, by the end of the 1820s, or possibly earlier, it is probable that Baur had abandoned the concept of a personal God and begun his search for a substitute which would fill the void. In Hegel's philosophy of religion he found his answer.

2. The Hegelian Period

For Hegel, as for Schleiermacher, there was no transcendent personal God who created the universe, as in the traditional view of the creation, and Baur's acceptance of Hegel's philosophy was largely determined by the need to find an explanation which would account for the existence of the world. Above all, what Baur wanted was a unified system; in Hegel he found what he was seeking.

The evidence shows quite clearly that in Hegel's philosophy of religion Baur found expressed what he had for so long sought without success, that he found here his resting place. Supernaturalism he had behind him; to rationalism, the standpoint of pure reason, he felt himself in a continually growing opposition; he had never been completely able to accept Schleiermacher's *Christian Faith*, he strove beyond its purely subjective standpoint after an objective one. . . . Everything that he possessed insecurely or still sought, he found in Hegel's philosophy of religion.[4]

[3] On Baur's understanding of the concept of a personal God see *Die christliche Lehre von der Dreieinigkeit und Menschwerdung Gottes*, III, pp. 929–31; *Die christliche Gnosis*, pp. 701 f.

[4] Fraedrich, *Ferdinand Christian Baur*, pp. 99–100.

What determines Hegel's whole philosophical system is his concept of God. If Hegel is to be understood he must be understood here. Many interpreters of Hegel failed to comprehend his thought in its entirety because they did not start at this point. It may be claimed that few have understood Hegel better than Baur and Strauss; to understand their interpretation is to understand Hegel correctly, for the whole centre of the Hegelian philosophy turns on the concept of God and the Person of Christ.

Hegel was not a pantheist in any of the three senses we have discussed above. The Hegelian concept of God is certainly not without difficulties and apparent contradictions, but taken all in all a generally clear picture emerges. The absolute and eternal Idea, or the Triune God, is essentially a process consisting of three stages or moments.

(i) God as he is in and for himself before the creation of the world is the infinite Spirit. The spirit is essentially thinking, a thinking Spirit which is not merely a static unity, but which includes within itself a self-distinguishing.

The actual essence of God opens itself to the thinking Spirit in thinking; God is essentially thinking, self-consciousness, Spirit, and all determining qualities through which thinking is essentially what it is are just so many moments in the idea of the Triune God. . . . In the pure thinking of the Spirit the relationship is a direct relationship, without a definite distinction; thinking is the pure oneness with itself where all obscurity and darkness vanish.[5]

Along with this unity there is also a distinction, without which there could be no process, no movement or life in the Godhead. God is not to be thought of without an inner movement which belongs to his nature as Spirit, as thinking activity, as living concrete God.[6] God is Spirit and it belongs to the nature of the Spirit to reveal and objectify itself, to distinguish itself from itself, to set up itself as another over against itself while in this process remaining identical with itself.[7]

If thinking is the substantial essence of the Spirit, then in it there also exists an immanent principle of activity, of movement, of the life which mediates itself with itself. As thinking, God is the one who

---

[5] *Dreieinigkeit und Menschwerdung*, pp. 890; 894–5.

[6] *Die christliche Gnosis*, p. 700.

[7] *Die christliche Lehre von der Versöhnung*, pp. 712–13.

differentiates himself, who determines himself, who sets himself as finite consciousness. In that the Spirit differentiates itself within itself, the finitude of the consciousness enters into its being, but this finite consciousness is a moment in the Spirit itself and the finite world is a moment in this Spirit.[8]

(ii) The Spirit must come to self-consciousness, to conscious-ness of its own nature as Spirit. But this is only possible when the distinction within itself finds definite and concrete form; and so in the second stage of the eternal process the Spirit distinguishes itself from itself, separates itself from itself, comes out of itself, and sets itself over against itself by dirempting[9] itself into finite forms—the world, nature, and the human spirit, which are simply different forms of the finite Spirit. Nature now becomes the stage upon which the world-drama is played out and where the finite spirit evolves towards perfection and final reconciliation with the infinite Spirit. The world is both nature and finite spirit, and the finite spirit in its direct form is the spirit of nature. In other words, the Spirit sets nature and finite spirit as its other self over against itself, and this stage of the process, in Hegel's thinking, corre-sponds to the Biblical idea of the second Person of the Trinity, the Son, taking human form. It is in this process of diremption that the infinite Spirit becomes conscious of itself; it observes itself in its other self, in its finite form, and the whole process unravels itself and evolves in history. 'History is the eternally clear mirror in which the Spirit views itself, considers its own image in order to be what it actually is, to be for itself, for its own consciousness, and to know itself as the motivating power of all history.'[10]

(iii) Through the diremption of the infinite Spirit there occurs a division within the Spirit itself, a separation, even though the finite form is still united with the infinite Spirit. In nature, the spirit is a sojourner in a strange land; it is aware of its unity with

---

[8] *Dreieinigkeit und Menschwerdung*, pp. 890–1.

[9] The technical term for this philosophical process is 'diremption'. The Spirit diremps itself when it separates itself from its original state, proceeds out of itself, and enters into a lower state. The complementary process in which the diremped spirit now sheds its finite clothing and returns to unity with the infinite Spirit is designated by the German word *Aufhebung*. This word carries the sense of raising or taking up into something higher while the original state of that raised or taken up is abolished in the process. The German words *aufheben* and *Aufhebung* are best rendered by the English verb 'subsume' and its correlate noun 'subsumption'. These words are used here with the meaning we have defined.

[10] *Lehrbuch der Dogmengeschichte* (Tübingen, 1847), pp. 55–6.

the infinite Spirit but aware also that it is separated from its true self, immersed in a world where it does not truly belong.

The world is both nature and finite spirit and the finite spirit in its direct form is the natural spirit. But as natural spirit the spirit is still in its incongruous form; in order to become the Spirit in its true form it must step out of its natural and finite form. To accomplish this it is necessary that the spirit become conscious of this incongruity, of this separation between its true form and its finite form. Thereby the splitting, the antithesis, the opposition within itself becomes actual. The spirit becomes conscious that it is not as it should be, that according to its nature as merely natural spirit it is bad; yet it also knows that it must not remain in its natural being, but through the will should become good. It feels within itself the infinite pain of the splitting of itself, its descent into sin, and its opposition to the world of evil, the consequence of sin.[11]

In the consciousness of this separation, the spirit is also conscious of the necessity of reconciliation. It knows that it must return to itself and become identical within itself once more as the Absolute Spirit; it cannot remain in its finite form but must free itself from the world in which it dwells. The opposition which would hold it back from rising to its former unity must be abolished,[12] so that the Spirit may be subsumed back into the Godhead, thus completing the whole process of reconciliation.

It belongs to the nature of the Spirit to take back into itself what is foreign, the other, that which is separated from itself, to reconcile itself with itself, just as the idea dirempted itself, fell away from itself in order to bring this falling away back to its own true nature and then itself to return from its appearance in nature. This return of the Spirit into itself, however, takes place only when the Spirit—in that it enters into finitude only to come to a knowledge of itself through its becoming finite, in order to subsume the finite consciousness and abolish its finiteness—knows itself as the Absolute Spirit, knows of its identity with God as an identity communicated through the negation of finitude. As God is the movement towards the finite, so he returns to himself in the ego as the one who abolishes his finite self and who is God only after his return.[13]

This, in brief, is a simplified summary of Hegel's concept of God. When we delve somewhat deeper into Hegel's views we

[11] *Versöhnung*, p. 715.
[12] This abolition is the negating of the finite nature, i.e. the negation of the negation.
[13] *Die christliche Gnosis*, p. 679.

find many perplexities and difficulties which are hard to explain, but the essential concept of God which we have outlined should be sufficiently clear. And for fifteen years, during the period in which the Tübingen School originated and came to fruition, Baur gave his unreserved allegiance to these ideas. It is this allegiance which constitutes him as a Hegelian. He may have differed from Hegel with regard to points of Christology, but these differences never affected his relationship to the speculative philosophy in its essential aspects.

3. The Ethical Period

Late into the 1840s Baur still held fast to his Hegelian views and only slowly did he follow his pupils in abandoning them.[14] It was, above all, the influence of Feuerbach which brought about Hegel's demise; for Feuerbach simply maintained that Hegel's infinite Spirit had no existence in reality. The whole speculative philosophy was just a great bubble of illusion, which had now been finally burst. And it was able to be burst because it was ultimately only a piece of unnecessary metaphysical sophistry which had no historically ascertainable point of contact in the world. It was abstract speculation, interesting and fascinating no doubt, but in the last resort mere speculation. Strauss, Zeller, and Schwegler all abandoned the new philosophy and Baur gradually saw himself compelled to follow suit. Now there was only a great void which had previously been filled by the speculative ideas. Everything was back to the original standpoint from which Baur had crossed over into the Hegelian camp—the rejection of a transcendent personal God.

THE PERSON OF CHRIST

The development of Baur's views concerning the historical Jesus and the Person of Christ may be divided into three periods which correspond to the three periods already outlined in dealing with Baur's concept of God.

1. The Orthodox Period

We have seen how up until the early 1820s Baur remained essentially in agreement with the orthodox theology of the time.

---

[14] Fraedrich (*Ferdinand Christian Baur*, p. 108) quoted the conclusion of J. Haussleiter: 'Baur held fast longer than others to the illusion that the traditional doctrines of the Church could be harmonized with Hegelian speculation' (Herzog's *Realencyklopaedie*, II, p. 478), and commented: 'No further words are necessary.'

This was on account of the fact that he saw no other alternative to the traditional beliefs, which were not unreasonable granted the presupposition of a transcendent personal God. Probably he had at first no serious doubts regarding the orthodox Christology, but slowly a more rationalistic trait makes itself felt and it is possible that even in the early 1820s he turned more and more towards the Enlightenment view of Jesus as a great ethical teacher.

2. *The Hegelian Period*

For Hegel, as well as for Baur, the Absolute Spirit is the identity of God with man, the unity of the Infinite with the finite. But it was essential that this unity should appear in the world, that it should be manifested in concrete form to the human race.

The human consciousness of God develops first in nature, in which the finite spirit raises itself to itself. But in order to attain to the knowledge of its true self, its consciousness must raise itself above nature. This can only occur through the finite spirit itself. But only through God can the spirit attain to the consciousness that God is near it and one with it. Thus God must reveal himself to it, not merely externally, but also through an essential and inner bond, i.e. the actual oneness of the divine and human nature can only be revealed to man in an objective way through God becoming man.[15]

The most difficult part of the whole problem was to explain how this unity was actually manifested and wherein it actually consisted. Hegel had left the whole question vague. The unity was indeed manifested in Christ, but it was a unity merely symbolized, and not a real unity of natures as had been formulated in the traditional doctrines of the Church.

Hegel distinguished three separate moments or stages:

(i) The purely external and historical moment sees Jesus merely as a historical figure, an ordinary man, a martyr for the truth like Socrates. Who and what Jesus was in himself, however, was regarded by Hegel as a purely historical problem—in actuality the question of the historical Jesus—which he preferred not to discuss.

(ii) The second moment is that of faith: Jesus is the God-man for those who believe in him; whether Jesus was the divine Son of God in reality, however, as believed by the early Church,

---

[15] *Versöhnung*, p. 716.

whether in him a real unity of God and man was actually present, is left undetermined. The unity exists for those who believe it exists—a rather dubious formulation whose equivocal nature was lucidly exposed by Geiger.

In Christ appears the oneness of the divine and human nature. With this statement the traditional Christological dogma is again restored to honour for the first time since Kant, Fichte, and Schleiermacher. But in this process these categories receive a completely different meaning. The above sentence does not signify that in the Person of Christ divine and human nature were uniquely united once for all time—although Hegel in his philosophy of religion, characteristically, nowhere directly criticizes this ecclesiastical dogma directly—but that the Church, humanity—in so far as it believes in Christ—sees this unity represented in him, sees that humanity itself is 'actually' united with God and part of the divine nature. An independent Christology has no place in Hegel's philosophy of religion. In the act of reconciliation between God and man, Christ is not the subject but the object, the mere point of reference for the Church, the catalyst which is necessary to enable the process to take place but which has no part in the act itself. As regards historical reality this means that we are left in the dark as to whether Jesus was really the God-man or whether he was only designated as the Son of God by the Church.[16]

(iii) The third moment is constituted by the speculative view of Christ. The actual truth, the unity of the infinite and finite, the divine and human, had to become conscious in the consciousness of the finite spirit. In this process the appearance of Jesus marks that point in history where the finite spirit becomes conscious of its identity with the infinite Spirit. It is at this point that the consciousness of the unity of God and man, as this unity exists in actuality, enters into the consciousness of man through the Person of Christ.[17] In this third moment faith must be raised to knowledge, belief must enter into the thinking consciousness, must be manifested through the philosophical concept as the actual truth. Just as it was impossible to remain standing by the merely historical event, just as faith raised the historical Jesus into the Person of the God-man, so belief itself must be raised into knowledge of the actual truth. But the actual truth is the Absolute Spirit, God as the Triune God, the identity of man with God.

---

[16] W. Geiger, *Spekulation und Kritik* (Munich, 1964), p. 66.

[17] *Dreieinigkeit und Menschwerdung*, p. 908.

The knowledge of Christ as the God-man is therefore nothing other than the knowledge of this truth, the consciousness of the unity of the divine and human natures.[18]

With this acceptance of the Hegelian philosophy, Baur had also no hesitation in accepting the Hegelian Christological viewpoint and the threefold distinction which Hegel had formulated between speculation, history, and faith.

For faith the appearance of the God-man, the incarnation, God's birth in the flesh may certainly be a historical fact. From the standpoint of speculative thinking, however, the incarnation of God is no unique historical fact which happened once for all time, but an eternal determining of the nature of God by virtue of which God enters time and becomes man (becomes incarnate in each individual person) only in so far as he is man from eternity. The finitude and painful humiliation to which Christ as the God-man subjected himself, is borne at every moment by God as man. The finished act of reconciliation is no event in time, but God reconciles himself with himself eternally, and the resurrection and exaltation of Christ are nothing other than the eternal return of the Spirit to itself and to its truth. Christ as man, as God-man, is man in his universality,[19] not one particular individual, but the universal individual.[20]

But Baur also saw clearly the main difficulty which Hegel had left unexplained—the relation between the Christ of speculative philosophy and the Jesus of history. Hegel had attempted to make his Christology appear as orthodox as possible, declaring that Christ was the God-man, in whom the unity of the infinite and finite had been manifested. This unity, however, was never regarded by him as an *actual* unity, but merely as the manifestation of a unity which was already presupposed. In order that this unity of God and man might be manifested to mankind it was necessary for God to appear in the world in human form. By this statement Hegel did not mean that the incarnation was to be regarded as an actual objective event, as if God himself should have become a particular individual man, but as a subjective event where the consciousness, faith, or subjective conviction fastens on to a particular individual in the belief that in this individual, God became man and appeared in human form.

[18] *Die christliche Gnosis*, pp. 714–15.
[19] The universal man is the identity of the finite spirit with the absolute Spirit.
[20] *Die christliche Gnosis*, p. 715.

But how, asked Baur, could faith in Christ as the God-man ever have arisen if Jesus was not actually what faith believed him to be? 'The Hegelian philosophy of religion views Christ as the God-man only in his relation to faith, without expressing more precisely what objective point of contact in the actual appearance of Christ faith has for its presupposition. But how could faith in him as the God-man have arisen, unless in some kind of way he was also objectively that which faith accepted him to be.'[21]

This passage has been often misinterpreted, as if Baur were saying that Hegel was guilty of severing 'all essential or internal connections between the Christ of faith and the Jesus of history.'[22] But Baur is not arguing that Hegel's formulation of the problem is in itself incorrect—merely that it is not clear and does not go far enough. Baur perceived that Hegel's formulation was inadequate and unable to provide a satisfying answer to the problem; for Hegel had maintained only that the consciousness of the unity of God and man was first realized *with reference to* Christ, i.e. that the believers first became conscious that this unity had been manifested in Jesus. But now Baur goes on to answer his own question and provide the link between the ideal and the historical. This consciousness, maintained Baur, arose in the believers because Jesus himself first realized this unity and imparted this consciousness to his disciples. 'The necessary presupposition in each case is that the actual truth, the unity of the divine and human nature, first became concrete truth and self-conscious knowledge in Christ, and was expressed and taught by him as truth. Herein consists, therefore, the peculiar pre-eminence of Christ.'[23]

Baur's explanation provides that connection between the ideal and the historical which is absent in Hegel's exposition. One other fact which should here be noticed is that Baur was completely in agreement with Strauss's statement in the concluding

[21] Ibid., p. 717.   [22] Hodgson, op. cit., p. 62.
[23] *Die christliche Gnosis*, p. 717. Hodgson's translation of this passage: 'The necessary presupposition in any case is that the implicit truth, the unity of divine and human nature, must first come to concrete truth and self-conscious knowledge in Christ, and be expressed and learned from him as truth' (p. 62), is incorrect. The whole point of Baur's assertion is that the consciousness of the unity of the divine and the human first *came* to concrete truth and self-conscious knowledge in Christ, that Jesus was the first to grasp the truth of this reality and to mediate it to the consciousness of humanity (cf. *Dreieinigkeit*, pp. 908–9).

section of his *Life of Jesus*, that the Spirit was never poured out solely in one individual, but in humanity as a whole; in other words, that Christ was no unique, divine, supernatural being in the traditional sense, but a member of humanity, essentially no different by nature from other human beings, but exalted in understanding and the first to perceive the underlying unity of God and man. Thus in terms of Strauss's classification of the speculative theologians, Baur stood completely alongside Strauss on the left wing. This fact, to the best of my knowledge, has never been noticed.

With the collapse of the Hegelian concept of God, the divine pole in the God-man polarity had no more meaning and the whole speculative Christology crumbled to pieces. What remained among the ruins was the problem of the historical Jesus, how he had been able to exercise such a commanding influence upon his disciples, and above all how he had come to be viewed as the Jewish Messiah and Son of God.

3. The Ethical Period

With the abandonment of the speculative philosophy, Baur also abandoned the Hegelian wrapping which surrounded his Christology and turned back to a purely rationalistic view of Christianity with Jesus as the great ethical teacher.[24]

We know that from the time of the publication of Strauss's *Life of Jesus* Baur stood substantially behind Strauss's view of the historical Jesus. Christ as the Gospels portrayed him had never so existed; he was the creation of the Gospel writers who had invented the miraculous stories in order to demonstrate Jesus as the Messiah. Here was the explanation for the rise of the Gospel

---

[24] Cf. Julius Köstlin: 'Thus Baur's conception of the Person and Work of Jesus, in all its essential elements, gravitated back to the old rationalistic explanations in which Jesus is conceived as a man and teacher who raised himself to the highest ethical ideas. By means of these ideas, which he strove to follow and practise, he wanted to establish an ethical-religious community, and for these ideas he fell as a sacrifice' (*TSK*, 1866, p. 744). When Hodgson (against Geiger) argues that 'the return-to-rationalism thesis is also rendered implausible by Baur's thorough-going criticism of rationalist theology' (*Ferdinand Christian Baur on the Writings of Church History*, edited and translated by Peter C. Hodgson, New York, 1968, p. 8, n. 10), he appears to confuse the two meanings of the word 'rationalism'. As Geiger and Barnikol use the word it refers to the rationalism of the Enlightenment, to a Kantian view of religion and not to the rationalist explanations of H. E. G. Paulus who attempted to explain away the Biblical miracles with ingenious and fanciful explanations. It was this latter rationalism which Baur criticized.

stories but the problem remained: who was the historical Jesus? 'If Jesus in his whole appearance was not more than results from Strauss's investigation,' wrote Baur to his friend Heyd, 'then it remains all the more puzzling how the conviction of the disciples, that he *must* have risen from the dead, could have developed.' During his Hegelian years Baur simply ignored the problem; it was really of no consequence to him who or what Jesus was; that was a question for historical investigation, and the Gospel records, in Baur's opinion, were so untrustworthy that nothing concrete was ever liable to emerge. Strauss had said all that was worth saying on the subject, and although he did not support Strauss's views openly, Baur never contradicted what his pupil had written concerning the origin of the Gospel stories.

I. THE MESSIAHSHIP OF JESUS

Up until 1853 when his *Church History of the First Three Centuries* appeared in print, Baur had remained silent regarding the Person of Christ. But now Baur found himself compelled to give some explanation as to how the enigmatic figure of the historical Jesus had been elevated into the Christ of faith, and for the first time he expressed his views in a cautious discussion of Jesus' Messiahship.[25]

What Baur first had to demonstrate was that the New Testament designations of Jesus had, from the earliest time, been misinterpreted; that the Biblical terms as traditionally understood had not been so interpreted by Jesus himself. Baur, therefore, had to present a positive picture of the true character of Jesus— Jesus as he actually was.

He began by examining the two main appellations of Jesus— Son of man and Son of God. The first designation, maintained Baur, was clearly to be traced back to Daniel 7:13, but whether this expression in the time of Jesus had been understood as a direct reference to Jesus' Messiahship was highly doubtful. It was much more likely that Jesus had used this expression simply to emphasize his true humanity, the fact that he too was truly man.[26]

---

[25] We must here take into account the posthumously published lectures on New Testament theology which Baur delivered during the 1850s: *Vorlesungen über Neutestamentliche Theologie* (ed. F. F. Baur; Leipzig, 1864).

[26] *Neutestamentliche Theologie*, pp. 77–9.

One must therefore suppose that Jesus chose for himself the designation Son of man—which, to be sure, was taken from Daniel yet was not such a common and familiar designation of the Messiah—not with the intention of directly declaring that he was the Messiah, but rather to designate himself simply as man—in opposition to the Jewish conceptions of the Messiah which expected solely a glorious heavenly figure—not as man in the ideal sense, but as he who shares our human lot, *qui nihil humani a se alienum putat*.[27]

The designation Son of God was explained in a strictly ethical sense. The appellation itself is bound to the conception of the Messiah and in Baur's view it was therefore necessary to investigate in what sense Jesus understood himself as such. Jesus, claimed Baur, wanted to be no Messiah in the sense that the people expected,[28] and held himself to be the Messiah only in an ethical sense. He perceived that it was alone the ethical which had worth and if, in Baur's view, man can think of God only as the highest ethical perfection,[29] as the ethical idea in itself, then Jesus must have employed the designation Son of God in order to denote that in himself the ethical idea, or ideal, finds its highest realization, i.e. that he is the Son of God.

If now Jesus viewed and designated himself pre-eminently as the Son of God, then he himself can have conceived this relation from no other point of view than the ethical. In the depth of his ethical consciousness he perceived himself as the Son of God, in so far as the idea of ethical goodness was prominent in his mind in the purity in which he elaborated it, especially in the Sermon on the Mount, and in so far as he himself through his ethical endeavour was conscious of being the most perfect realization of this idea.[30]

Baur saw three stages in the development of the Messianic idea in the early Church. In the first stage Jesus used the appellation 'Son of man', obviously intending to eschew any possibility of being connected with the expected Messiah. It was a new ethical understanding which Jesus desired to bring to the consciousness of the people. Then came a turning-point. Having made little

[27] Who considers himself exempt from no human experience. *Neutestamentliche Theologie*, p. 81.
[28] Ibid., p. 94. This statement is deliberately ambiguous and may refer either to a political Messiah or to the Messiah prophesied in the Old Testament. Baur wanted it to be understood in both senses.
[29] Ibid., p. 117.
[30] Ibid., p. 118.

impression upon the people, Jesus realized that the only way to have his teaching accepted by the people was to appropriate for himself divine authority. For in Judea at that time the people were eagerly awaiting a Messiah, and nothing of higher significance could gain a foothold in the Jewish religion if it was not bound up with the Messianic expectation.

Had not the most national idea of Judaism, the idea of the Messiah, become so identified with the Person of Jesus that one saw in him the fulfilment of the old promise, the Messiah who had appeared for the salvation of his people, how could faith in him have become a world-historical power of such significance? Through the idea of the Messiah the intellectual content of Christianity received its first concrete form in which it could enter on to the road of its historical development.[31]

And so for the one great purpose of educating the Jewish people to the higher ethical and moral life, for the purpose of showing them that the Messianic concept was moral and spiritual rather than national and political, Jesus made his one great concession to the national Messianic consciousness[32] and consented to take upon himself the role of the Messiah in order that his teaching should find acceptance among the people and have enduring value. Accordingly, he decided to go up to Jerusalem and confront the religious leaders, for the crisis had become so acute that he resolved to bring the issue to its conclusion one way or the other.

After his long and uninterrupted ministry in Galilee and after all the experience he had gained concerning the acceptance of his doctrine among the people and the opposition evoked against it by his adversaries with whom he had at that time already come into contact, he reached the decision to leave Galilee and go to Judea to appear in the capital itself, at the seat of those authorities against whose whole system and traditions his ministry up to that time had been decisively opposed. Such a momentous step can only have proceeded from the conviction that it was absolutely necessary for his cause—now ripe for decision— to be immediately and finally decided. The time had come for his doctrine and Person to be either accepted or rejected; the whole nation had actually to declare whether it would persist in that traditional Messianic belief which bore the stamp of selfish, Jewish particularism, or whether it would acknowledge such a Messiah as he was and had shown himself in his whole life and influence to be. This was the

---

[31] *Das Christenthum*, p. 36.   [32] *Die Tübinger Schule*, p. 32.

question to which there was only one answer—the answer which he had himself given long previously with all the self-assurance of his inner consciousness.[33]

Alas, the daring confrontation did not succeed and the hopes of the disciples lay broken and shattered. No Messiah who had died such an ignominious death could be the long-expected Messiah who would bring Israel to national glory. For the disillusioned disciples it was an either/or. Either their faith must be completely extinguished or it must break through death into life. And just this latter possibility, according to Baur, is what actually happened. In the third and final stage of the process, the Messianic conception again burst into the full consciousness of the disciples through their belief in the resurrection of Jesus.

II. THE RESURRECTION OF JESUS

Baur did not believe that Jesus had actually been raised from the dead. Since miracles in the supernatural sense were for him incredible and as there was no transcendent personal God who was able to send his Son and raise him from the dead, it was only too plain that the resurrection of Jesus as an objective physical event could not have taken place. However, Baur could not state this openly and in his *Church History of the First Three Centuries* he contented himself with the assertion that the resurrection lies outside the sphere of historical investigation. It was not the factuality of the resurrection which was important, but belief in the resurrection.

The question as to the nature and reality of the resurrection lies outside the sphere of historical investigation. Historical consideration must be content with the simple fact that in the faith of the disciples the resurrection of Jesus came to be regarded as the most firm and unquestionable certainty. It was in this faith that Christianity first acquired a firm basis for its historical development. The necessary presupposition for the history and development of the Church is not so much the factuality of the resurrection of Jesus himself, but rather the belief that he was raised. However one may view the resurrection of Jesus—whether as an objective miracle which actually happened or as a subjective miracle which is to be explained psychologically— we may say that in so far as one assumes the possibility of such an inward experience, no psychological analysis is able to penetrate the

[33] *Das Christenthum*, p. 38.

inner mental processes in the consciousness of the disciples, by which their unbelief at the time of Jesus' death was changed into belief in his resurrection. Only through the consciousness of the disciples can we attain to that which was the object of their faith; and thus we can go no further than to say that however this process may have happened, the resurrection of Jesus became a fact in the consciousness of the disciples and possessed for them all the reality of a historical event.[34]

In his preaching Baur employed the orthodox Biblical language of the time. His sermons were primarily expositions which did not radically depart from the accepted Church teaching and were outwardly always impeccably orthodox.

The divine Lord who according to the will of the Father should sacrifice his holy life for the most holy cause, but who through the almighty power of the Godhead which was within him rose again from the dead in order to celebrate the glorious victory of life over death, of redeeming grace over the power of sin, of saving faith over the saddest, fatal error, appears anew to his despondent disciples and sets himself before them as the same Jesus whom they had seen dying on the cross at the hands of his enemies.[35]

We find the nearest approximation to Baur's actual views in

---

[34] Ibid., pp. 39–40.
[35] Sermon on Quasimodogeniti Sunday (UBT, Mh 969, pp. 311–13). It is a quite false procedure to accept Baur's sermons as representing his actual views. Baur could not state his beliefs openly in books, let alone before the pietists in the Tübingen *Stiftskirche*. All his sermons are in the orthodox language of the time and cannot be taken at face value. Hodgson is especially to be criticized here for not taking this fact into consideration. Thus he quotes passages from Baur's sermons which tend to give the impression that Baur's doctrine of the Person and work of Christ was that of orthodox traditional theology: 'Therefore only in him who was given by God for the forgiveness of our sins, and who has purchased us dearly through his reconciling death, can we grasp hold of the fatherly heart of God with almost childlike trust, which is the first condition on which love must rest' (quoted Hodgson, p. 113). 'Can [the Christian] believe in his Lord and Redeemer without having the certainty that he has come also for him, that he has suffered and died for him, in order to secure for him anew the grace and fatherhood of God, and with this fatherhood to consecrate him to the blessed inheritance of his heavenly kingdom?' (ibid., p. 115). Or, we may add: 'By his blood an eternal reconciliation has been accomplished which guarantees the eternal victory of grace over sin' (Sermon on Good Friday, Mh 969, pp. 304–6). All this sounds extremely orthodox, but by no honest stretch of the imagination could it be said that Baur believed these words. All traditional supernatural views of the Person and work of Christ were regarded by him as based on ignorance, as the product of primitive, unenlightened Jewish belief, which was scarcely better than superstition. For Baur, Jesus was an ordinary man who in his exemplary life and death might be an example to humanity, but no divine Saviour, Redeemer, or Mediator.

the posthumously published lectures on New Testament theology. Here Baur in thinly veiled fashion expresses his opinion that
the resurrection was merely a subjective and psychological event
in the religious consciousness of the disciples.

It is still more difficult with regard to the resurrection of Jesus to
answer the question as to what is objectively factual and what is
subjectively imagined. All those who do not believe in real miraculous
events can only presume that faith in the resurrection proceeded from
the whole mental process which took place in the minds of the disciples subsequent to the death of Jesus. After the whole impression
which Jesus' life and his final fate had made on them, it was absolutely
impossible for them to think that everything which through faith in
Jesus had now already been established in their minds as absolute
truth could perish in one moment with Jesus' death. Even in his death
they could still only think of him as the Living One. As the Dying One
he must also live, because everything that they believed and hoped
depended on his Person. How the disciples after the death of Jesus
persuaded themselves into believing in the necessity of his resurrection
is seen from the manner in which they sought to interpret his whole
faith to their religious consciousnesses by employing Old Testament
passages. He had to die but he also had to rise again because death
could have no power over him. Cf. Acts 2:24: 'God raised him up,
having loosed the pangs of death, because it was not possible for him
to be held by it.' Cf. also Luke 24:26. Once they had convinced themselves from the Old Testament that Christ was foreordained to suffer
and die, then in the necessity of his death was also contained the inner
necessity of the resurrection. If one can now imagine how this inner
necessity in its whole significance must have presented itself to the
minds of the disciples, and if one also considers that the religious
consciousness of this early period of Christianity was of an extremely
ecstatic nature, who then could hold it to be psychologically impossible
that the thoughts with which the disciples so busily occupied themselves in their minds were transformed into visions which they believed
to be appearances of the Resurrected One? What thrust itself into the
consciousness of the disciples in this way and caused them to believe
in the Resurrected One was the certainty—which represented itself
to them in the form of a given picture of the Person of Jesus—that
the cause of truth as God's cause could not be defeated. One can
therefore say that if Christ did not rise bodily, then he had to rise
mentally in the faith of the disciples. It was an inherent necessity in the
whole course of events that the thought of Christ's exaltation over
death, and the all-conquering power of truth for which he died had to

pass into their faith as the certainty of the factual reality of the resurrection.[36]

But now we must return to Baur's statement that the resurrection in itself lies outside the sphere of historical investigation. If this is really so then there is little purpose in even considering the question of whether in fact Jesus was actually raised from the dead; the event lies in a realm utterly outside our knowledge.

At this point one may certainly raise a question mark. Is the resurrection of Jesus as an objective event really so completely outside the sphere of historical investigation? Is it really so unique that it differs from every other miraculous event in history?[37] Is it really so etherial, so utterly other that it has nothing to do with history? For we have to do with a Jesus who lived, with a historical Jesus who was actually a part of history. His dead body was taken down from the cross and placed somewhere—according to the Gospels, in a tomb. If this body had been raised from the dead by a supernatural act, then the first piece of evidence which would have to be investigated would be whether or not the body could be found. If it still lay where it had been placed— or even elsewhere—then there could be no further argument about the matter; the most that could be claimed would be that Jesus's soul had been raised to a higher life—something that could never be verified. But a visible and tangible body is different

[36] *Neutestamentliche Theologie*, pp. 126–7. Hodgson's claim: 'Baur never implies that the reality of the resurrection is constituted simply by the faith in it' (op. cit., p. 236), is ambiguous and misleading. From at least his Hegelian period onwards Baur completely rejected the reality of Jesus' bodily resurrection and accepted the resurrection only as a subjective experience in the minds of the disciples. Thus, in whichever sense we understand the word resurrection, we may say that, contrary to Hodgson, Baur believed its reality was constituted *only* by faith in it. Hodgson's assertion that (for Baur) 'faith is the subjective acceptance and completion of an objectively realized, historically mediated process of reconciliation' (op. cit., p. 236) can only be understood as being true for Baur's Hegelian period.

[37] Hodgson is inconsistent when he claims that 'the historical theologian has access only to faith in the resurrection, not to the event itself' (op. cit., p. 144 n. 4) while at the same time maintaining that 'historical theology can determine whether in fact [Jesus] corresponds to what faith has claimed for him as the mediator of reconciliation' (p. 236). If it is possible to determine whether or not Jesus was the Son of God, i.e. divine (I take Hodgson's words at their face value), why then should it be impossible to determine—i.e. weigh up the evidence for (which in the last resort is all that anyone can do), with regard to any historical event—the factuality of the resurrection? The Person of Christ in the traditional belief of the Church is a divine supernatural Person and not merely a human; his appearance is an event in history, just as his resurrection is an event in history. Why then should what is possible as regards his Person, be impossible as regards his resurrection?

from an invisible and intangible soul or spirit. And the body of Jesus was never found.[38] That is a historical fact which has never been disproved. What actually happened to the body may of course be explained in other ways, but the fact remains that the body disappeared and was never discovered. But this is then an event *in history*, a part of history, however one seeks to explain the body's disappearance. And therefore, it is open to historical investigation. Thus the hypothesis of a supernatural resurrection to account for the disappearance of the body may be weighed against other theories—that it was stolen by the disciples, etc. And this piece of evidence is just one of a number of pieces—the change in the disciples from unbelief to belief, from despair to joy, their testimony that they had seen the risen Christ, the witness of Paul, etc., etc.—which may also be weighed against evidence to the contrary and alternative explanations. Moreover, if there were no objective resurrection of Jesus, if the resurrection were not an actual event—and it could not be other than *in history*— then the logical consequences, that the disciples were deceived, that they simply imagined the whole affair, were victims of psychological hallucinations, must be fairly and squarely faced, and their probability evaluated in comparison with other alternatives.

Thus, there is no ground for claiming that the resurrection lies outside the sphere of historical investigation. It did not lie outside this sphere for the disciples and Paul. It lies at second hand *for us* through the New Testament writings, but that is entirely different from saying that it lies outside the sphere of historical investigation, that we can know nothing about the resurrection as a historical event.

[38] It might of course have been found, but never reported. However there was never any claim to that effect, not even from his enemies.

12. The Rise and Decline of the Tübingen School

BAUR'S REPRESENTATION OF THE STRUGGLE BETWEEN PAULINE AND JEWISH CHRISTIANITY

The year 1831 marked the beginning of Baur's investigations into the historicity of the New Testament. In his long examination of the historical situation in the Corinthian church[1] he enunciated for the first time those views which were to form the basis of that total perspective of the early Church which may broadly be called the Tübingen perspective. In itself Baur's historical investigation was not new; others before him had examined the problems and to a very large degree Baur stood on the shoulders of his predecessors, but with this difference: that he presented not just new solutions to individual questions but a new total-view, a comprehensive picture of the situation in the early Church, and a new standard by which the New Testament narratives might be appraised. It was a new methodological approach which Baur pioneered, a new interpretation of the historical evidence. Upon this foundation the whole future investigation of the Tübingen School was established and maintained.

The cornerstone of this new approach was found in the opposition between Pauline and Jewish Christianity. From Paul's letters it was not difficult to perceive that on his travels he was met with hostility in many places and that the source of this hostility arose from the implacable hatred of the Jews (and later, Jewish Christians) towards the gospel which he preached. According to Baur, this bitter confrontation between Gentile and Jewish Christianity, between Paul and the other apostles, between the universalism of the gospel and the bondage of the law not only dominated the apostolic age, but continued after Paul's death late into the second century. Only at the end of this century did the opposition diminish, when in the face of dangers from outside the Church a con-

---

[1] 'Die Christuspartei in der korinthischen Gemeinde . . .', *TZT*, 1831: IV, pp. 61–206.

ciliatory movement gained ascendency which brought the two hostile parties together, both being finally absorbed into the higher unity of the emerging catholic Church.

The starting-point of Baur's investigations into the Corinthian church was 1 Corinthians 1:11–12, where Paul refers to the quarrels in the church and to four rival parties: 'For it has been reported to me by Chloe's people that there is quarrelling among you, my brethren. What I mean is that each one of you says, "I belong to Paul", or "I belong to Apollos", or "I belong to Cephas", or "I belong to Christ".' The problem was to account for the origin of these four parties and the differences which separated them from each other. It was not difficult to explain the parties following Paul and Peter and it was generally agreed that the opposition here lay in the Gentile and Jewish groups within the congregation; but it was hard to perceive the distinction between the Apollos party and the Pauline party. As for the origin of the Christ party—that was a riddle which baffled everyone. Eichhorn believed that it was a neutral party, while Storr thought it had James for its head. Baur was satisfied with neither of these suggestions but he could see little better to offer and contented himself with accepting the suggestion of J. E. C. Schmidt, that there were in fact only two parties—the pro-Pauline Gentile believers and the pro-Petrine Jewish Christians. The Apollos party was therefore to be viewed as pro-Pauline, but with minor differences, and the Christ party as consisting of Jewish Christians adhering to Peter, who wanted to stress their direct relationship to Christ through the apostles whom Christ had appointed.

Baur found the hypothesis of a hostile opposition between Jewish and Gentile Christians confirmed by two other New Testament letters—Romans and Galatians. In the former there are no obvious traces of the conflict, but Baur argued that the whole tenor of the letter showed it to have been written to the predominantly Jewish-Christian church in Rome. The evidence for this assertion was only briefly touched upon in his discussion of the church at Corinth, but five years later Baur expounded his views more fully in a long article[2] dealing with the origin and purpose of the letter.

In Baur's day the generally accepted theory held that Romans

[2] 'Über Zweck und Veranlassung des Römerbriefs ...', *TZT*, 1836: III, pp. 59–178.

was pre-eminently a letter written for the doctrinal instruction of the Christians in Rome, who were predominantly Gentiles. Baur, however, found this explanation unacceptable and regarded the letter as a polemical-apologetic treatise of Paul, written to a predominantly Jewish-Christian church in order to defend his apostleship. The evidence for this new hypothesis was discovered not in the first eight chapters of the letter, but in chapters 9–11 where the primary subject is the relation between Israel and the Gentiles. It is these chapters, argued Baur, which form the central theme of the letter, and not the dogmatic material in chapters 1–8, which is merely an introduction to the main problem in the Roman church—the relation between Jewish and Gentile Christians. At this point two main difficulties in Baur's solution became evident, the first being that nowhere in the letter, as Baur himself conceded, was there any evidence of a dispute within the church, either between Paul and the church or between Jewish and Gentile Christians. This objection, however, was simply set on one side and Baur argued that since the other Pauline letters (with the possible exception of Ephesians and Colossians) were all written with a definite purpose in view, then it was highly probable that the originating cause of Romans was the relationship existing between the two parties in the church. The second difficulty in Baur's hypothesis consisted in the fact that of the list of names found in the final chapter of the letter none is obviously Jewish; all are Gentile names—Greek or Roman. But if the church consisted predominantly of Jewish Christians, as Baur asserted, and if Paul was writing to Jewish Christians in order to defend his apostleship and to mediate in the dispute, was it not then strange that he should greet none of the Jewish Christians? Did not that fact completely contradict Baur's hypothesis? This objection was really of little concern to Baur who simply argued that the last two chapters of the letter were an unauthentic addition to the original letter, and not from Paul's own hand.

Most of all it was the letter to the Galatians which provided the confirmation which Baur required for his views. Here the bitter dispute with the Judaizers was at its height and Baur assumed that this hostility was to be found everywhere among the Jews to whom Paul carried the gospel. Nor did this hostility abate, but continued with undiminished intensity throughout the whole of Paul's life. To his gospel of freedom from the law was opposed the Jewish-Christian fanaticism for keeping the law, and the authentic Paulinism, according to Baur, was to be found where the opposition between the two factions was most evident. Where no evidence of such a struggle was to be seen in the writings of the early Church, the conclusion was to be drawn that such writings dated from a later period. Thus in Baur's view the only genuine letters from the hand of Paul were Romans, Galatians, 1 and 2 Corinthians; all other letters traditionally accepted as Pauline were unauthentic.

According to Baur, the opposition to Paul did not die down immediately after his death, but continued unabated, so that the whole Church was continually torn by the strife between the two opposing Jewish and Gentile-Christian factions. The crucial piece of evidence which Baur adduced in support of this view was drawn from the *Clementine Homilies*[3] which Baur attributed to an Ebionite[4] author. In Baur's opinion the *Homilies* were written about A.D. 170. This early date fitted in well with his other observations concerning the development of the early Church and he viewed the Clementine writings as an attack against the Pauline party, whose influence in the Church had become an ever-increasing factor with which the Jewish Christians had been forced to reckon.

[3] The *Clementine Homilies* and its sister book the *Recognitions* (probably a later working-over of the *Homilies*) are now generally held to have been composed in the third century. The *Homilies*, which has sometimes been described as a didactic novel, narrates the story of the life of Clement—how he went to Judea and met St. Peter whom he accompanied on his journeys. In the course of the narrative Peter takes part in a three-day dispute with the heretic Simon the magician, who is defeated and put to flight. The romantic story, however, is only the framework for the doctrinal teaching which reveals the influence of Jewish-Christian views. These portray Christ as a prophet and teacher, but not as the divine Son of God.

[4] The Ebionites were Jewish Christians who emigrated to Transjordan and Syria about A.D. 66–7, just before the siege of Jerusalem by the Romans. The sources for the history of Ebionism are very meagre and even the origin of the name is obscure. Epiphanius and Tertullian believed it to have been derived from a certain Ebion, reputedly the leader of the sect, but another explanation finds the origin in the Hebrew word *Ebionim* or 'poor men'. Although it is necessary to take into account that ideas within the movement were continually developing, there are still some general characteristics which may be noted. The Ebionites represented a syncretistic Judaism combining theosophical speculation with ascetic tendencies. They practised ritual ceremonies, the most important of which was baptism, and according to Irenaeus they insisted upon the observance of the whole Jewish law. Christ was regarded as a mere man—as a prophet and teacher, but not as divine. They rejected the doctrine of his virgin birth and were utterly hostile to Paul whom they regarded as a false apostle deluded and deceived by a devil-inspired hallucination.

The *Clementine Homilies* may be described as a religious novel in which the Apostle Peter confronts Simon the magician (cf. Acts 8:9–25) in a number of debates about the Christian faith. Wherever Simon journeyed spreading his heretical views, there Peter also followed in order to confute him with the truth of the gospel. The story itself is set in the same period in which it occurs in the book of Acts, i.e. before the conversion of Saul, so that there is no actual mention of Paul himself. Baur, however, saw the Clementines as a thinly disguised attack on Paul. In Baur's opinion, Paul was presented in the guise of Simon the magician. Thus Peter's declaration to Simon, that true revelation comes not through visions and manifestations but rather through external communication and teaching, is taken as an attack on Paul's apostleship and his claim to have met Christ on the Damascus road. It is James and Peter who are the attested and true apostolic witnesses, and when Simon's beliefs are condemned by Peter as utterly heretical and blasphemous, Baur views this as an Ebionite attack on the Pauline doctrines. Thus according to Baur, the conflict between the two parties was still raging with undiminished intensity during the second half of the second century, and in order to strengthen its authority, the Jewish-Christian or Ebionite party invented the story that Peter actually resided at Rome and was martyred there—a story which in Baur's opinion has not a shred of supporting evidence. Only in the last decade of the century, under the papacy of Victor, was the struggle ended when the Pauline party finally gained the upper hand and the opposition was abolished in the unity of the catholic Church.

BAUR ON THE PASTORAL EPISTLES

In 1835 Baur published his investigation into the Pastoral Epistles which were in his opinion unauthentic and to be dated late in the second century. The main grounds given for this later dating were as follows: first, that the heretics mentioned in the letters were in Baur's opinion the Gnostics of the second century, the letters being a polemic directed against the Marcionites. Secondly, Baur maintained that the letters presupposed a church constitution which is nowhere in evidence in the four authentic Pauline letters. In the Pastoral Epistles Paul speaks to bishops, presbyters, and deacons while in the Corinthian letters, where the organization of the church comes in for discussion, these offices are never mentioned. Was it likely, argued Baur, that the apostle Paul, who had shown no interest in a constitution for the Corinthian church, had now in the same period become so bureaucratic in his ideas? Thirdly, Baur could see no period in Paul's life where the historical details mentioned in the Pastorals could be fitted into the framework of historical events ascertainable from the four authentic letters and Acts. A fourth missionary journey after Paul's first imprisonment at Rome, followed by a second imprisonment and trial, remained, in Baur's view, quite out of the question. This third objection, however, loses much of its weight when it is remembered that Baur rejected the book of Acts as a trustworthy historical source.

The long review of Rothe's book on the beginning of the Christian Church[5] appeared in the *Tübinger Zeitschrift für Theologie* in 1838[6] and provided a much more detailed discussion on the origin of the episcopate in the early Church. Rothe had argued that in every church established during the apostolic age there had been a body of presbyters who governed the affairs of the congregation, and that the apostles still living after A.D. 70 appointed bishops in various towns and cities as a bulwark against the heresies then infiltrating the churches. Baur, on the contrary, maintained that the episcopate was not something instituted from above by the apostles, but was rather a purely democratic institution which grew naturally out of an increasing need for an administrative and central authority which would have the oversight of a whole district. In his view the bishop was elected by the other presbyters as *primus inter pares* and only gradually did he take on a more monarchical function. Nor, argued Baur, could the Ignatian letters be used to support Rothe's claims, as these letters were themselves unauthentic and written at a date much later than was generally supposed.

SCHWEGLER'S MONTANISM AND ITS REPERCUSSIONS

During the following five years Baur devoted himself to his dogmatic studies and wrote his long work treating the development of the doctrine of the Atonement (1838); this was followed by his even longer three-volume treatise on the doctrines of the Trinity

---

[5] *Die Anfänge der christlichen Kirche und ihrer Verfassung* (Wittenberg, 1837).
[6] 'Über den Ursprung des Episcopats in der christlichen Kirche', *TZT*, 1838: III, pp. 1–185.

and Incarnation (1841-3) in which he traced the history of these doctrines from the Fathers down to the nineteenth century. The investigations into the historicity of the New Testament and the writings of the post-apostolic age were now bequeathed to his younger disciples and not until 1844 did Baur return to this field. The study of the early Church, however, did not decline, but blossomed in a quite unexpected manner as the younger members of the School eagerly seized their opportunity for independent investigation and advanced the research which Baur had already begun. In the years 1841-6 the Tübingen School came to fruition.

The work which initiated the new interest in the post-apostolic age was Schwegler's book on Montanism[7] which appeared in 1841. Here was a learned and conscientious attempt to penetrate the cloud which hung over the second century and to shed some light on the origin and development of the early Christian doctrines. Who were the Montanists? What were the distinctive ideas which separated them from the main stream of Christianity? In what ways did they influence the Christian Church and the formation of Christian doctrines? These were some of the questions which Schwegler set himself to answer.

The book was divided into three parts, the first discussing the character of Montanism, the second treating the relationship between Montanism and the other religious systems of the time—Ebionism, Gnosticism, and Paulinism—and the final part dealing with the history of Montanism—its origin, development, its struggle with the church at Rome, and its later history. Although little is known about the origin of Montanism, Schwegler was of the opinion that it arose out of a legalistic Ebionism. Rejecting the traditional view that the leader of the new sect was a certain Montanus, who was accompanied by two prophetesses, Maximilla and Priscilla, Schwegler also viewed all other information regarding the time and origin of the movement with great suspicion. Nevertheless, he thought it extremely probable that it began about the middle of the second century, that it had its roots in Asia Minor and that its distinctive features were the acceptance of new revelations through visions and prophecies, a strict asceticism, and a fanatical emphasis on the second coming of Christ. What differentiated the new sect from Ebionism was the new teaching on the Trinity. Schwegler argued that although the

---

[7] *Der Montanismus und die christliche Kirche des zweiten Jahrhunderts* (Tübingen, 1841).

concept of Spirit (*pneuma*) appeared in Ebionism, it had in fact a feminine form in its connection with the Old Testament idea of wisdom (*sophia*), whereas in Montanism the Spirit appears in the masculine form (*parakletos*). In analogous manner Christ himself, who was reported to have appeared to Maximilla in the guise of a woman, was able to be transposed into the masculine category of the Word (*logos*). The two concepts *logos* and *parakletos* now emerged in the forms of the second and third Persons of the Trinity.

This hypothesis provided Schwegler with the necessary ground for setting the composition of John's Gospel (which in Schwegler's opinion betrayed a certain Trinitarian tendency) in this period. From the days of the apostle John, who had lived in Ephesus (Schwegler held that John had written the Apocalypse, but not the Gospel), there had been a strong Johannine circle, but about the middle of the second century an anti-Jewish reaction in Asia Minor began to make itself felt, the first representative of this new Pauline upsurge being Bishop Apollinaris of Hierapolis. It was in this circle, with its anti-Ebionite tendency, that the Gospel of John was most likely to have been composed, the emphasis on the Word and the Spirit, according to Schwegler, being undoubted references to the Montanist movement.

The first review of Schwegler's book was written by Planck[8] who took occasion to point out a number of faults, his main complaint being that Schwegler had identified Montanism too closely with Ebionism. The essential principle of Ebionism, according to Planck, was tradition, and Montanism severed itself from Ebionism in that it made prophecy the central point in its movement.

On the whole Planck's criticism was friendly and favourable but in the following year (1842) a highly critical review appeared in the *Deutsche Jahrbücher*,[9] written not by an orthodox theologian, nor by a pietist, but by one of the Tübingen camp itself, by one of Baur's own pupils, a close friend of Strauss: Louis Georgii. It was a comprehensive and penetrating criticism which Georgii made and Schwegler's whole book was carefully and systematically torn to pieces. Almost everything came under fire—his interpretation of the sources, his identification of Ebionism with

Jewish Christianity, his argument that the Montanists had conceived not only the Spirit, but Christ himself, in a feminine form, and especially that the doctrine of the Trinity had originated within the Montanistic movement. But the most damaging feature of the whole review was Georgii's denial that the reaction against Montanism was essentially a struggle between Paulinism and Ebionism, since Georgii conceived the controversy as taking place within an essentially Pauline church where a free spirit had set itself against a more rigid and restricted conception of the Christian faith. Georgii then went even further and applied his axe to the root of the whole Baurian hypothesis, declaring that the supposition of a continuing struggle in the post-apostolic age between Pauline and Jewish Christians was quite untenable.

We meet here again the hypothesis of the author which has such undue importance, that all these events are to be subordinated to the opposition between Jewish and Gentile Christianity. This hypothesis is the principal defect of the whole representation; it entangles the author in contradictions with himself (thus the free-thinking Marcion, according to his asceticism, would have been a zealous Jew), leads him astray into arbitrary interpretations of many events, to arbitrary explanations of obscure happenings through motives of his own imagination, in short, to a treatment of history which would horrify anyone versed in the patristic and early Church writers.[10]

Zeller also reviewed the book in the *Theologische Jahrbücher*, but while agreeing with many of Georgii's criticisms he rejected Georgii's assertion that Schwegler's whole view was basically false. Zeller's arguments, however, were weak and ineffective and only called forth an even stronger rebuttal from Georgii, who again stressed the untenability of Schwegler's views. As far as he could see, declared Georgii, not only was there no trace of any anti-Paulinism in the post-apostolic Church but the hypothesis of a continuing struggle between Pauline and Jewish Christians was utterly without foundation.

The hypothesis of an opposition between Paulinism and anti-Paulinism in the Church, which runs through the first two centuries still seems to me nothing more than a hypothesis which has no other ground than the ingenuity of its defender. An ecclesiastical document in which that anti-Paulinism appears openly and undisguised, in which Paul is

[10] *DJWK*, 1842, p. 150.

really attacked as an apostate and named as such, does not exist. For the defenders of this hypothesis, therefore, there remains no other course than to find, or rather, divine this polemic against Paul in indirect references, in subterfuges, in veiled allusions contained in isolated writings of this period. But even this procedure is still highly doubtful and not at all favourable to the hypothesis. Why, one must ask, did the anti-Paulinists use such circumlocutions? What hindered them from attacking the apostle to the Gentiles openly and just as the strict Ebionites did? If the views which the Clementines put into the mouth of Peter are anti-Pauline, if Paul's opponents dared to find sanction for their views by using the name of the Prince of the apostles, how does one explain the cowardice with which they attack the hated enemy by portraying him in disguised form and using a different name? And how inconceivable is this procedure, when, according to Schwegler's extension of this hypothesis, this anti-Paulinism was not just an isolated fraction of the Christian world, but rather the whole Church in the first two centuries was under the sway of this anti-Pauline Ebionism. Did somehow the mighty spirit of the apostle to the Gentiles weigh upon the life of the Church like a ghost with magic power, which they indeed dared to fight but not to call by name? Certainly an enigmatic, unintelligible situation! Is it really possible to find the historical Paul in the character of Simon the magician as he appears in the Clementines, the Simon who denied the resurrection of the dead? (*Clem. Homilies*, II. 22).[11]

Schwegler was not impressed with Georgii's views. 'Georgii's article is weak', he wrote to Zeller, 'and his obdurate reasoning completely unbearable.'[12] Georgii's criticism struck not only at Schwegler but also at Baur himself, and from this time forward Georgii was in particular disfavour with Baur.

Schwegler replied in the following year with a brief rejoinder but he did not debate the main issue, that the continuing hostility between Pauline and Jewish Christianity continued through the second century; this hypothesis was simply referred back to Baur's interpretation of the evidence, and at this point the controversy within the camp came to a close.

ZELLER ON THE APOCALYPSE

The Tübingen hypothesis of a continuing struggle between Jewish and Gentile Christians rested on slender foundations and

[11] 'Über den Charakter der christlichen Geschichte in den ersten zwei Jahrhunderten', *DJWK*, 1842, p. 919.
[12] To Zeller, 20 Oct. 1842.

every argument which could in any way strengthen the case was especially welcome. One such argument was found in the book of Revelation, at that time commonly referred to as the Apocalypse. In 1842 Zeller's friend Schnitzer contributed an article on the Johannine writings to Zeller's newly founded journal. In discussing the Johannine authorship of the Gospel, Epistles, and Apocalypse, Schnitzer expressed his support for the view that while the Gospel could not be attributed to the apostle it was extremely probable that the Apocalypse was from his hand. Zeller was impressed and quick to see that here was a new argument which could lend support to the Baurian hypothesis. He at once set to work and appended a long article on the Apocalypse[13] to that of Schnitzer's.

Zeller proceeded from the assumption that knowledge of future events was impossible and that the Apocalypse had to reflect the history of the time in which it was written—in his opinion, the time between Nero's death and the fall of Jerusalem. In Zeller's view the Apocalypse was probably written by the apostle John, either in Patmos or in Asia Minor, i.e. it was a genuine apostolic document in contrast to the Gospel of John which (with Schwegler) he held to have been written late in the second century. Zeller found two main arguments to support his assertion that the Apocalypse was an anti-Pauline polemic written from an Ebionite standpoint. He maintained that (1) the emphasis on the fixed number of twelve apostles (Rev. 21:14) was intended to exclude Paul from the apostolic corpus; (2) the polemic against the Nicolaitans (Rev. 2:2–6) expressly referred to the Pauline Christians. From Rev. 2:14 Zeller deduced that the Nicolaitans were those who ate food sacrificed to idols and practised immorality, i.e. fornication. Possibly, he argued, this identification was not entirely justified, but may have arisen through a misunderstanding of Paul's teaching on the freedom from the law which may in turn have led to excesses among the Pauline Christians. Nevertheless, in Zeller's opinion John was making the most of an opportunity to polemicize against the Pauline Christians and attack Paul's apostleship with veiled and insidious allusions. It was only one step further to identify Paul with the false apostles mentioned in Rev. 2:2: 'I know your works . . . and how you cannot bear

---

[13] 'Einige weitere Beiträge zur Einleitung in die Apokalypse', *TJ*, 1842, pp. 654–717.

evil men but have tested those who call themselves apostles but
are not, and found them to be false.' Zeller did not make this
identification, but four years later in his book on the post-
apostolic age Schwegler took this final and logical step.

PLANCK ON THE PRINCIPLE OF EBIONISM

Whereas Baur and Schwegler had so far left the problem of Jesus'
attitude to the law untouched and pushed the question of Jesus
as the founder of Christianity into the background, Planck's
article on the principle of Ebionism[14] was an important step forward in defining these two important aspects of early Christianity
more clearly. Why was it, asked Planck, that for so long the Jewish
Christians in the early Church held the upper hand over the Gentile Christians who followed the teaching of Paul? Fundamentally,
he answered, it was because of the influence of the other apostles
who attacked Paul's authority and maintained that the Jewish
law remained in force for Jewish and Gentile Christians alike.
The law had been given by God through Moses, and the Ebionites maintained that Jesus had said or done nothing to abolish its
validity: He had come not to abolish the law, but to fulfil it.

But if Jesus had had no intention of abolishing the law, in what
sense had he intended to fulfil it? According to Planck, Jesus
desired to free his people from their restricted nationalistic
understanding of the law and to lead them to that higher understanding of it which formed the content of his own religious
consciousness—a consciousness manifested supremely in the
Sermon on the Mount.

Jesus perceived that the rulers of the people would oppose his
teaching and that they would finally bring about his death.
Nevertheless, for the sake of the people he sacrificed himself.
His death was the negation of their restricted nationalism, the
necessary completion of his Messianic work and the final necessary step in freeing his disciples from the Jewish nationalistic
ideal. Because he expected the end of the world to come in the
immediate future and the sound of the gospel to have gone out
into all lands, Jesus did not reflect upon the problems which
would arise with regard to the Gentiles and particularly with
respect to the keeping of the law; but had he once foreseen the

---

[14] 'Das Princip des Ebionitismus', *TJ*, 1843, pp. 1–34.

problems which Paul would have to face, argued Planck, he would never have demanded that the Gentiles should observe the Jewish law. For Jesus, then, the law was only of temporary validity, but Ebionism made Jesus' consciousness of this validity into a fixed dogma. What in Jesus was a living unity, became in Ebionism rigid tradition. According to Planck, it was Paul who first pressed through to the conception of unity in the Spirit and freedom from the law, and for this reason he was everywhere opposed by the Ebionites as a false teacher and apostle.

BAUR ON THE GOSPEL OF JOHN

With the completion in 1843 of the final volume of his work on the Trinity and the Incarnation, Baur again returned to his investigations into the New Testament and in the following year his long treatise on the Gospel of John appeared in the *Theologische Jahrbücher*.[15] Eight years earlier in his 'Compelled Explanation' (1836) he had protested that as he had had no opportunity for a full investigation into the Gospel, he had no reason to deny its authenticity. But even at this early date it is almost certain that he had already been convinced by Strauss of the Gospel's unauthenticity and in 1838 he wrote to Strauss thanking him for sending the third edition of his *Life of Jesus*.

The new edition of your work is very welcome to me since I am now making a special study—occasioned first of all by preparation for lectures—of the Gospel of John. To be sure, I haven't yet got beyond the first few chapters but this little has already made upon me the most decided impression that historical truth, i.e. relatively speaking, can be sought only on the side of the Synoptics, and it almost appears to me that in this latest edition you have already conceded too much to your critics.[16]

In his treatise of 1844 Baur denied that the Gospel was to be attributed to the apostle and argued that all indications pointed to a date near the end of the second century. Naturally he was at great pains to emphasize that in his opinion the worth of the Gospel was entirely independent of its authorship, that the book possessed outstanding literary merit and moral insight even though the events narrated were not historically true. Against the

[15] 'Über die Composition und den Charakter des johanneischen Evangeliums', *TJ*, 1844, pp. 1–191; 397–475; 615–700.
[16] To Strauss, 29 May 1838; *ZKG*, LXXII (1962), p. 104.

traditional view of authorship Baur brought forth four cardinal objections which may be briefly stated.

(i) It was unlikely that John, who was obviously so immersed in the narrow Jewish view of Christianity and had been named along with Peter and James as one of the 'reputed pillars' (Gal. 2:9) of the Church, could later have developed such a universal outlook as is shown in the Gospel.

(ii) Although he had never set foot in Palestine, Baur thought that he was able to detect a number of geographical and historical errors in the Gospel; these, in Baur's opinion, showed plainly that the author was not a Jew by birth, that he was unfamiliar with the Jerusalem locality, and had little knowledge of the historical and political situation in Palestine at the time of Jesus. According to Baur, Bethany probably never existed; the description of the pools of Bethesda and Siloam were to be regarded as fictitious, and John's knowledge of the office of High Priest was clearly deficient, since Caiaphas was High Priest for ten years and not, as the writer implied, only in the year that Jesus was crucified.

(iii) A more important objection was found in the debate concerning the date of the Last Supper. According to John's Gospel Jesus was crucified on the fourteenth day of the month Nisan, i.e. on the day of the Passover. However, the Church in Asia Minor observed that day as the day on which Jesus ate the Passover meal with his disciples. Since the Asia Minor Church claimed support for their practice from the apostle John himself, in that John, while he was in Ephesus, had also observed the fourteenth Nisan as the day of the Passover meal, Baur argued that the contradiction between tradition and the Gospel of John showed that the Church in Asia Minor had no knowledge of the Gospel, because it had not then been written.

(iv) The fourth main objection to the Gospel's apostolic authorship lay in its dissimilarity with the Apocalypse. Baur's view (following Zeller) was that the apostle had written the Apocalypse somewhere near the end of the first century, and that as the two books were so basically different, this fact automatically excluded apostolic authorship of the Gospel.

What then did Baur hold regarding the Gospel's origin and date of composition? Baur was not specific about time and place but he pointed to four features in the book which reflected the situation in which the Gospel was composed—the presence of Gnosticism, Montanism, the doctrine of the *logos*, and the controversy on the passover. These elements, in his opinion, reflected a period late in the second century. He thus tentatively accepted Schwegler's view that the Gospel was written in Asia Minor about A.D. 170, but he also held open the possibility of an Alexandrian origin.

BAUR'S PAUL, THE APOSTLE OF JESUS CHRIST

Among all Baur's writings his book on Paul[17] was the work that he most prized. It marked the conclusion of a long period of study on Paul and the early Church, which Baur had pursued during the previous fifteen years. With this book Baur's representation of the Apostolic Church received its final form, and was never altered in any essential points.

The book itself falls into three parts: a historical account of Paul's life and work, a critical investigation of his epistles, and a summary of his doctrinal teaching.

1. The most important critical question in depicting Paul's life and work concerned the relation between the historical sources—the historical details contained in Paul's own letters and the biographical sketch recorded in the Acts of the Apostles. The older method of expounding the Bible had simply assumed the historical material in both sources to be historically true and that it was simply a matter of harmonizing any alleged discrepancies. Baur, however, discovered in the book of Acts not just minor discrepancies, but differences and contradictions too great to be harmonized, to say nothing of many incidents whose historical credibility was unacceptable. The following are just a few of Baur's objections, which, in his opinion, showed conclusively the unhistorical nature of Acts.

(i) Baur found in Acts a number of events which he considered to be historically inconceivable or impossible: the attitude of the Sanhedrin to the apostles and to Stephen; the apostolic decree; Paul's doubtful behaviour with regard to the magistrates in Philippi and his ambiguous conduct and skilful diplomacy in Jerusalem.

---

[17] *Paulus, der Apostel Jesu Christi* (Stuttgart, 1845); ET: *Paul, the Apostle of Jesus Christ* (London and Edinburgh, 1876).

(ii) A more substantial objection was Baur's allegation of contradictions between Acts and the Pauline epistles, as well as within Acts itself. Thus there were said to be differences in chronology with regard to Paul's visits to Jerusalem; even more serious was the silence in Acts over the dispute between Peter and Paul at Antioch and the failure of Paul to mention the council of Jerusalem in his letter to the Galatians. Baur also pointed out differences in the three accounts of Paul's conversion experience.

(iii) Fabulous and mythical stories were rejected outright by Baur as unhistorical. These included Paul's encounter with the risen Jesus—according to Baur, simply a subjective, psychological experience; the visions of Peter and Ananias, the miraculous healings and releases from prison, and the raising of Tabitha from the dead.

In 1841 Matthias Schneckenburger in Bern had published a book dealing with the aim and purpose of Acts[18] in which he had argued that Acts had been written by Luke as an apologetic defence of the apostle Paul. Although he disagreed with Schneckenburger in ascribing the authorship of Acts to Luke, Baur was very much impressed with Schneckenburger's arguments and had no hesitation in adopting them. According to Schneckenburger the idea which runs through the whole book is that of a parallel between the two apostles Peter and Paul. Its purpose was to represent the differences between them as being of no significance. Thus in the first part of Acts Peter is made to appear as much as possible like Paul, and Paul in the second part, as much as possible like Peter. Both work miracles: Peter opposes Simon the magician, Paul Elymas; both raise the dead, both lay hands on the disciples with miraculous results, and later tradition asserts that both were martyred at Rome. All this, according to Baur, shows the mediating and conciliatory character of the book and stamps its origin as belonging to the middle decades of the second century. Baur did not deny that the book had some historical basis. It was possible, he thought, that the final redactor had used some narratives which Luke had written; but in his opinion the canonical Acts was a highly untrustworthy historical source which required careful critical examination in order to sift the historical events from the fictitious.

---

[18] *Über den Zweck der Apostelgeschichte* (Bern, 1841).

2. In the second part of the book Baur examined the Pauline epistles in the light of the historical framework which formed the basis of the Tübingen perspective. The thirteen letters were divided into the three classes already employed by Eusebius: *homologoumena* (acknowledged writings), *antilegomena* (disputed writings), and *notha* (unauthentic writings). The first class consisted of Romans, Galatians, 1 and 2 Corinthians; in the third class Baur reckoned the Pastoral Epistles, and the remaining six Pauline letters were placed in the category of disputed letters; these, for various reasons, were finally all rejected as unauthentic. None of them reveals the conflict betwen Paul and the other apostles; Ephesians cannot have been written by him since the author writes to the church as one who is a stranger, and Paul would never have referred to the apostles as holy when he elsewhere refers to them in scathing terms. Ephesians and Colossians stand in a special relationship to one another and show a Gnostic background which is far removed from the apostle Paul. Thus there are continual references to principalities, thrones, and dominions, and other expressions such as wisdom, mystery, and knowledge. According to Baur, Colossians was written first and Ephesians is a later working over of it. These same Gnostic ideas are also found in Philippians, and Philemon, which Baur regarded as highly fictional, is also rejected on the ground of its close relationship with the other prison epistles. This leaves the two Thessalonian letters which Baur found lacking in content and purpose as well as being devoid of any originality. Moreover, in his opinion, the central theme of the letters—the proclamation of the second coming of Christ—was not in harmony with 1 Corinthians 15, while the greeting at the end of 2 Thessalonians could scarcely have been written at a time when probably no other letters of Paul's had made their appearance in the world.

The authenticity of the Pauline letters remained a disputed point within the Tübingen School during the next fifteen years. Hilgenfeld accepted the Baurian corpus plus Philippians, I Thessalonians, and Philemon; Ritschl accepted all the letters with the exception of I Timothy; Volkmar (and later Holsten) clung to the four undisputed epistles.

3. In the third and final part of the book Baur analysed Paul's theological views, beginning with an examination of Paul's own

personality and religious consciousness. Based only on the four epistles which Baur regarded as being from the hand of Paul, this examination sought to show the centrality of the doctrine of justification by faith as the outward representation of Paul's inner religious consciousness. In his description of Paul's life Baur had ascribed Paul's conversion to an inner psychological experience, which Paul himself had believed to be a miracle. Important, in Baur's opinion, is not the objective factuality of the event, i.e. whether Paul *actually* met the risen Jesus, but the factuality of the subjective experience, i.e. that Paul experienced a change in his life—the whys and wherefores being of secondary importance. The doctrine of justification, according to Baur, is simply an analysis of the Christian consciousness, and Jesus is the Christ in that in him alone this Christian consciousness first came to full fruition—a representation scarcely different from Schleier-macher's conception of Christ as the archetype of the Christian ideal. Following this discussion of justification by faith Baur treats in rather cursory fashion the doctrine of the Church, the relation of Christianity to Judaism and heathenism, and minor points of doctrine in which are included the doctrines of God, Christ, angels and demons, predestination, and the heavenly state.

What one notices in reading through this third part of the book is the dichotomy between Baur's objective presentation of Paul's own statements and his desire to interpret these statements from a completely different point of view. In outward appearance this third part presents an impression of a traditionally orthodox treatment, but its content is essentially that of Schleiermacher's Dogmatics (here and there Hegel also appears) in that Baur wishes to interpret everything from the viewpoint of Christian conscious-ness. Thus the spirit of man's Christian consciousness is identical with the Spirit of God, and the knowledge of one's Christian consciousness is the knowledge of God himself. This third part is the least convincing and most unsatisfying part of the whole book and reveals Baur groping for a consistent interpretation, which he attained to in some measure only after his return to the rationalism of *The Church History of the First Three Centuries* (1853).

SCHWEGLER'S POST-APOSTOLIC AGE

If Baur's writings had laid the foundations of the new Tübingen perspective it was in Schwegler's work on the post-apostolic age[19] that this perspective was most clearly and concisely set forth. Schwegler's work marked the highest point of the Tübingen School; it was the crowning achievement, the summit, from which the path could only lead downwards. For although Baur's writings had provided a basic and detailed investigation of the early Christian documents, they were somewhat long and rambling and concerned with establishing the basic Tübingen hypothesis of a continuing struggle between Jewish and Gentile Christians, rather than presenting an over-all summary of the apostolic and post-apostolic age. Schwegler's book, on the other hand, was a comprehensive survey of the whole period; in this survey all the relevant writings were examined and allotted their proper place in the framework which Schwegler had erected from the pioneering investigations of Baur, Zeller, and Planck, and not least from his own studies on the nature and character of Montanism.

Schwegler's whole presentation was based on the principle already formulated by Baur—the continuing struggle between Jewish (Ebionite) and Pauline Christianity. The old catholic method of treating the history of the Church had regarded the New Testament as a closed canon, had allowed no room for development, and treated all doctrines appearing after this time as heretical when they did not agree with the teaching of the canonical scriptures. But there are obviously different types of teaching within the New Testament—in Matthew there is no mention of the pre-existence of Christ; in 1 Peter nothing about the *logos;* in James no hint of the Trinity; in Revelation no emphasis upon justification by faith. All this, according to Schwegler, simply revealed a development of views within the early Church, and it was only one step further to dissolve the canon on the ground that many New Testament writings did not actually belong to the New Testament period, i.e. the apostolic age. In Schwegler's opinion the so-called canonical and extra-canonical writings were simply moments in the development of Christian history, writings which reflected the period in which they had been written, but so hopelessly jumbled up in the New Testament that all understanding of their historical and chronological setting had been completely lost, and needed to be restored. Schwegler now set himself to this task of restoration, which was indeed

[19] *Das nachapostolische Zeitalter* (2 vols.; Tübingen, 1846).

the whole basis of the Tübingen perspective. The origin and date of each writing was to be determined by its tendency, i.e. by deciding the historical period into which the character of the writing was best fitted.

The balance sheet must be checked by adding up the figures backwards and it must be able to be shown that a writing which must be torn free from its ostensible and supposed context because of its historical, dogmatic, or personal incongruencies, is able to be fitted more appropriately into another context, and that through this transposition there originates a more closely knit line of development, a more harmonious and historical total picture.[20]

This was the basis of the Tübingen perspective. With this new method, criticism was to be set on a purely historical basis, thus doing away with the old traditional approach which regarded all the New Testament writings as inspired by God, and all extra-canonical writings as uninspired. In Schwegler's truly scientific tendency-approach there were to be no presuppositions—i.e. no supernatural presuppositions. The Scriptures were to be treated as purely historical documents and each particular writing fitted into the historical framework which had previously been determined by the moving ideas and events of the time—the current state of affairs within the Church, Church order, the theological and ecclesiastical controversies, the factions, the party delineations, and the political relations between Church and State. This historical framework into which the New Testament writings were to be fitted according to their teaching, was evolved and formulated in the three main steps already outlined by Baur.

(i) The four Pauline letters, Romans, Galatians, 1 and 2 Corinthians, were pronounced authentic in that they alone showed the hostility between Paul and the other apostles, and the controversy with the Jewish Christians concerning the law. From these letters Schwegler was able to portray the situation in the early Church. The only difference between the Jewish Christians and the Jews themselves was that the former regarded Jesus as the Messiah while the latter still awaited the Messiah's coming. Had not Paul appeared on the scene, Christianity would have remained simply

[20] Ibid., I, pp. 10-11.

an internal sect of Judaism. What Paul brought, according to Schwegler, was a universality which required the abolition of the Jewish law in order that Christianity might spread beyond the borders of a faith limited to Israel alone. Christianity was to embrace believers from all nations in the new Israel of God. Thus Paul's teaching, as could be foreseen, was to bring upon him the hatred of the Jews, who could not see beyond their own nationalistic aspirations.

(ii) Schwegler's second step was to assume that this controversy was not a fleeting one, that the struggle did not quickly die down after Paul's martyrdom, but continued unabated down to the end of the second century. Schwegler found no evidence to support the view that Paulinism triumphed shortly after Paul's death; on the contrary, in his opinion it was Jewish Christianity which gained the upper hand, and so powerful was the influence of the Ebionite Christians that Paulinism was driven underground. Only in the middle of the second century, when a reaction against Jewish Christianity began to set in, did Paulinism again begin to assert itself, finally gaining control of the Church during the last decade of the century when Victor was bishop of Rome.

Paulinism, which in its essential points was basically opposed to the existing Jewish Christianity and lacked the necessary traditional attestation, could in the earliest Christian times appear only as an unjustified innovation. Completely in opposition to the basic principles advocated by the original apostles, neither endorsed nor backed by the authority of an apostle who had been a direct disciple of Christ, it was inevitable that it should be resisted from every side by the existing, traditional, and established Jewish Christianity.

When we consider the circumstances of the time when Paul first came to prominence and the basic beliefs which he preached and fought for, we will certainly find it credible that as his position became known in the early Church, he was everywhere received with mistrust. The validity and value of his apostleship were doubted; even his personal character was not spared from misrepresentations; his teaching was repudiated as an unaccredited and unauthorized innovation; his missionary activity was basically disapproved of; and for all this opposition, the authority of the older, original, and accredited apostles was claimed . . .

Certainly the fire he had kindled continued to flicker, but the existing traditional Jewish Christianity flooded everywhere, even into the neighbouring regions where Paulinism was established; and how much more after Paul's death must it again have whittled down the results of his tireless exertions.

Because Christianity continued to be restricted to the lower classes of society and still remained outwardly connected with the Jewish synagogue, it was inevitable that the Christian faith would retain its materially Jewish character; and even if for a short time it was shaken out of this rut, it quickly sank back again. Generations had to pass by and the whole internal and external situation of Christianity had to change before the spirit of the great apostle to the Gentiles could again arise and spread its wings victoriously over the Roman world.[21]

(iii) Schwegler now traced the development of Christianity in the two centres where an abundance of literature allowed this process to be followed in detail—in Rome and in Asia Minor. In this examination he discarded the traditional views regarding the date and origin of the New Testament writings and reordered them according to the controversies of the time (Gnosticism, Montanism), the various key-words, concepts, and doctrines (*logos*, pre-existence, justification by faith, etc.), and not least, whether the writings revealed a Pauline or Ebionite, a polemical or irenical-mediating tendency.

We shall follow Schwegler through his analysis as concisely as possible.

A. The History of the Church at Rome

1. The Jewish-Christian Development

The situation in the church at Rome during Paul's own lifetime is first depicted, and here the letter to the Romans is the keystone. Schwegler following Baur holds that the letter was written to the Jewish Christians in a predominantly Ebionite congregation where the Pauline Christians could do little against the powerful opposition which claimed Peter as its authority. The secondary non-canonical literature is then investigated—Hermas, Hegessipus, and Justin—from which Schwegler thought himself able to discover traces and hints of the prevailing Ebionite opposition to the Apostle Paul. Then follows a summary of the *Clementine Homilies*, clearly Ebionite in viewpoint and utterly hostile to Paul in portraying him as Simon the magician; in this class are also found the letter of James, which in its attack on the Pauline

[21] Ibid., I, pp. 156–7.

doctrines of justification by faith reveals a 'polemical-irenical' (!) tendency, and 2 Clement. Finally come those writings which symbolize the last stage in the development of Ebionism, which exhibit neutrality and attitudes which may be viewed as revealing overtures for peace: the Gospel of Mark, written late in the second century, was the last of the three Synoptic Gospels and subordinated the Ebionite viewpoint to its epitomatorian character; the *Clementine Recognitions*, in which may be seen the last stage of the transition from Ebionism to catholicism, were a working over of the early *Clementine Homilies;* and the keystone of the whole Ebionite development which found its consummation in the catholic Church was 2 Peter. 'The keystone of the Ebionite line of development is the second epistle of Peter. In this letter the two opposing viewpoints celebrate their peace-treaty and the two apostles, Peter and Paul, their names formerly the rallying-call of the two contending parties, give each other a brotherly handshake. Ebionism has now attained the standpoint of catholicity.'[22]

2. The Pauline-Christian Development

Schwegler now describes those writings possessing a Pauline tendency and ascertains that parallel to the development of Ebionism runs a similar development in Pauline Christianity. He distinguishes three phases—a decisively Pauline, a mediating and conciliatory, and finally a catholicizing phase. In the first phase the Pauline party is characterized by the fundamental views of Paul himself and the writing which typifies this period most fittingly is—astonishingly!—1 Peter. Of course this is not as surprising as might appear on first sight, since Schwegler argued that the letter was not written by Peter, but composed by a follower of Paul who had the ingenious idea of attributing it to Paul's opponent in order to heighten the reconciling element which occupies such a central position in the letter. According to Schwegler its composition was probably to be dated in the reign of Trajan (A.D. 98–117) 'since it was psychologically improbable that Peter could have written such a letter only ten years after his dispute with Paul at Antioch'.

The second phase of the development is characterized by a neutral and conciliatory tendency. At that time the Jewish-Christian party was the dominant power in the church at Rome

[22] Ibid., I, p. 490.

and the Paulinists, through concessions, renunciations, and attempts to smooth over the differences which lay between the two parties, sought to gain recognition. The most important writings in this phase are those customarily attributed to Luke, in which the Pauline universalism plays a leading role. In Acts especially, Schwegler observes a mediating tendency which paints Paul as far as possible in Petrine colours, while Peter is painted correspondingly Pauline. The traditional Lucan authorship was rejected as untenable and Schwegler suggested that the unknown author had composed his works in Rome somewhere between A.D. 110 and 130. From this period the Pauline party had begun to increase in influence and take its place more and more alongside the Jewish-Christian party, whose influence had now begun to decline. Thus both writings were written with the interests of the Pauline party in view and Schwegler made it clear that no reliance could be placed on the historical veracity of the events recorded. In his eyes the book of Acts was valuable only in that it provided a source of information concerning the time in which it had been composed.

The purpose, now, for which the author of the Acts of the Apostles remoulded the real course of events into the alleged, introduced unhistorical or half-true material, omitted essential facts, generally slurred over the opposition between Paul and the church at Jerusalem, and cast a reconciling veil over the vehement struggles, the passionate negotiations, differences, and misunderstandings, which according to any normal course of events must have taken place between the new apostle and the older 'pillars', is the irenical-apologetic purpose of a Pauline Christian. Only by such means and sacrifices did the author know how to create acknowledgement for the Pauline universalism in a time still predominantly inclined to Jewish Christianity and among a generation still constricted by prejudices against the person, doctrine, and activity of the apostle to the Gentiles. The Acts of the Apostles is—as we have already remarked in the introduction to this work and as we now reiterate on the basis of its conclusions—a defence of the apostle and of his apostolic activity among the Gentiles, an overture for peace, and an attempt to mediate in the form of a history—*in the form of a history*—for even if there are old sources and reports lying behind the first part at any rate, and probably also the second, there remains, notwithstanding, exceptionally little which is historically tenable, even when everything improbable, impossible, demonstrably unhistorical, or which is connected with unhistorical material—

especially the freely-composed speeches and the numerous repetitions
—is taken away. Against the whole historical credibility of the book of
Acts speaks its frequent tendency to omit events and to pass over them
in silence. But whoever remains intentionally silent about important
incidents and facts in order to set the principal characters of his representation in another light, whoever intentionally leaves out characteristic features of a portrait in order to give it another appearance will
no longer be able to be considered honest and conscientious, and it lies
all the more in the interest of such a person to permit himself also the
luxury of positive distortions of history and unhistorical fabrications.
We can with certainty now say this much about our author, that in the
use, the fashioning, and the remoulding of the material which was
handed down to him and at his disposal he went to work in a thoroughly arbitrary and wilful way . . . Thus as a whole, the Acts of the
Apostles has only the worth of a historical document for that time,
those relations, and that situation to which it owes its origin, and in
this regard it warrants us at any rate to draw far-reaching consequences.[23]

Belonging also to this time and possessing the same conciliatory
tendency are the final two chapters of Romans, 1 Clement, and
Philippians.

In the third and final phase the Pauline party sought to produce
a union, a coalition of the two opposing parties on the basis of a
'catholic' Church. This was to be achieved partly through doctrinal agreement, partly through the foundation of an episcopate
and a hierarchical constitution for the Church, which would provide a secure basis for the future against the inroads of heresy
and lax discipline. To this phase belong the Pastoral Epistles,
which Baur had already shown to contain an anti-Gnostic polemic
against the Valentinians and Marcionites, together with a Church
order presupposing the election of bishops and elders. Of a
slightly later date were the unauthentic letters of Ignatius, which
were the final documents written from a Pauline standpoint and
probably composed during the last decade of the second century
in the primacy of Victor (A.D. 189–98).

It was Rome that became the focal point of Christendom at the
end of the second century and here the decisions were made which
determined the future of the Church. According to Schwegler,
all signs pointed to the pontificate of Victor during which this

[23] Ibid., II, pp. 113–15.

final unification of the opposing parties was effected. The Pauline concept of the universality of the Church was united with the Petrine emphasis on the unity and uniformity of the hierarchical organization, thus forming the gradual establishment of a body of catholic teaching and tradition, the exclusion of dissentient views under the name of heresies, and the collection of a New Testament canon.

B. *The History of the Church in Asia Minor*

The second locality which Schwegler now watches is Asia Minor. Here he traces through a similar development in the Church and depicts the step-by-step process by which Ebionism evolved into catholicism. As in the church at Rome this process begins with the sharpest antagonism between the Ebionite and Pauline parties, and the letter to the Romans finds its parallel here in Asia Minor in the letter to the Galatians, while at the other end-point the Ignatian letters are paralleled by the Gospel of John. It is at this period especially that the difference between the two churches becomes most noticeable, in that the church at Rome is concerned with ecclesiastical unity—the unity of the hierarchical structure of the Church—while the Church in Asia Minor centres its basis on theological and doctrinal unity; its end-point is characterized in the concept of the *logos* and the catholic teaching on the Trinity.

The letter to the Galatians is the first piece of evidence for the hostility between Paul and the Jewish Christians in Asia Minor and this opposition, maintained Schwegler, was further strengthened with the arrival of the apostle John in Ephesus. From this time onwards begins the Johannine period which was marked by the domination of a Jewish apocalyptic Christology typified by the Apocalypse, which Schwegler ascribed to the apostle John. For over half a century this Johannine Ebionite Christianity held sway, but about the middle of the second century an anti-Jewish reaction set in against the Ebionite Christianity and especially against Montanism.

In this period also belong the epistles to the Hebrews, Colossians, and Ephesians, which manifest in varying degrees a polemical attitude towards Ebionism. These writings contain the concept of Jesus as the pre-existent Word of God as a principal counter to the Ebionite teaching which saw Jesus as merely a man. Hebrews, the earliest of the letters, was probably written to Jewish Christians at the end of the century by a Paulinist attempting to mediate between the two parties; Colossians was a freer and more Pauline letter written later in the second century, and Ephesians was a working-over of Colossians from a more developed standpoint. Finally came the Gospel of John which Schwegler regarded as the end-point of the whole process of development in Asia Minor. Here, in Schwegler's opinion, were evident the Montanist concepts of the *logos* and the Trinity, the passover controversy, and Gnostic concepts, all of which reflected a date of composition about A.D. 170.

Schwegler's book was a brilliant and sparkling work which impressed through its concise, sharp, and clear representation of the early Church during the first two centuries. It was beautifully written, in scintillating prose—Schwegler was undoubtedly the most talented of the whole Tübingen School in this respect—and the organization of the material was so logical and well thought out that the reader has no difficulty in finding his way through its 900 pages.

But although the author's talent and diligence were willingly acknowledged, his representation of the post-apostolic age found hardly a single supporter outside of the School itself. There were two main criticisms. The first was that, for Schwegler, the Person of Christ had almost no significance. Jesus was scarcely ever mentioned, except in a footnote where Schwegler stated that he avoided speaking about Christ because the historical sources were so untrustworthy that nothing definite could be said about him. Thus, in effect, Christianity begins with Paul rather than with Jesus, who might be regarded as the stimulator of the Christian faith but not its founder. The second main criticism was that Schwegler had interpreted the early Christian writings according to his previously formulated ideas—that he highlighted and emphasized obscure hints and allusions which fitted in with his views, while playing down or omitting all relevant evidence to the contrary. This criticism, unfortunately, was only too true. Schwegler found what he wanted to find and overlooked or avoided everything which did not harmonize with the representation he had previously decided upon.

RITSCHL ON THE GOSPEL OF LUKE

Baur's book on Paul marked a provisional end to investigation in the Pauline field and in 1846 attention shifted to the Gospel of Luke, which up until this time had been somewhat neglected. Apart from a short study of the Gospel by Zeller in 1843 and Schwegler's discussion in his 'Post-apostolic Age', there had been no thorough investigation of its origin by a member of the School. The new impetus in this direction was provided by the arrival of Ritschl in Tübingen.

The discussion centred primarily around Marcion's edition of Luke and the 'mutilation hypothesis', which had hitherto found general acceptance. This hypothesis, put forward by Olshausen and defended by Hahn, maintained that the original Gospel written by Luke, the companion of Paul, had been wilfully mutilated by Marcion in order to propagate his anti-Jewish and Gnostic views. Schwegler in his 'Post-apostolic Age' had rejected this hypothesis but had not gone so far as to assert that Marcion's edition was actually the source of the canonical Luke. This step was taken by Ritschl. He had come for the winter semester 1845/6 to Tübingen where he wrote his first major work, 'The Gospel of Marcion and the Canonical Gospel of Luke',[24] in which he maintained that the canonical Luke was a working-over of the Marcionite version of Luke which in turn was derived from a proto-Luke composed in the last decades of the first century.

Ritschl's argument ran roughly as follows: the canonical Luke shows a neutral and conciliatory tendency with a mixture of Pauline and Jewish elements, the basis, however, being Pauline. The redactor introduced a Jewish-Christian tendency into the original Pauline narrative, softened the Pauline element where it appeared too favourable to the apostle Paul, and also made concessions to the Jewish Christians, such as the introduction of the birth and infancy stories which presented Jesus as the Jewish Messiah. Ritschl examined the external testimonies relating Marcion's Gospel to the canonical Luke and argued that they were of no historical worth. Since the Gospel revealed an anti-Marcionite tendency it was only one step further to suppose that the unknown redactor had used Marcion's edition and that this in turn was

---

[24] *Das Evangelium Marcions und das kanonische Evangelium des Lucas* (Tübingen, 1846).

based on a proto-Luke with which Marcion must have been familiar.

This hypothesis of Ritschl was now adopted by Baur in his long article[25] which appeared in 1846, following the publication of Ritschl's book. On only one major point did they not agree—Ritschl's assertion that the final composition was motivated by an anti-Marcionite interest. In defending his position,[26] Ritschl made the point that in the time of Marcion the reconciliation between Jewish and Pauline Christians was already accomplished and that this reconciliation was not the objective for which Luke's Gospel had been written, but rather its presupposition. Baur, however, in his 'Critical Investigation of the Canonical Gospels'[27] which appeared in that same year (1847), remained unconvinced. Nevertheless, the general unanimity which prevailed over the whole hypothesis was not greatly impaired by the disagreement and Baur basically accepted the validity of Ritschl's solution.

BAUR ON THE SYNOPTIC GOSPELS

With the appearance in 1847 of Baur's work on the Gospels, interest within the Tübingen School switched to the field of the Synoptics. Baur's investigations were, so to speak, a companion work to his book on Paul and contained his former studies on John and Luke along with two shorter chapters devoted to Matthew and Mark. A long introduction dealt with the history of Gospel criticism, beginning with the 'dogmatic conception' of the Biblicists, who believed in the equal inspiration of every part of the Bible and the possibility of harmonizing the apparent differences in the Gospel narratives. In the second phase of the historical development—a phase which Baur designated 'the abstract-critical conception'—the Gospels were viewed as purely literary products with little or no understanding of their historical nature. The pioneer of this approach was Eichhorn who, following a suggestion of Lessing, developed the theory that the close relationship between the Synoptics was to be explained by the existence of a proto-Gospel from which the common element in the Gospels was derived. In Baur's opinion this theory was quite

[25] 'Der Ursprung und Charakter des Lucasevangeliums . . .', *TJ*, 1848, pp. 453–615.
[26] 'Das Verhältnis der Schriften des Lucas zu der Zeit ihrer Entstehung', *TJ*, 1847, pp. 293–304.
[27] *Kritische Untersuchungen über die kanonischen Evangelien* (Tübingen, 1847).

inadequate and he regarded the later modifications of Hug, Gieseler, and Schleiermacher—the last of whom postulated not just one, but a number of original sources—as being of no more value than Eichhorn's original hypothesis. The third approach was the 'negative critical' or 'dialectic' approach of Strauss who had simply played off one Gospel against another; this method, in Baur's eyes, was also unacceptable in that Strauss had criticized the Gospel history without any real consideration of the Gospel sources. But Baur's hardest strictures were reserved for Bruno Bauer, who maintained that the author of Mark (which Bauer, following Wilke, regarded as the original Gospel) had invented the whole Gospel narrative, as Shakespeare had created King Lear. The fourth approach which Baur named 'the historical conception' was his own. The literary approach was indecisive, claimed Baur, for the Gospels were products of a certain time and revealed the historical situation not of the time which they purported to represent, but of the time in which they were actually written. As such they were tendency writings and once the tendency had been determined, the writings could be fitted back into the historical period in which they had been created, in order that the time and origin of the composition might be ascertained more accurately. Only by such an approach was the true literary relationship between the Synoptics able to be firmly established.

Three factors determined Baur's solution to the Synoptic problem: the tendency of each Gospel, the literary relationship between the corresponding passages, and the external testimony respecting authorship, date, and place of writing. The decisive and controlling factor, however, was the Gospel's tendency, and the second two factors were both subordinated to the first.

The principal grounds on which Baur based his conclusions to these questions regarding authorship were as follows: Mark showed a definite neutral tendency which suited a date of composition late in the second century, while Matthew was definitely the most Jewish of the three Gospels and presupposed an earlier date—probably at the end of the first century. For this last view Baur found confirmation in the external testimony of Papias, who had handed down the tradition that Matthew had written his sayings (*logia*) in Hebrew, as well as in the testimonies of others who had spoken of a Gospel to the Hebrews. Baur saw no reason to deny that Matthew might have composed such a Gospel, which at a later date was translated into Greek along with various additions to the original core composed by Matthew. The earliest date for the final composition was determined by the little Apocalypse, the twenty-fourth chapter of Matthew. Baur argued that the events mentioned in this chapter referred not to the destruction of Jerusalem in A.D. 70 but to the Jewish uprising of A.D. 132 when Bar Kokhba led his followers against the Romans in a futile revolt which was mercilessly crushed and after which the city of Jerusalem was razed to the ground. The time in which Baur set the final composition of Matthew thus falls within the years A.D. 130–4.

This result having been ascertained, Baur now found confirmation for the priority of Matthew from the literary investigation. It was much more credible, he argued, for Mark to be a rounded abridgement of Matthew and Luke than for Matthew to be an expansion of Mark, in that Mark gave no appearance of being an independent source but appeared rather to be the work of an intelligent redactor whose intention was to give a more neutral character to the Jewish Matthew and the basically Pauline Luke.

If we take into consideration everything which has been mentioned here, then the general opinion will thereby be adequately established that even in the passages peculiar to the Gospel of Mark there is nothing of independent historical value, but only the peculiarity of a writer who in an artful manner was clever enough to conceal the emptiness of his historical material, the poverty of his own information, on the one hand by abridging and summarizing a detailed portrayal, on the other hand by filling out and amplifying certain facts, by interweaving pronounced features, highlighting circumstances and motives of various kinds. There can be nothing more erroneous and false than the procedure of those who in their apologetic interest desire to see in a writer such as Mark the historical faithfulness of an eyewitness in every descriptive detail which is to be found in his portrayal, and who believe themselves to be able to extract the most important data for the construction of the Gospel history from passages where in actuality there is nothing except stories empty of any historical reality and full of subjective invention and imagination. What great illusions one so often makes in this respect is demonstrated by no more pertinent example than the Gospel of Mark, when it is considered according to its true character.[28]

[28] Ibid., p. 560.

Baur's conclusion postulated that Matthew was the earliest Gospel, the canonical Greek version dating from A.D. 130–4; this was then followed a few years later by the canonical Luke and finally by the Markan rearrangement of the Gospel material. Drawn from both Matthew and Luke, Mark's Gospel was written late in the second century when the controversy between Pauline and Jewish Christians had entered upon the period of reconciliation.

One important objection to Baur's hypothesis still remained to be dealt with: tradition was unanimous in ascribing the apostolic origin of Mark to St. Peter, whose words were reputedly written down by his companion, Mark. This was a real problem for Baur to overcome, for were this tradition true, not only his view of the second Gospel, but his whole tendency approach in general, stood in jeopardy. And just at this point Baur's answer was unconvincing. He attempted to cast doubt on the tradition by arguing that the witnesses contradicted themselves as to whether Mark had written his Gospel before or after Peter's death, but he was extremely reticent about the great weight of external testimony and passed over the whole question as quickly as possible.

Fraedrich[29] suggested that Baur might have accepted the Markan-priority hypothesis put forward in 1838 by Wilke, had he not been prejudiced against it by the fact that C. H. Weisse and Bruno Bauer had both come out in its support. For in 1836 Weisse had written an extremely critical review of Baur's book on Gnosticism and in his review[30] of Weisse's 'Gospel History' Baur had returned the compliment and set himself solidly against the priority of Mark. This prejudice was doubtless also strengthened by the fact that Bruno Bauer had adopted Wilke's hypothesis in his radical view that the whole Gospel had been concocted, with no historical basis whatsoever, in the mind of a single individual— a theory upon which Schwegler in 1843 had already poured out his scornful disgust. Thus Fraedrich's suggestion that before 1847 Baur was already prejudiced against the Markan-priority hypothesis, was not without ground, but on the other hand Baur had good reasons for not accepting it. For one thing he found the literary grounds unconvincing, but more important was the fact

[29] *Ferdinand Christian Baur*, pp. 200–3.
[30] *JWK*, 1839: I, pp. 161–99; 585–621.

that had he accepted this hypothesis on a basis for which he himself could find no evidence, he would have been forced to revise completely his whole tendency approach; for if he had misjudged the tendency of Mark, how could his judgement about the other New Testament books have been trusted?

BAUR ON THE LETTERS OF IGNATIUS

In 1828 the English Egyptologist Lord Proudhoe visited a Coptic monastery in the Nitrian desert some three days' journey northwest of Cairo, where in a dark cell in the depths of the monastery he discovered some ancient manuscripts which even the monks could no longer read. Because the monks were suspicious, he was unable to return to England with more than a few of the parchments. However, his search was not in vain and in 1839 the Revd. Henry Tattam, a distinguished Coptic scholar, undertook a journey to the monastery and brought back forty-nine of the precious manuscripts, among which William Cureton discovered a sixth-century Syriac copy of Ignatius' letter to Polycarp. The value of this find did not go unnoticed and in 1842 Tattam was commissioned by the British Museum to return to the monastery and buy the remaining manuscripts at any price. He succeeded in accomplishing this objective and in 1843 the rest of the treasure passed into the hands of the British Museum. Among the 246 parchment and seventy paper manuscripts, Cureton discovered a seventh- or eighth-century manuscript containing three letters of Ignatius—those to Polycarp and to the churches at Ephesus and Rome.

Little is known about the life of Ignatius apart from those facts which may be gleaned from his letters. He was apparently of Syrian origin and Lightfoot thought that before his conversion he may have been a pagan and a persecutor of the Christians. He was born about A.D. 35 and became either the second or third bishop of Antioch. Just after the turn of the century he was arrested and brought to Rome where he was martyred about the year A.D. 107. On the journey to Rome he was received with great honour by Polycarp at Smyrna, from where he wrote letters of encouragement to the churches of Ephesus, Magnesia, and Tralles. In a fourth letter, written to the church at Rome, he begged that the Christians there should not deprive him of martyrdom by intervening with the authorities. He was then taken to Troas where he wrote three further letters—to Polycarp and to the churches at Philadelphia and Smyrna.

There are in all fifteen letters which bear his name, of varying age and value. The seven already mentioned are found in a shorter and a longer Greek recension. Of the remaining eight spurious letters, three are found only in a Latin text and are quite worthless, while the other five found in the longer Greek recension were, until the early nineteenth century, regarded by Catholic scholars as authentic, and rejected by anti-episcopalian Protestants because of their emphasis on the episcopal order.

Fresh interest in the whole question was aroused by Cureton's publication of the Syriac manuscript in 1845. Cureton maintained that the three Syriac letters were the only genuine ones and that the other four of the now accepted seven had been added later. This view was adopted by C. C. J. Bunsen, the Prussian ambassador to Britain, who in 1847 published the texts[31] along with a commentary, and a discussion composed in the literary form of seven letters to his friend Neander.

It is at this point that Baur enters into the picture. Bunsen had sent him a copy of his book, with which Baur was not impressed. His brother-in-law Robert von Mohl had urged him to write a refutation, and Baur's reply provides us with an interesting insight into his reaction to Bunsen's work.

What you tell me about Bunsen is most interesting and agrees completely with the impression I received from his writings, which I read a short time ago. You want me to treat him as gently as possible. I'll do my best, but it's a delicate matter. You are probably not aware of it, but his latest book is for the most part directed against me and in his polemic he falls completely into the usual adverse tone of the North-German theology which is hostile to the newer criticism. To be sure, he did not fail to include some nice statements of acknowledgement concerning me, but the whole is so hard and harsh that I cannot actually comprehend how one can send a book of this kind to another, even as a gift. The hypothesis itself which he proposes is so untenable that the enormous importance which he ascribes to the question contrasts far too much with the whole tone of the book. It will be no great trouble to refute it. I will do this as far as possible and thereby show him that I know well how to maintain my standpoint against his. He has dared to enter a field in which he is a mere dilettante and

[31] *Die drei ächten und die vier unächten Briefe des Ignatius von Antiochien* (Hamburg, 1847).

appears generally to be a man whose feelings outweigh his judgement. I enjoy dealing with such people, one can easily rout them with their own weapons.[32]

It may be asked why Baur thought the authenticity of the Ignatian letters so important. The reason is that the outcome of the investigation had important consequences for Baur's whole historical perspective. For if, as Baur claimed, the controversy between Pauline and Ebionite Christians continued unabated down to the end of the century, then one would expect to find traces of the controversy in the letters, if their traditional dating in the first decade of the second century were correct. But the letters reveal no trace of such a controversy: therefore either there was none—in which case the whole Tübingen perspective was imperilled—or else the letters were fabricated much later, after the struggle for power had been settled. Other explanations —that Ignatius was unaware of such a bitter struggle or that he chose to say nothing—are quite improbable.

For ten years Baur had emphatically denied the authenticity of all the Ignatian letters and in 1848 he published his refutation of Bunsen's arguments.[33] In his introduction Baur remarked on one important point which had specially impressed him: he had formerly been criticized for his rejection of all seven letters, and now what does he find but that his critics themselves have suddenly changed their minds and now argue that four, i.e. the majority, of the letters are spurious. It therefore seemed to him only a question of how long it would be before they also rejected the other three letters to which they still desired to cling!

There were four main grounds for Baur's rejection of the letters: 1. The historical data in them harmonized badly with the time in which Ignatius was supposed to have written them. 2. Baur argued that certain phrases in the letters presupposed a knowledge of Valentinian Gnosticism, which was later than the first decade of the second century. 3. A more important ground was the emphasis on the episcopate, which Baur regarded as evidence of a much later period, since in his view the episcopal system only came into existence about the middle of the second century. 4. Baur was not at all impressed with the personality of Ignatius as it was reflected in the letters and he especially objected

[32] Baur to Mohl, 31 Dec. 1847.
[33] *Die Ignatianischen Briefe* (Tübingen, 1848).

to the false heroism which Ignatius showed in wishing to be martyred.

The final amusing touch to the whole book concerned Bunsen's denunciation of the unscrupulous forger of the four unauthentic Ignatian letters. Baur replied that the moral consciousness of the second century was not to be judged by that of the nineteenth, and then asked gently whether Bunsen's seven letters to Neander (covering some 220 pages of quarto) had actually been written to Neander as letters, or whether it was simply a literary form which Bunsen had chosen to use.

Herr Bunsen has published his investigation of the Ignatian epistles in the form of letters, in seven long letters to Neander. I may be permitted to ask whether these letters which are dated at Oakhill and Stoke were sent to his friend Neander singly, as real letters, as one must accept according to their form, or whether they first came into his hands as a published book. I can scarcely believe that this former alternative is really the case, although Herr Bunsen also speaks of a correspondence (pp. 151, 233); but a correspondence can only take place where the writer is not merely always the same. Among these letters not only is there none from Neander, but not once does one perceive in them anything which could be viewed as an answer from the recipient. The supposition is quite probable that these letters were not written as actual letters. But is this not also a literary fiction? Certainly it is of such an innocent kind that surely no one will reproach Herr Bunsen with the charge of immorality, but at the same time this form of representation is indeed fictitious and if Herr Bunsen could permit himself this fiction, without thereby having any deceitful intention, then he may be so fair as to concede that others also may have permitted themselves such a fictitious representation—and that in a time in which there were no such enlightened beliefs as we possess —in the same good faith, without on this account having to be regarded as deceivers.[34]

Baur really had much the better of the argument and it was possibly his finest piece of writing. Bunsen did not reply and the debate slowly faded away into the background. Not until a quarter of a century later were Baur's arguments decisively answered by Theodor Zahn[35] and independently by J. B. Lightfoot[36] who established conclusively the authenticity of all seven letters and demonstrated that Cureton's text was a crude abridgement of the original letters.

[34] Ibid., pp. 139–40. [35] *Ignatius von Antiochien* (Gotha, 1873).
[36] *The Apostolic Fathers* Part II, Vol. I (London, 1885).

THE ORIGIN OF EARLY CHRISTIANITY

For all its brilliance Schwegler's representation of the early Church possessed two highly problematical theses: (1) that there was nothing supernatural or miraculous about the Person of Christ, so that with his appearance there was no absolute beginning of Christianity; (2) that primitive Christianity was essentially Judaism while traditional Christianity in effect begins with Paul. Such controversial theses could hardly have remained unchallenged for very long, and while the Tübingen School were united upon the first they were divided upon the second.

The first member of the School to take Schwegler's representation to task was Planck, who in 1847 wrote a long article on Judaism and early Christianity.[37] For Planck the central question was to determine exactly wherein lay the decisive new element which separated Christianity from Judaism. According to Schwegler this new element was the belief in Jesus as the Jewish Messiah, and had it not been for Paul, whom Schwegler considered to be the real founder of Christianity, then Christianity would have simply remained another opinion within the walls of Judaism; at best a Jewish sect. Planck went deeper into the matter and maintained that if Christianity originated with Jesus then there must have been some new principle, teaching, or idea not found within the old Judaism. This positive new element which, according to Planck, had its seat in Jesus' consciousness, was the thought of the perfect righteousness. In the time of Jesus the Jewish religion had become a legalistic observance of the Mosaic law and the shibboleths which had formed around it. But although the Jews might keep the outward letter of the law, they failed to perceive that its true fulfilment concerned an inward observance from the heart. What Jesus proclaimed, according to Planck, was an objective righteousness which lies outside of man; the righteousness which belongs to God. To attain this righteousness man had to renounce self and serve God, wherein lay the perfect fulfilment of the law and the essence of true Christianity.

But what for Jesus was the consciousness of an objective righteousness outside himself, became for Paul the consciousness of a subjective righteousness within.

The distinction between the original Christian consciousness and

---

[37] 'Judenthum und Urchristenthum', *TJ*, 1847, pp. 258–93; 409–34; 448–506.

the Pauline consciousness of righteousness may now be defined in its different aspects more precisely. The basic distinction is simply that the Synoptic Christ understands the true righteousness still in its Old Testament objective aspect, while Paul conceives righteousness in its subjective aspect, more according to its indwelling in the ego, as a new essential power.[38]

The essential character of Jewish Christianity (which was the original form of Christianity) consisted in attempting to fulfil the law perfectly. But in this attempt the Jewish Christians failed to perceive the inward and spiritual demands of the law, and the futility of a rigid external observance. According to Planck it was Paul who first expressed consciousness of the fact that it was impossible for man to fulfil the law without divine aid. Even Jesus had not understood the necessity for the grace of a transcendent God; he had believed that man was able to fulfil the law and required no new transcendent power of reconciliation with God to enable this fulfilment. The thought of a perfect dedication to God carried within itself the possibility of fulfilment. Paul, however, was unable to grasp what Jesus had preached—that dedication to God carried within itself a new power—and he therefore derived this new power from a transcendent source and through a sinless 'man from heaven'. Thus it is hardly too much to say that Planck viewed Paul's teaching as a perversion of the original Christianity which had its beginning in Jesus. Whereas Jesus concerned himself with man's inward relation to the law, Paul introduced a complex supernatural system in order to demonstrate what Jesus had only dimly perceived.

In passing, it only needs to be pointed out that Planck's views were divorced from any sound exegesis of the New Testament. Planck took it for granted that Jesus was no supernatural figure, and his attempt to interpret Jesus' significance was based entirely upon this presupposition. But the question which Planck attempted to answer and which lies somewhat submerged under Planck's complex and difficult style was of vital importance: If Jesus was not divine, who was it who turned the non-supernatural Jesus into a supernatural figure—the disciples or Paul?

With Schwegler traditional Christianity began with Paul; with Planck true Christianity was Ebionism, which originated in the

---

[38] Ibid., p. 281.

life of Jesus, and Pauline Christianity was a revisionist super-natural form. Köstlin now advocated a third solution:[39] the catholic Church was descended from neither Ebionism nor Pauline Christianity; these were simply the two extreme forms of the Christianity actually dominant in the second century. According to Köstlin there was a middle party to which the majority of believers belonged and from which the catholic Church finally emerged.

Thus early Christianity was not Ebionism, and it was also not simply and solely a struggle between Ebionism and Paulinism as two rigidly defined parties, incapable of any development and which finally, by means of mutual concessions, concluded an outward peace.... Those parties formed only the outermost extremes of the Christianity of the second century, while among the majority of the Christians the simple Christian interest which rose above all those controversies was the most predominant. Therefore, from the beginning there formed among the majority of Christians a Christianity which pursued a middle path between the two extreme parties and the differing apostolic points of view, a mediating Christianity from which the catholic Church finally emerged.[40]

There was indeed, according to Köstlin, a struggle between Ebionism and Pauline Christianity, but this broke out in full ferocity only twice—in the last years of Paul's life and then in the second century, during the struggle between the Ebionites and the Gnostics. In between these two points there flourished a Christianity neither Jewish and nationalistic nor Pauline, but a universal Christianity based on the principle of law and works which may be traced back to Peter and James.

What Köstlin criticized most trenchantly was Schwegler's identification of Jewish Christianity with Ebionism. This identi-fication, maintained Köstlin, was completely false. The earliest Jewish Christianity of James, John, Peter, and the church at Rome was not Ebionite, because it acknowledged that in Christ something new had appeared which was not to be found in Judaism. Jewish Christianity attempted to hold this new element (Jesus as the Messiah) in harmony with Judaism, while Ebionism, on the other hand, sought to stress its Jewish origin. In adding

---

[39] 'Zur Geschichte des Urchristenthums', *TJ*, 1850, pp. 1–62; 235–302.
[40] Ibid., pp. 60–2.

dualistic and ascetic elements, which tended to lead to a complete withdrawal from the world, it proceeded beyond Judaism and degenerated into a sect.

Jewish Christianity is the endeavour to harmonize Christianity with the Jewish consciousness, which is still steadfastly adhered to. Ebionism is the endeavour to lead Christianity back to Judaism; the essence of the former is Christianity, of the latter, Judaism; Jewish Christianity is Christianity as it is for the Jews, and not for the non-Jewish man in general; Ebionite Christianity is Judaism that knows and asserts itself as Judaism just by means of a Judaizing of the new Christian element.[41]

Another attempt, quite independent of Köstlin's, to correct the deficiencies in the Tübingen perspective was made about this same time and from within the Tübingen School itself by Ritschl. Shortly before Köstlin's article appeared in the *Theologische Jahrbücher*, Ritschl's 720-page book on the beginning of the early Church[42] was published in November 1849. The book marked a break with the Tübingen perspective, although this break was somewhat hidden in that the significance of Ritschl's arguments was not fully perceived. For Ritschl did not press his views to their logical conclusions but allowed his essentially anti-Tübingen conclusions to stand within an essentially Tübingen framework, so that his book, for all its deviations from the views of Baur and Schwegler, still appeared to remain within the limits of the School. Right from the beginning Ritschl had made Schwegler the butt for his criticism, while Baur was mentioned only in favourable references—a manoeuvre which did not escape Baur's notice. Baur was naturally displeased with Ritschl's veiled attack on the Tübingen principles.

I have now also read our friend Ritschl's thick book on the old catholic Church—he even sent it to me himself along with a few lines, according to which I am supposed to consider the whole book as directed to me rather than against me. The book is infinitely long, self-complacent, petty, one-sided; but now he sets himself so much upon the other side that he in fact completely denies that Judaism is capable of developing. He has been extremely cunning in leaving out the development of the Johannine concepts and the whole Johannine question generally—by which, incidentally, he gives us to understand that he stands on our side. What has annoyed me most of all is the

---

[41] Ibid., p. 298.   [42] *Die Entstehung der altkatholischen Kirche* (Bonn, 1850).

way he treats Schwegler and makes him the scape-goat for us all. He misses no opportunity to criticize him in a downright venomous way. In my reply to him I could not refrain from expressing my displeasure about it. His representation can certainly serve the purpose of finally bringing the historical material into clearer view, as it has been worked over from such different standpoints.[43]

Previous to the appearance of Ritschl's book, Baur, Schwegler, and Köstlin had avoided all discussion of the Person of Christ, and the only member of the School who had made any attempt to deal with the problem was Planck. Ritschl was impressed by Planck's ideas and with a little modification adopted them as his own. He perceived that the root of the controversy between Paul and the Jewish Christians concerned the keeping of the Jewish law; for, as Ritschl observed, Jesus' working among the people was the common ground from which both the Jewish-Christian and Pauline parties derived justification for their own particular standpoints.

Planck had argued that Jesus had held it possible for men to keep the law, by renouncing self and serving God with undivided heart. But with this view Planck remained, in Ritschl's opinion, still within the Old Testament framework and failed to explain what the radically new element was which had made its appearance in Jesus and which had been able to break through the bounds of the Old Testament consciousness. This new element, according to Ritschl, was 'that the fulfilled righteousness which Jesus demanded over against the Pharisees as the condition of entrance into the heavenly kingdom, was actually represented in his life'.[44]

It was not Jesus' teaching alone which was important (as Planck had maintained) but Jesus' personality—and herein for Ritschl lay the explanation of Jesus' claim to be the Son of God—which was inseparable from his teaching. But as Jesus himself, according to Ritschl, did not analyse this concept of sonship, the unveiling of the secret of Jesus' inner life was not possible by ordinary historical methods, and Ritschl rejected any attempt to justify the statement by dogmatic or philosophical explanations. 'In summarizing the historical picture of Jesus we may say only this much, that he could not have professed to be the Son of God

---

[43] Baur to Zeller, 21 Dec. 1849.
[44] *Die Entstehung der altkatholischen Kirche*, p. 45.

if he was not, if he did not actually stand in that relation to God which remains eternally unattainable by keeping the fulfilled law, as long as that fulfilled law is not accompanied by the fulfilled life in God'.[45]

This sentence should not be understood as indicating an acceptance of the traditional supernatural views about Jesus' Sonship and Messiahship, which Ritschl had abandoned some years previously. Faith in Jesus, according to Ritschl, had arisen in Jesus' disciples, who viewed him as much more than a teacher whose teaching could be separated from his Person: 'The real Jesus is only he who with his teaching of the fulfilled law moves within the bounds of his people's horizon of knowledge and by his personality actually creates a new centre, without—through a reflective analysis of his new relationship to God (in whatever form one may conceive it)—offending the way in which his contemporaries thought, and repelling them from himself'.[46]

Ritschl's explanation was somewhat more satisfying than Planck's and certainly a step forward from Baur, Schwegler, and Köstlin who had all omitted any discussion of the Person of Christ. Beginning from this point Ritschl was able to show that Jewish and Pauline Christianity had both been able to derive their legitimacy from Jesus.

Schwegler had seen only two hostile parties which had struggled for supremacy; Planck had maintained that Paulinism was a heterodox form of true Christianity, i.e. Jewish Christianity, and Köstlin had proposed a middle party. Ritschl disagreed with all these alternatives and put forward his own solution. In that both Paul and the original apostles had found their justification in the working of Christ, they held certain points in common—the concept of God, angels, and demons, the distinction between present and future worlds, and eschatological conceptions. Thus there was a neutral basis shared by both. After Paul had perceived that the keeping of the law was totally unable to bring about a new relationship between man and God, he set himself in opposition to the law and emphasized the new concept of justification by faith; in taking this attitude he believed that his views were in agreement with the divine promise given by God; but the apostles also believed themselves to be maintaining the continuity of the

[45] Ibid., p. 46.   [46] Ibid., p. 48.

Old Testament revelation when they stressed man's obligation to keep the law and the commandments, which Jesus had never abolished. However, Jewish Christianity soon forgot Jesus' command to evangelize the heathen, turned in upon itself, and, possessing no ability to develop and expand outside its own limited natural boundaries, finally died. Thus the catholic Church was actually a product of Pauline rather than Jewish Christianity.

Ritschl also raised other important objections against the Tübingen perspective. The first was that Baur and Schwegler had overestimated the hostility between Paul and the other apostles. The speeches at the council in Jerusalem, according to Ritschl, were certainly unhistorical, but Ritschl saw no reason to suppose this of the decree sent out by James and the church at Jerusalem, which laid the Gentile Christians under the obligation to keep certain regulations pertaining to the law. Ritschl believed that Paul was not involved in this decision and that in all probability it was this decree which caused Peter to give up his practice of eating with the Gentiles. The dispute between Paul and Peter arose subsequently, but according to Ritschl this neither increased the opposition between the two parties nor led to any long-lasting break between Paul and the other apostles. Only later did a strict Judaizing party in Galatia arise which attacked Paul's apostleship and demanded that the Gentiles should keep the Jewish law. In the Johannine Apocalypse Ritschl thought that a milder form of Jewish Christianity could be observed, but the authenticity and origin of the letter of James with its hostile polemic against the Pauline doctrine of justification was in Ritschl's view a riddle which could only be solved with great difficulty.

The second important point in which Ritschl diverged from the Tübingen School was found in the *Clementine Homilies*. Baur and Schwegler had identified the person of Simon the Magician with the apostle Paul; Ritschl now rejected this identification and maintained that Simon had been characterized as the representative of all Gnosticism.

In these two criticisms lay the seed of the Tübingen School's destruction, although Ritschl did not take the second step and show how false were the assumptions on which the School was founded. Rather, he treated them as parts of the whole, parts which were indeed incorrect, but which did not necessarily invalidate the whole Tübingen perspective. As yet he was not ready to make any final devastating critique, preferring to wait and see what further investigation might bring to light.

Three years later came Baur's *Church History of the First Three Centuries* (1853) which was essentially a summary of all his former writings on the origin of Christianity. However, apart from a discussion of the Person of Christ, in which Baur presented Jesus as a moral teacher who, for the sake of gaining authority for his teaching, consented to take upon himself the role of the Messiah, there was nothing essentially new introduced into the discussion. Baur simply contented himself with repeating the views which he and Schwegler had put forward previously, modifying details and grounding the whole with a more thorough and rounded discussion of the historical evidence.

The next contribution which brought a new element into the existing state of the investigation, in which the Baur–Ritschl lines were now firmly drawn, came from Hilgenfeld who in 1855 entered as third party into the debate between Baur and Hase. In his small 135-page monograph on early Christianity Hilgenfeld declared that he preferred not to be counted as a member of the Tübingen School, although acknowledging that he had found his starting-point in the works of Dr. Baur. There were too many points, he asserted, in which he had to differ from the Tübingen perspective, for apart from his acknowledgement of the genuineness of 1 Thessalonians, Philippians, Philemon, and the two final chapters of Romans, he was of the opinion that the opposition between Pauline and Jewish Christianity was not as great as Baur had asserted it to be. The church at Rome consisted not of strict Judaizing Christians but, on the contrary, the majority were Gentile Christians, although Jewish-Christian ideas were prominent among them. Thus at the beginning the controversy between Paul and the other apostles was not as hostile as Baur and Schwegler had maintained it to be, but it became exacerbated in the dispute at Antioch where Paul 'threw down the glove to the whole Jewish-Christian community. . . . Is it any wonder, then, that from now on the Jewish Christians recognized in Paul their deadly enemy and began to attack his activity?'[47]

The new feature which Hilgenfeld introduced into the discussion lay in his assertion that the Gnostic movement had played a far larger part in the formation of the catholic Church than had

[47] Hilgenfeld, *Das Urchristenthum* (Jena, 1855), p. 59.

generally been supposed. It was not simply that the Church had become more united through having to defend the apostolic faith against the Gnostic heresies; Gnosticism, according to Hilgenfeld, was a movement actually *within* the Church. Alongside of Jewish and Pauline Christianity, Gnosticism formed a third movement which flowed into the catholic Church through the Gospel of John, which in Hilgenfeld's opinion was a product of Gnosticism, full of Gnostic teaching about sons of God and sons of the devil and riddled through and through with Gnostic conceptions of the world.

The second edition of Ritschl's *Entstehung* was published two years later in 1857 and marked publicly and formally his break with the Tübingen School, which had actually taken place in the previous year. New in the book was his acceptance of Mark as the eldest of the Gospels, and his attitude of conscious opposition to the Tübingen perspective. Jesus, maintained Ritschl, had aimed to establish an order for living which should be kept by those who believed in him and who thus became his brethren in the kingdom of God. For his first and most important task was to establish the kingdom through the representation of his personal worth as the Son of man and through the awakening of faith in his Person. Jesus declared invalid everything in the Jewish law that did not conform to the highest moral principles of the kingdom of God, and led his followers towards the more ethical understanding which formed the basis of that kingdom. Nor did the original apostles have any disagreement with Paul on this question, and both parties acknowledged the absoluteness of the revelation in Christ. Paul, who derived true ethical behaviour from faith in Christ, rejected the Pharisaic demand that the Gentiles keep the law. However, in arguing that the Gentiles were not obliged to keep the law, he stood over against the apostles, not in a fundamental, but only in a practical opposition. While part of the church at Jerusalem, in which were many former Pharisees, desired to place the Gentiles under the obligation of keeping the whole Mosaic law, the apostles rejected this demand and agreed with Paul and Barnabas upon the sending of an apostolic decree which enjoined only the necessity of keeping the laws given to Noah. And although there were differences of opinion between Paul and the other apostles—and especially between Paul and James—there was no long-lasting opposition, let alone hostility. Thus Ritschl abandoned his former view that Acts 15 and Galatians 1 stood in irreconcilable contradiction, and sought to bring the two passages into harmony.

Apart from numerous smaller divergences from the first edition, which cannot be considered here, the other main point of departure from the Tübingen perspective was found in Ritschl's opposition to Baur's rejection of the authenticity of the New Testament writings. Thus, while Baur acknowledged as genuine only four Pauline epistles and the Apocalypse, Ritschl accepted the Gospel of John and the first Johannine letter, 1 Peter, James, and all thirteen of Paul's letters with the exception of 1 Timothy. The acknowledgement of these letters and the rejection of the Tübingen historical perspective signalized, in Baur's own words, Ritschl's 'unfurled flag of apostasy' from the School.

The second edition of Baur's *Church History of the First Three Centuries* which appeared in 1860 remained essentially unchanged from the first edition. Baur's views had never commended themselves outside of the School and in later years they were almost universally ignored or rejected. Hilgenfeld went his own way as did Volkmar, and after Baur's death the investigation of the early Church returned to the outline sketched by Ritschl. In the writings of Ritschl's protégé Adolf Harnack the discussion of the post-apostolic age found its most outstanding continuation.

THE DEBATE ON THE SYNOPTICS 1847–52

Ritschl had propounded the hypothesis that Marcion's version of Luke's Gospel was not a mutilation of the canonical Luke, but that the canonical Luke was an irenical working-over of Marcion's anti-Jewish version, which in turn was derived from a Lucan writing circulating at the end of the first century. Even Baur had been convinced by the daring hypothesis and in his work on the Gospels, which appeared the following year (1847), he had supported Ritschl's views with such words and phrases as 'indisputable', 'without doubt', 'quite evident', and 'as sure as anything'. However, the new hypothesis was not as certain as it had appeared and in 1850, in an article published in the *Theologische Jahrbücher*,[48] Volkmar subjected it to a penetrating criticism and mercilessly exposed its flaws, errors and improbabilities.

---

[48] Über das Lucasevangelium . . ', *TJ*, 1850, pp. 110–38; 185–235.

Whereas Ritschl and Baur had accepted that the differences between Marcion's text and the canonical Luke could be explained as additions to Marcion's version by the hand of a redactor who desired to interpolate a Jewish element into the text in order to satisfy the Jewish party, Volkmar showed conclusively that the differences could only be accounted for as omissions from the canonical Luke, and that the presence of a large Judaistic element, as held by Ritschl and Baur, was in fact scarcely at all evident. So convincingly did Volkmar argue his case that Ritschl and Baur both conceded that they had been wrong, and although Baur later had second thoughts, he never again explicitly defended the validity of the hypothesis.

Coming from inside the Tübingen School Volkmar's article created a good deal of surprise and sparked off a further concerted debate on the Synoptic problem. In autumn of the same year (1850) Hilgenfeld's book on the Gospel of Mark appeared, in which he argued that the canonical Mark was an abridgement of an earlier 'Gospel of Peter'. Hilgenfeld based his assertion on three main arguments: (1) that since the canonical Mark possessed no specific Petrine character, the Petrine or anti-Pauline passages must have been omitted by a later irenical redactor; (2) that Luke is the best-planned of the three Gospels whereas Mark is 'without plan', 'incoherent', and 'absurd'; (3) that a transition was necessary between Matthew and Luke, this transition being the Gospel of Peter.

To be forced to admit that he had erred in accepting Ritschl's Lucan hypothesis was, for Baur, especially disagreeable and only grudgingly did he acknowledge the validity of Volkmar's refutation. On the other hand, he was not at all impressed with Hilgenfeld's argument that Luke had made use of a Gospel of Peter, and in his investigation of Mark's Gospel published in 1851, he again strongly defended his views that Mark was the last of the three Gospels to be composed and that its author had used both Matthew and Luke.

It was now Ritschl's turn to re-enter the discussion. He had been completely convinced by Volkmar and Hilgenfeld that his Lucan hypothesis was invalid; and now he himself sought a new answer to the problem. In all probability it was the desire to find a solution different from those advocated by Baur and Hilgenfeld which led him to adopt the hypothesis that Mark was prior to both Matthew and Luke, a hypothesis recently supported by Ewald.

I have given up my Lucan hypothesis and in that I set the formation of the three Synoptics in the first century, I have been led by my friend Sommer on to the right track; I now hold Mark to be the eldest among them. For this hypothesis I find confirmation and further ideas in a work by Ewald which has just recently appeared. On the other hand I grumble and rage inwardly at my friend Hilgenfeld, who in the same book in which he liberated the world from my Lucan hypothesis wants to bind it with a new fable about a Gospel of Peter, which he again wants to perceive in the citations of the Gospels in Justin the Martyr, and which in the Gospel family is supposed to be the daughter of Matthew and mother of Mark.[49]

Ritschl decided to write an article for the *Theologische Jahrbücher* and communicated his plan to Baur, who surprisingly enough had decided that Ritschl's former hypothesis had not yet been overthrown and deserved at least a new investigation. 'I am, as you see, a far more faithful adherent of your view than you yourself.'[50]

Ritschl's article[51] was completed in May 1851 and appeared in the fourth issue of the journal, but it was not well written and it was not convincing. Ritschl began by conceding the invalidity of his former Lucan hypothesis and then attempted to disprove Hilgenfeld's view of a proto-Mark in the form of a Gospel of Peter. However, when it came to adducing evidence for the priority of Mark, Ritschl ran into difficulty and his grounds were exceedingly weak. Three main arguments were urged: (1) that in Mark, Jesus orders that his Messiahship is not to be made known, whereas in Matthew this negative attitude is absent; (2) that in Mark the disciples are portrayed as incapable of understanding Jesus' teaching, whereas in Matthew they are able to comprehend it; (3) that the Old Testament citations in Matthew reveal a dependence upon Mark. But all these arguments, as Baur later demonstrated, were really quite inadequate to bear the whole weight of the Marcan-priority hypothesis.

Hilgenfeld wrote another article[52] in 1852, replying to Baur's

[49] Ritschl to his father, 24 Jan. 1851; OR, I, pp. 180–1.

[50] Baur to Ritschl, 1 Feb. 1851; OR, I, p. 181.

[51] 'Über den gegenwärtigen Stand der Kritik der synoptischen Evangelien', *TJ*, 1851, pp. 480–538.

[52] 'Neue Untersuchung über das Markusevangelium . . .', *TJ*, 1852, pp. 102–32; 259–93; 304.

criticisms and defending his view that the Gospel of Peter occupied a mediating position between Matthew and Luke; and Baur, who was now in the happy position of being able to play off Hilgenfeld (Matthew before Mark) against Ritschl (Mark before Matthew), replied in the following year[53] with a penetrating criticism of them both and the affirmation that he found nothing in the arguments so far put forward which would lead him to change his present views.

THE QUARTODECIMAN CONTROVERSY

The controversy over the Quartodecimans dragged on intermittently for fifteen years and was the longest controversy which engaged the attention of the Tübingen School. The importance of the discussion went far beyond the controversy in itself, for the really central issue concerned the authenticity of the fourth Gospel, which in turn held far-reaching consequences for Baur's whole tendency approach. It was for this reason, therefore, that the Tübingen arguments were so stubbornly defended by Baur and Hilgenfeld.

The Gospel of John presents Jesus as being crucified on the fourteenth Nisan, the day on which the Jewish passover lamb was being slain. The Synoptic Gospels, however, represent him as eating the passover meal with his disciples on this day, from whence it was inferred that Jesus was crucified on the fifteenth Nisan, i.e. on the day following the Jewish passover. This variation in the dating of the crucifixion was the source of a lively dispute in the second century between the church at Rome and the churches in Asia Minor. The problem was to determine when Easter should be held. If the celebration of Easter was to be dated from the day of the crucifixion, i.e. from the day of the Jewish passover, the fourteenth Nisan, then the day of the resurrection might fall on any day of the week; if, however, the determining day was to be the day of the resurrection, then the crucifixion would always be celebrated on the previous Friday and thus be independent of the Jewish passover observance. This latter practice was adopted by the church at Rome; the churches in Asia Minor however, clung to the former practice in which the Easter events were reckoned according to the day of the month, and not

[53] 'Rückblick auf die neuesten Untersuchungen über das Markusevangelium', *TJ*, 1853, pp. 54–93.

according to the day of the week. In taking this stand the Quarto-decimans claimed the support of their tradition, according to which the Quartodeciman practice had been observed by the apostle John himself, who had resided in Ephesus, the apostle Philip who had died in Hierapolis, Polycarp of Smyrna who had known the apostle John, and other notable Christians.

Shortly after A.D. 150 Polycarp had come to Rome and spoken about the matter to Bishop Anicetus, with whom he failed to agree. Nevertheless, they parted on cordial terms and the peace of the Church was not disturbed. It was another story, however, in A.D. 170 when a heated controversy broke out in Laodicea. The church in Asia Minor was divided on the issue: on the Quarto-deciman side stood Bishop Melito of Sardis; opposing him was Bishop Apollinaris of Hierapolis supported by Clement of Alexandria. The final encounter between the church at Rome and the church in Asia Minor erupted about A.D. 190. The latter church, represented by Bishop Polycrates of Ephesus, held that the fourteenth Nisan should be observed as the day on which Easter should begin; the church at Rome with Bishop Victor at its head and supported by the churches of Palestine, Gaul, and Greece attempted to excommunicate the Asia Minor churches, but were in turn censured by Irenaeus and others who, while supporting the Roman view, were of the opinion that the mystery would be finally solved only at the Lord's return.

One of the main grounds advanced by Baur to justify his dating the origin of the fourth Gospel late in the second century was that in his opinion the Gospel reflected this controversy concerning the time of the Last Supper and the crucifixion. The church in Asia Minor claimed that its tradition—that Jesus had kept the Passover with his disciples on the fourteenth Nisan—was derived from the apostle John himself. But according to the fourth Gospel, Jesus was already dead and lying in his grave by the evening of this day. Therefore, maintained Baur, this contradiction simply proved that the Gospel had not been written by the apostle John. Moreover, since the Gospel made no mention of any passover meal, its silence, according to Baur, was to be understood as a direct repudiation of the Quartodeciman practice.

A new representation of these events was put forward in 1848 by K. L. Weitzel who, in a carefully detailed book,[54] maintained

---

[54] *Die christliche Passafeier der drei ersten Jahrhunderte* (Pforzheim, 1848).

that there were actually two passover controversies in the Asia Minor church and that in each case the disputed points were different. In the first controversy at Laodicea about A.D. 170 the question was how great a role the Jewish passover should play in the Christian Easter celebrations. In this matter the minority Jewish-Christian party, which desired to retain the Jewish form of the commemoration feast as a continuation of the Jewish passover, were opposed by the rest of the church, which followed a more Pauline practice and desired that a break should be made with the Jewish observance. The second controversy between the churches of Rome and Asia Minor about A.D. 190 was over an entirely different matter, as the specifically Christian practice had now been distinguished from the Jewish. In this second controversy it was a question of the chronology of the passover—whether the crucifixion or the resurrection should be determinative in setting the date, i.e. whether the commemoration of the Easter events should begin on the fourteenth Nisan, as the Quartodecimans desired, or on the Friday preceding the day of the resurrection. Weitzel further maintained that the Easter celebration in Asia Minor was not a Jewish passover meal, but a commemoration of the suffering and death of Christ, and that Baur's claim that the church in Asia Minor observed the passover meal on the evening of the fourteenth Nisan was in fact incorrect. In Weitzel's opinion there was no contradiction between John's dating of the Easter events and the practice of the church in Asia Minor.

The ensuing discussion revolved around the nature and chronology of the Easter observance in the Asia Minor church. Baur, in his reply,[55] refused to accept Weitzel's contention that the Gospel of John was acknowledged as apostolic by the church in Asia Minor, and reiterated that it had originated during the Quartodeciman controversy. Hilgenfeld, on the other hand, while agreeing with this judgement, argued[56] that the Gospel did not originate because of the controversy, but rather fostered it, in that it provided the opponents of the Quartodecimans with an important weapon. And with this contribution from Hilgenfeld the discussion was temporarily concluded.

[55] 'Das johanneische Evangelium und die Passahfeier des zweiten Jahrhunderts', *TJ*, 1848, pp. 163–97.
[56] 'Der Paschastreit und das Evangelium Johannis . . ', *TJ*, 1849, pp. 209–81.

Further articles on the topic continued to trickle into publication in the ensuing years: Ritschl, in the first edition of his *Entstehung* (1850), supported Weitzel's views; Baur discussed the subject further in his *Church History of the First Three Centuries* (1853); Hase in his book on the Tübingen School disagreed with Baur, and Baur in his reply simply restated his opinions. But the next significant contribution which brought something new into the discussion came from the Frankfurt pastor G. E. Steitz, a friend and later brother-in-law of Ritschl. While generally agreeing with Weitzel, Steitz argued[57] that the church in Asia Minor did not keep the fourteenth Nisan as the day on which Christ had eaten the passover, but, in harmony with the fourth Gospel, as the day on which he had been sacrificed. According to Steitz, a distinction had to be made between the 'specific' Quarto-decimans—those holding that Christ was sacrificed on the fourteenth Nisan—and the Judaizing Quartodecimans, who held that the Easter celebration should begin on the fourteenth Nisan, but with the passover meal and not with the observance of Christ's death. Steitz defended these views with the assertion that Apollinaris was opposing the Judaizing Quartodecimans and that this opposition lent weight to the claim that the 'specific' Quartodeciman view of Apollinaris was in fact the dominant view in the Asia Minor church.

Since Steitz's solution had received Ritschl's warm approval in the second edition of his *Entstehung* (1857), it was only to be expected that it would find no favour with Baur and Hilgenfeld. Baur wrote two rebuttals of Steitz's views[58] and Hilgenfeld had the last word in his extensive investigation of the controversy.[59] Not until ten years later, when Schürer looked afresh at the whole question,[60] was the subject again discussed in any extensive way.

THE DEBATE ON THE SYNOPTICS 1852–7

Köstlin, who had long been out of sympathy with the views of Baur and Schwegler, wrote a long criticism of Baur in his book on the Gospels[61] which was published in 1852. The know-

---

[57] 'Die Differenz der Occidentalen und der Kleinasiaten in der Paschafeier', *TSK*, 1856, pp. 721–809.

[58] *TJ*, 1857, pp. 209–57; *ZWT*, 1858, pp. 298–312.

[59] *Der Paschastreit der alten Kirche* (Halle, 1860).

[60] Emil Schürer, *De Controversiis Paschalibus secundo* (Lipsiae, 1869).

[61] *Der Ursprung und die Komposition der synoptischen Evangelien* (Stuttgart, 1853).

ledge of the doctrinal tendency of a writing, argued Köstlin, was not enough; it certainly provided information regarding its course, but not about the finer details. For this, literary criticism was necessary and here Baur had scarcely touched upon the question of the literary relationship between the three Synoptic Gospels. Using this literary criticism Köstlin now reached the conclusion that Mark formed the basis of the other two Gospels, that in its canonical form it was, to be sure, the youngest of the three, but that a proto-Mark, which was the earliest Gospel, had been used by both Matthew and Luke. Köstlin's view, however, found generally no acceptance either inside or outside the School.

The final, new, and original development in Synoptic criticism came from Volkmar, who went beyond Baur and Schwegler in propounding entirely new ideas concerning the origin of the Gospels.[62] For Volkmar, practically nothing in the Gospels is historically true. He does not deny a historical core—that there was a person named Jesus who was crucified—but more than this core lies in the realm of speculation. The resurrection of Christ is 'ideal history', by which Volkmar gives us to understand that it is 'essentially' true, i.e. true for those who believe it. But now, how did the Gospel stories originate if, as Volkmar maintains, they have no historical veracity?

Volkmar takes us back into the historical situation of the apostolic and post-apostolic age. The Gospels, he tells us, are products of the controversy between the Paulinists and the Jewish Christians. The anti-Pauline, Jewish-Christian Apocalypse, which was in all probability *not* written by the apostle (against Baur), was composed—Volkmar knows the date precisely!— between August A.D. 68 and January A.D. 69. The reaction against Paul which was vigorously beaten back during his lifetime rose to new heights after his death. His friends and disciples grew ever more timid, for the anti-Pauline Apocalypse with all its prophecies appeared to have been given by God. But soon the hopes and expectations among the anti-Paulinists, that the Messiah would return to elevate the Jewish Christians to the place of honour, proved to be vain. The fall of Jerusalem, the destruction of the temple, and the failure of Israel to turn to their Messiah contradicted the prophecies of the Apocalypse and it now became clear that God had not spoken through the author of

[62] *Die Religion Jesu* (Leipzig, 1857).

Revelation and that he had not rejected his apostle Paul. Now, in consequence, was the time to see the *parousia* of Christ, not as a second coming, but in the glory in which it had already appeared in the first coming of Christ. Now was the time to proclaim the validity of the truths which Paul had taught. This was the hour in which the original Gospel was born.

According to Volkmar it was a Paulinist who undertook to write the first Gospel—a 'Pauline-Christian epic'—relating the glory which had appeared in the Person of Jesus, a truth which had been preserved by Paul. This 'epic', the canonical Gospel of Mark, is not a history of Jesus but rather a biography of Paul, and a mirror of the apostolic age. Thus the feeding of the five thousand is a fictitious story invented to portray Paul's preaching of the Gospel to the Gentiles—i.e. their spiritual feeding, and Christ's walking upon the water represents Paul's taking the Gospel across the sea to the Gentiles. 'What are even seas as obstacles, for Christ in his apostle to the Gentiles! Calmly and confident in God he crosses the wild waves of the sea (Mark 6:47f).'[63] Paul of course is not mentioned in the Gospel, but Volkmar has no doubts that the idealized epics portray not Jesus, but Paul. Moreover, while the author of the Apocalypse had excluded Paul from the twelve apostles, the author of Mark makes room for him through the betrayal of Jesus by Judas. Such a betrayal, according to Volkmar, could never have actually taken place because (1) it would have made Judas a bestial figure; (2) there was no reason why Judas should betray him; (3) the Apocalypse mentions twelve apostles, i.e. knows nothing of any betrayal. It is only fifty years after the crucifixion that the Paulinist author has the ingenuity to denounce Judas as the betrayer, in order to create the vacant place among the the apostles which Paul shall fill. Mark, then, is the original Gospel, the first formation of the Gospel stories. 'The poetic Gospel could not fail to make the deepest impression on all—even Jewish-Christian—circles'.

But unfortunately the Gospel found no favour; it was too one-sided and a reaction arose from among the Jewish Christians who, although not constituting the majority in the Church, were still strong enough to form a powerful opposition party. Thus there were a number of revisions of this original Gospel and the new rise of the Jewish-Christian spirit reached its peak in one

[63] Ibid., p. 213.

such Judaizing version called 'The Preaching of Peter' consisting of the Gospel of Mark and the first half of Acts. Volkmar adduced the evidence for the existence of this revision, which is no longer extant, from Acts and the *Clementine Homilies*. The Judaizing author of this writing added a genealogy, which attempted to trace Jesus' descent from David, and the Sermon on the Mount, in which Essene ideals find their place; Paul's authority is challenged by excluding him from the apostolic circle through the election of Matthias, and his person defamed in the story of Simon the magician, in that Simon's offering of money actually refers to the collection which Paul brought to Jerusalem for the relief of the poor. On the other hand, Peter appears as the appointed apostolic leader.

This one-sided picture now resulted in a reaction against the Jewish-Christian party and a Paulinist took upon himself to compose a more resolute Pauline apology—Luke and Acts. Since it was essential to cut the nerve of the Jewish claim which described Jesus as the son of Joseph, who in turn was descended from David, the author portrayed Jesus as God's son, born of a virgin, without human, i.e. Jewish, father. In order to weaken the influence of the other apostles the author depicted Jesus as appointing seventy others. In the second part of Acts, which was a new addition to counterbalance the first part as contained in 'The Preaching of Peter', Paul is placed on equal terms with Peter. Thus Paul's apostleship is defended and justified, even though some of his historical character is surrendered.

By this time the reader may be finding Volkmar's picture of reaction and counter-reaction in the early Church somewhat involved. Still more is to come. The Lucan stories were not well received since they were clearly understood as Pauline and rejected as too one-sided. Thus a Jewish Christian, sympathetic to the Pauline viewpoint and in opposition to the exclusiveness of Jewish Christianity, undertook a new revision with the aim of mediating a truer and more neutral picture. This was the canonical Matthew. According to Volkmar it originated in the time of Trajan and is the first harmony of the Gospels, a combination of the two foregoing Gospels and with a thoroughly mediating tendency. 'It completely ousted the former Judaistic forms of the Gospel and as the Jewish-Christian and Pauline Gospel of the true middle path it became, from that time on, of all the Gospel forms, the "chosen" one. It became and has remained the first Gospel, although the zenith of development within the Gospels was not yet attained.'[64] This zenith was attained in the Gospel of John, which, according to Volkmar, was the prophetic Gospel of the true Gnosticism. About A.D. 160 its author took up the struggle against the enslaved and enslaving Judaism, i.e. Jewish Christianity, which hated the light and attempted to exclude all Gnosticism from its ranks.

Such, in brief, was Volkmar's explanation of how the Gospels originated. The framework was essentially that of the Tübingen School, but the details within this framework bore little resemblance to the representation of Baur and Schwegler. With Volkmar the personal aspect plays a far greater role than with Baur; instead of seeing merely ideas, doctrinal opinions, and struggle for party supremacy, Volkmar sees individual personalities who are engaged in doctrinal disputes, ecclesiastical intrigues, and personal animosities. With Volkmar, Baur's whole chronological tendency evaluation was turned upside-down. Thus the speeches of Jesus in the Synoptics, which Baur held to be the eldest strata, are, according to Volkmar, the youngest, and sentences such as 'blessed are the poor in spirit', which were formerly regarded as genuine sayings of Jesus, are now counted as late additions from an Essene source. Mark, which in Baur's view was the last of the Synoptics and bore a neutral character, is now held by Volkmar to be the earliest Gospel and classified as definitely Pauline. Acts, which had previously been regarded as conciliatory, is now in consequence of the Lucan Gospel also held to be Pauline; and Matthew becomes the epitomator in place of Mark. At last the key to unlock the mysteries of the Gospels—a key, in Volkmar's opinion, lost for 1,800 years—had been discovered, and Volkmar regarded it as his great merit to have finally lifted the veil from the 'crystal-clear' 'poetical inventions' and to have demonstrated that the Gospels were actually epics.

Volkmar's solution was never accepted by anyone of repute, but it did show where Baur's views might lead when taken further than the Master had been prepared to go. The investigation of the Gospels, however, turned not to the left but to the right and followed the path championed by Ritschl in his espousal of Mark

---

[64] Ibid., p. 384.

as the earliest Gospel—a view which H. J. Holtzmann later carried through to its victorious acceptance.

BAUR'S DATING OF THE NEW TESTAMENT WRITINGS

In conclusion it may be found helpful to summarize Baur's opinions on the dates and tendencies of the New Testament writings.

Matthew	c. 130–5;	Jewish Christian
Mark	c. 140–50;	mediating, neutral
Luke	c. 130–40;	Pauline, mediating
John	c. 170;	originates in the Montanist/ Quartodeciman period
Acts	c. 130–40;	Pauline, conciliatory
Romans 1 Corinthians 2 Corinthians Galatians	c. 50–60;	genuine letters of Paul
Ephesians Philippians Colossians	c. 120–40;	Pauline, mediating, Gnostic influences
1 Thessalonians 2 Thessalonians	c. 70–5;	no special tendency, empty of thought
1 Timothy 2 Timothy Titus	c. 150–70;	written against the Marcionites
Philemon	c. 120–40;	mediating
Hebrews	c. 70–5;	Pauline
James	c. 130–50;	Jewish Christian, anti-Pauline
1 Peter	c. 120–40;	Pauline, mediating
2 Peter	c. 130–40;	Pauline, catholicizing
1–3 John	c. 170;	originate in the Montanist/ Quartodeciman period
Jude	c. 130–40;	eclectic, catholicizing
Revelation	c. 70;	Judaizing

13. The End of the Tübingen School

THE year 1846 saw the Tübingen School at its height. Baur's 'Paul' had appeared in the previous year; Schwegler's 'Post-apostolic Age' in the same year, and Baur's 'Critical Investigation of the Canonical Gospels' saw the light in the following year. The sun was at its zenith, but 1847 marked the beginning of its slow decline and Baur spent the last thirteen years of his life trying to hold the school together.

From 1846 attacks against him were mounted with increasing frequency. In the same year Thiersch published his polemical criticism, and Ebrard in his articles and books continually availed himself of every opportunity to attack the Tübingen views. Ewald, after his departure from Tübingen, waged a bitter and vitriolic campaign which raged on intermittently until after Baur's death.

Of even more importance in the decline of the School, however, was the loss of Baur's two most esteemed and trusted pupils. Schwegler bade farewell to theology in 1846 and contributed nothing more to the School; Zeller's departure for Bern in the following year depleted the Tübingen circle and his enforced transfer to the philosophical faculty in Marburg three years later caused a great gap in the ranks. True, three new members— Ritschl, Volkmar, and Hilgenfeld—had taken their places in the School, but Zeller's loss was inestimable in that he was the one person who might have been able to hold the School together. The other members of the School all held him in respect and through his editorship of the *Theologische Jahrbücher*, he, even more than Baur, was responsible for the growth and formation of the School. Indeed, without Zeller it is doubtful if there would ever have been a Tübingen School, as the School in its formative years revolved around the *Jahrbücher*.

In the first half of the 1850s things took a quieter turn. Baur's relationships with Hilgenfeld and Ritschl became at times strained, but never broke; Planck and Köstlin were still in Tübingen; Zeller's commentary on the Acts of the Apostles

appeared in 1854; Ritschl visited Tübingen and effected a reconciliation with Baur, and if Schwegler wanted nothing to do with
him, Köstlin was ready to stretch out a friendly hand. Outwardly
—and, of course, those outside the School knew little of the
internal differences—everything was in respectable order and the
School appeared to be stable and relatively unified. Within four
years all was changed.

What really started the final process of dissolution was Ritschl's
defection in 1856. But Baur's relations with Hilgenfeld had
deteriorated in the previous two years to such an extent that when
the review of Schwarz's book appeared in the *Centralblatt*, in
which was contained the provocative statement: 'The Tübingen
School has fallen to pieces', Baur immediately concluded that the
reviewer was Hilgenfeld. The fact that Ritschl was the author was
all the more serious in that Baur was in danger of losing not just
one, but two of his pupils, and only the most apologetic letter on
Baur's part staved off Hilgenfeld's defection also. The second
edition of Ritschl's *Entstehung*, which appeared in the following
year (1857), signalized that its author no longer desired to be
known as an adherent of the School and from this point onwards
Ritschl set himself in direct opposition to the Tübingen perspective.

Thus by 1857 Ritschl's statement appeared to have been proved
correct. Planck had left Tübingen and was busying himself in
Ulm with his philosophical treatises; Köstlin remained in
Tübingen but had transferred to the philosophical faculty;
Schwegler had died at the beginning of the year, and only Volkmar, pursuing his own path in Zürich, remained unaffected by
any changes. In this year also, the *Theologische Jahrbücher*, which
had been steadily losing subscriptions, finally had to cease publication.

And now in 1858 came the hardest attack against the School—
the hardest because it was the most objective and fairest criticism
which had yet been mounted. It was contained in an article[1] by
the Göttingen theologian and Court-preacher in Hanover,
Gerhard Uhlhorn, and even Baur admitted that Uhlhorn was 'no
unfair judge' of the School. Uhlhorn began his article with a
review of Baur's own writings and then went on to deal with the

---

[1] 'Die älteste Kirchengeschichte in der Darstellung der Tübinger Schule', *JDT*,
III (1858), pp. 280–349.

writings of the younger members of the School. He showed that the School had in fact fallen to pieces—that Ritschl had maintained the dispute between Paul and the other apostles to be of short duration and of no great consequence; that Hilgenfeld had progressed beyond Baur in claiming Gnosticism had been an important influence in causing the Jewish-Christian and Pauline parties to draw together; and that Volkmar had passed even beyond Hilgenfeld, with his theory that the Gospels were 'epics' portraying the controversies of the early Church. The two lines of development which proceed from Baur find their end-points, according to Uhlhorn, in the works of Ritschl and Volkmar, and Uhlhorn concluded his representation of the School with the following verdict.

If Baur with his tendency criticism did not press the matter to its logical conclusion, in that he contented himself with generally defining the tendency of the fourth Gospel, without designating its doctrinal standpoint more accurately, so Hilgenfeld has done this for the Gospel of John, and Volkmar, accepting Hilgenfeld's view of the fourth Gospel, has accomplished the same for the other three Gospels. If a caricature has resulted from this, then it is the sure proof that its basic axioms must already lie in Baur's views. Of the two lines which proceed from Baur and Schwegler, the one which passes through Planck and Köstlin ends with Ritschl in the abandonment of the Baurian principles, the other line which progresses logically through Hilgenfeld ends with Volkmar in this caricature of the early Church. According to both sides the goal has been attained and when we survey the works of the Tübingen School we will not be able to escape the conclusion that the School has finished its course. This conclusion is also indicated by many other signs, by Baur's summarizing of his earlier works, as well as by the undeniable unproductivity of the School which has set in during the last few years. We do not mean unproductivity in the sense that the School has not produced any more works at all; in this the School has not failed, but the works offer little that is new. The old investigations are revised, the old fields once more ploughed up, here and there the results modified, grouped, and combined in some other way, but by and large everything remains the same as it was before. Thus the Tübingen School will perhaps continue its investigations for a time, agitating the problems back and forth, certainly, not without also advancing our understanding of individual questions; but by and large we are convinced that the School has completed its mission and that one can confidently close the account without fearing that the result could be essentially changed through any new factors.

If we now balance the books, we can summarize the reckoning as follows. The development of the School, which we have described, is its best criticism, and we need only draw out the consequences. The task which the School set itself was to portray the origin of Christianity and the Christian Church from finite causes, without the intervention of an absolute causality. The history of the School shows that it was not able to accomplish this task. It made a number of attempts, devised ever new combinations, but nowhere did it succeed in finding such a combination of finite causes which on the one hand could be verified by the historical sources and on the other hand was able to solve the riddle of how Christianity originated. And finally, on the one side, it turned back again with Ritschl into the old roads, on the other side it produced writings which completely dissolved history in arbitrary hypotheses and which in the capricious treatment of the historical material can scarcely be counted any more among the historical investigations.[2]

Baur was deeply wounded by Uhlhorn's portrayal and wrote his brochure on the Tübingen School.[3] The School as consisting of individuals, he admitted, was no longer a School; however, it was not, he maintained, a question of individual personalities, but of the 'spirit' of the School.

Here also Herr Uhlhorn holds the personal element and the substantial essence of the School too little apart. The persons are certainly changing and transitory. If one judges the value and significance of historical events only with respect to the persons with whose names they are connected, then one can err greatly in one's judgement. Herr Ulhorn, too, may believe that with his critical survey he has so easily disposed of the School, by demonstrating in each of its different members now this, now that principal defect, by reckoning the one among the apostates, the other among those who have run completely astray, and by determining the character of the School as a whole according to the most non-essential features of particular individuals; but all this belongs to the personal aspect and does not touch the essential character of the School itself. Its actual essence still consists in the basic axioms and basic views from which it has proceeded, in the direction it followed—quite apart from the by-ways taken by the one or the other—most persistently and decidedly from the beginning, in the whole way and manner in which it comprehended its task—to investigate the early Christian age—and in the three demands which characterize the School as a historical critical School: 1. Above all, not to be bounded by any dogmatic presuppositions and consideration for

<hr>

[2] Ibid., pp. 346–7.   [3] *Die Tübinger Schule* (Tübingen, 1859).

traditional views which darken the impartiality of judgement. 2. To accept nothing as historical truth which cannot be demonstrated as such from the sources at our disposal, but emphatically and decidedly to accept everything that must be acknowledged as having actually happened in history, without letting oneself be led astray by attempts at mediation, confused, imaginative explanations, and uncertain, insignificant traditions. 3. Finally, never to lose sight of the fact that a general total-view of Christianity consists in the complementary oneness of the parts and the guiding basic-view, and that this total-view results from the investigation of the individual and special events.

Further, although Herr Uhlhorn may still estimate the positive results which have been obtained in this way up until the present time as being of little worth, the basic axioms and basic views of the School are still thereby not refuted; it would simply be a case of carrying them through more strictly and precisely. This could, indisputably, only take place when everything in the first form of their conception and representation (and in their former advocates) which had given them a too individualistic stamp and a too one-sided direction, was stripped away from them. Thus far from the School, with the persons by whom Herr Uhlhorn balances his books, having already completed its course there lies in its historical view nothing which would not fully justify accepting that it will have a definite and decisive influence upon all future investigations in the field of theological science.[4]

Relations with Hilgenfeld now reached their lowest ebb. Hilgenfeld had been satisfied with Uhlhorn's portrayal of the School in that Uhlhorn had emphasized clearly Hilgenfeld's independent position over against Baur. After Baur's reply to Uhlhorn, however, Hilgenfeld, in an article which appeared in the second issue of the *Zeitschrift für wissenschaftliche Theologie* for 1859, distanced himself from Baur even further. If Baur's views were the measuring-rod for adherence to the Tübingen School, wrote Hilgenfeld, then he could no longer consider himself a member of the School; he had no desire to be saddled with views which he did not hold, and, moreover, why should he, a North German who had never been south of Thuringia accept involvement in a name bound to a particular Swabian town, which he had never even visited?

Baur was furious and wrote a letter in which he bitterly resented Hilgenfeld's attempt to distance himself from the School.

[4] Ibid., pp. 56–9.

Tübingen, 27 March 1859

Honoured Herr Professor,

It is not very long since I received the second issue of your journal . . . In consequence of your earlier statement, I see that I have erred, in that I did not expect the remarks about my latest brochure in the manner in which I now found them in this issue. In good faith in your disposition towards me I called you a true co-worker. You took this in good part, but I must almost believe that it would have pleased you even more had I said that I had been with you in your School. But now, since according to the language in common currency—which was none of my doing—there is no Jena School, but a Tübingen School, you reproach me with School-coercion. I would like to know wherein I have deserved this reproach, especially with respect to yourself. And now in order to cut the relations to the so-called Tübingen School from your side, you depreciate the Tübingen School to a purely local significance in order to be able to ask justly how you then, a good North-German who has never been south of Thuringia, has never seen Tübingen, can be a Tübingen man! Everyone who has any knowledge at all of such questions knows that when at the present time a Tübingen School is spoken of, above all I am meant. You say in your letter of 20 February that above all you are for openness and clarity. But if you believe yourself obliged to protest so earnestly against an association with a Tübingen School, why do you not say so plainly and openly instead of hiding behind an innocent place-name: I no longer know this man! I'm sorry that I must express myself in this way, but this meaning of your explanation compels me. You say, pp. 277f., you do not see how such a free viewpoint can bear the name of a particular locality, to which it is no longer bound, and not the personal name of its founder. What difference is there, then, whether the viewpoint in question is called by my name or by the name of the town from which it proceeded and in which he still lives, whom you yourself name the founder of the School?

Is it not clear that it is not here a question of the mere name of a locality, but of the viewpoint designated by the name, and of my personal relation to this viewpoint? What is true of the one is also true of the other! Since you so gladly seize the opportunity to give me to understand by the name Tübingen, that which I understand right well, then I must reserve myself the right to explain myself once more also regarding this relation.[5]

A second letter followed some three weeks later in answer to Hilgenfeld's reply.

[5] Baur to Hilgenfeld, 27 Mar. 1859.

Tübingen, 21 April 1859

Honoured Herr Doctor,

... With regard to the main content of your last letter which concerns the name 'Tübingen School', you say, 'I can easily imagine that the name "Tübingen School" could be pleasing to no one who had not himself proceeded from Tübingen and who, because of that name, is thus, without further ado, placed in the mere appendices.' As if this hinged on the name 'Tübingen' and not much more, so far as it can be said, on the concept of the School. Why then do you not rather dispute that anything at all which can be called a School and which also accordingly could have had any influence upon you, had proceeded from Tübingen? Only in this way would everything connected with the name Tübingen be thoroughly eradicated.[6]

The matter was then allowed to drop. Relations resumed some months afterwards but the letters were formal and cool. Then in June 1860 Hilgenfeld sent Baur a copy of his book on the Passover controversy, in the foreword to which he had spoken of Baur as the 'Lord of the house', the 'Lord of the School', of 'School-dogmas' and 'School-views'. Baur was offended and said so plainly.

Tübingen, 1 July 1860

Most-honoured Herr Professor,

Please accept my warmest thanks for the valuable gift, your book on the Passover controversy, which you sent me. You have given an extremely comprehensive, clear, well-ordered representation of the course of this remarkable historical question, which on account of its completeness is to be highly recommended. But why have you spoilt my pleasure in your work by the postscript to the preface? Why can you still not refrain from wounding me by always printing something of this kind? Must it not wound me when you reproach me with just that very thing against which I expressly defended myself, when you describe me as the Lord of the School and my views as School-dogmas, when you speak of a School-mentality, and also indicate a disapproval of further investigations, which the unconversant and ill-disposed may understand how they like? Must it not wound me when you represent me as the one over against whom the work—which, to be sure, was founded by me but is still burdened by ties of locality and School-constriction—first had to be raised to the free, universal standpoint of science? You speak of being bound to a locality, but how can one comprehend the relationship in question in a more local way than you do, when you reject everything which could somehow have passed

[6] Baur to Hilgenfeld, 12 Apr. 1859.

over from me to you, and deny every appearance of such a relationship with the declaration that you have never been to Tübingen. When you maintain that Mark is the second Synoptic Gospel, I the third, you call my view a School-dogma and reproach me with the weight of evidence which, according to you, has not been refuted, As if I also could not say the same thing about my point of view; but I would never avail myself of this way of speaking as I know well that one so often leaves unrefuted what one thinks is too insignificant to take further notice of. You say that, notwithstanding, even now I still hold fast to my view; should I then let myself be compelled to change by your views and by you, you who still want to be so free from every School-coercion? What you say otherwise in my favour, your assent to what I have said, the respect which you show for my advanced years, the predicates which you otherwise bestow upon me—all this in my eyes does not make the matter any better ... I conclude with the wish that this may be the last time I will have to express myself to you about matters which I so unwillingly make the object of a correspondence.

Yours respectfully,
Dr. Baur.[7]

On 15 July Baur suffered his first heart-attack. In a final letter to Hilgenfeld on 16 October he sympathized with the difficulties continually confronting Hilgenfeld, reported on his health, and invited Hilgenfeld to Tübingen to visit him. Baur's death in December brought the brittle relationship to an end; and with Baur's death, it may be said that the Tübingen School also completed its course.

Two questions remain to be discussed: 1. What constituted the distinctive character of the School? 2. What was the essential qualification which constituted one as a member of the School?

1. There was no single feature which characterized the School, but rather four main features may be distinguished.

(i) The name of the School was derived from and tied inseparably to a small university town where Baur spent the last thirty-four years of his life as professor of theology. It was in Tübingen that Strauss had written his *Life of Jesus* and thereby caused Tübingen to be regarded by the orthodox as a centre of unbelief; it was in Tübingen that the five Swabian members of the School had completed their university studies and were

[7] Baur to Hilgenfeld, 1 July 1860.

employed on the staff of the University; here also the Tübingen School circle had gathered together and resolved to publish the *Theologische Jahrbücher*. Thus, it was in no wise unfitting that the name of the School should be linked with the town of its origin and the town in which it was centred.

(ii) The School was linked, secondly, with the name of its head, Ferdinand Christian Baur. It would be too much to say that Baur was the founder of the School as the School itself owed probably as much to Zeller and Schwegler as to Baur; but Baur was its acknowledged head in that he stood behind everything and provided it with the authority and patronage which it required. Thus the School might also be called the Baurian School, in that Baur's views provided the School with its foundation and its guiding principles.

(iii) Thirdly, the Tübingen School was based on a definite theological principle, namely, the purely historical, non-supernatural, and non-miraculous interpretation of Christianity. Christianity as a historical religion was to be investigated as such; from this point of view everything else had to be interpreted accordingly. It was therefore clear that this involved a radically new approach to the investigation of the early Church and the authorship of the New Testament writings. Henceforth, all scientific investigation was to be presuppositionless, i.e. the Scriptures were to be evaluated by a free investigation untrammelled by the old traditional supernatural presuppositions. This purely historical investigation constituted the central and fundamental dogmatic principle on which the School was grounded.

(iv) Under the aegis of this dogmatic principle Baur evolved and constructed his total-view of the history of early Christianity, which may be described as the Tübingen perspective. The thesis which Baur put forward was that the opposition between Paul and the original apostles continued on as the opposition between Pauline and Jewish Christianity until late in the second century. Not only was the history of the early Church to be determined by this total-view, but also the origin and authorship of the New Testament writings. On this Tübingen perspective hinged the validity of Baur's whole investigation of the New Testament.

What was the essential qualification which constituted one as a member of the School? It was not a matter of being resident in Tübingen; Hilgenfeld never set foot in the town; Volkmar only visited it and Ritschl was there for only one semester. Neither was it the fact that one had studied under Baur, although all the seven younger members of the School had either attended the University at Tübingen or had been greatly influenced by Baur's writings; for there were many other Swabians who had been pupils of Baur and yet were not included in his School. Neither was it a question of sharing Baur's views on the non-supernatural character of Christianity, for others, such as Lipsius, who were never reckoned among the members of the School, were absolutely at one with Baur on this point. Nor was it a matter of being in full agreement with Baur's Tübingen perspective, for Köstlin was never completely in sympathy with it and Ritschl was finally led to break with it. The theologian who could best lay claim to Baur's mantle was Carl Holsten, who only became well known twenty years after Baur's death.

We may summarize by saying that there were actually two qualifications which constituted the basis of the School's membership. The first was the acceptance of the principle of a *purely historical* interpretation of Christianity and the New Testament writings. On this point everyone was agreed. The second qualification was that each member made an *essential contribution to the historical development of the School.* This is why Ewald (in the early years) and Alexander Schweizer could be reckoned only as adherents and not as members, in that their reviews and articles did not contribute *essentially* to the character and development of the School. For the same reason Strauss and Vischer are not numbered among the eight members, for although playing a large part indirectly in the School's formation, they made no *essential* contribution to the investigation of the apostolic and post-apostolic age, an investigation which characterized the School.

Nor can those theologians who were sympathetic to the Tübingen viewpoint and who rose to prominence after Baur's death be included among the members. Carl Weizsäcker, who succeeded to Baur's chair in Tübingen, was at the beginning of his professorship numbered among the more conservative mediating theologians, and only years later did he draw much closer to Baur's views; Karl Theodor Keim named Baur with unreserved respect as his great teacher, but his rise to fame as professor of theology in Zürich came after Baur's death, and he too contributed nothing to the School's historical development. Lipsius, Pfleiderer, Holtzmann, and Hausrath were all agreed with the Tübingen principle of a scientific investigation of the historical sources of Christianity, but were never reckoned as belonging to the School. Only Carl Holsten, who pronounced all the Pauline epistles except Romans, Galatians, and the two Corinthian letters to be unauthentic, really held fast to the Tübingen historical perspective originally formulated by Baur and Schwegler.

When everything has been taken into consideration it would not be too much to say that the School died with its head. It is true that former members of the School were still living and active: Zeller wrote a long appreciation of his father-in-law, showed up Ewald's unsavoury character, and debated with Ritschl over Baur's historical investigations; Schwegler was in his grave; Planck teaching in Ulm; Köstlin lecturer in Aesthetics; Ritschl was still in Bonn and shortly to move to Göttingen; Hilgenfeld in Jena editing his theological journal; and Volkmar in Zürich. But these last three had all gone their own way and had little more in common with the Tübingen perspective originally evolved by Baur and Schwegler. Time had not stood still and theological investigation had not remained static. The Tübingen perspective had been superseded, and with the passing of Baur the School as a School ceased to exist. A few months after Baur's death, Köstlin pictured the new situation in Tübingen: 'Tubingen is changing so much lately through the continual coming and going of new lecturers that one would think one belonged to two completely different generations'[8]; and two years later the Tübingen School was just a memory. 'With regard to your question as to how things stand here, there is little to tell you that is good; the old "Tübingen School" is now here again, just as it was before Baur.'[9]

[8] Köstlin to Hilgenfeld, 29 July 1861.
[9] Köstlin to Hilgenfeld, 18 Apr. 1863.

14. The Tübingen School: An Evaluation

It would not be too much to say, that after Strauss's *Life of Jesus* the Tübingen School exerted the greatest influence on the course of theology in the nineteenth century. Its influence was in some respects more extensive and enduring than that of Strauss, but this was possible only because Strauss's book had first created the possibility of a Tübingen School. Strauss and the Tübingen School belong together: the first is the presupposition of the second and the second the continuation of the first.

Only when we look back after more than a century is it really possible to assess the full importance of the School. Both Mackay[1] and Berger[2], who wrote in the decade following Baur's death, were unable to perceive the total impact which the School would have on theological and Biblical studies. They were too immersed in their time and could not see how dramatically the Tübingen investigations had changed the whole course of Biblical criticism. Within a generation from the appearance of Strauss's *Life of Jesus* the critical investigation of the Bible had established itself. Every other theological direction, be it conservative or mediating, Lutheran or Reformed, was compelled to take issue one way or another with the Tübingen School, and to defend its own position. It was the Tübingen School which really instigated the whole critical investigation of the New Testament. True, others before had made a beginning with such investigations—we need only think of Michaelis, Ernesti, Semler, Eichhorn, and Schleiermacher—but all these worked within a broadly theistic view of the Bible and on particular aspects of Biblical interpretation. They did not, however, attempt to formulate any comprehensive total-view such as constituted the basis of the Tübingen School.

It was Baur who established the principle of a purely historical interpretation of the Bible, a principle which hitherto had been expressed with great caution and with reference only to particular

---

[1] R. W. Mackay, *The Tübingen School and its Antecedents* (London, 1863).
[2] S. Berger, *F. C. Baur: les origines de l'école de Tubingue et ses principes, 1826–44* (Strasbourg, 1867).

problems of Biblical exegesis. This principle became the rallying-point for all who rejected the old traditional view, and the Tübingen School became the focal point of all *avant-garde* Biblical investigations. It initiated and established the historical-critical investigation of the Bible, which made it possible for others to branch out on their own lines of thought and pursue the more specialized aspects of Biblical research.

Although the Tübingen School itself was 'damned' by the orthodox and often eschewed by liberals and rationalists, it exerted an influence out of all proportion to its contemporary disrepute. All theologians of the later nineteenth century lived under its shadow and were influenced by it to varying degrees, either positively or negatively. And not only in the field of New Testament studies was the School so influential; for the critical investigation of the Old Testament, although in time preceding Strauss and Baur, followed in their wake, in that the Tübingen School provided the methodological tendency-approach which was simply adapted and applied to the Old Testament by Graf, Wellhausen, Duhm, and Buddle. Only when we think of the Zürich tradition beginning with Alexander Schweizer (who was a faithful contributor to the *Theologische Jahrbücher*), Volkmar, Keim, and Biedermann; the influence of Hilgenfeld's *Zeitschrift für wissenschaftliche Theologie* which continued right down to the First World War; the Heidelberg theologians Holtzmann, Holsten, and Hausrath; Lipsius at Jena; Pfleiderer at Berlin; and above all, the descending line from Albrecht Ritschl through Harnack, Herrmann, Johannes Weiss, Albert Eichhorn, Gunkel, Bousset, and the history of religions school, to Bultmann, do we gain any adequate idea of how influential the School really was.

What Baur desired and strove after was a free investigation of the New Testament, an investigation uninhibited by the traditional supernatural presuppositions—in short, a presuppositionless investigation. But that, as Ernst Käsemann remarked, was quite impossible to attain.

That leads to a second reflection. If there is anyone who demonstrates that there is no such thing as presuppositionless theology, then it is Baur. In every detail of methodology we are chained to our dogmatic premises. Not the presuppositionless theology is possible, but the theology which radically questions and is continually ready to correct itself. That means, however, that we must give an account of the dogmatic tradition from which we come and in which we find ourselves at the present time.[3]

The importance of presuppositions was also stressed by Klaus Scholder.

It has become abundantly clear—even when this is not explicitly emphasized—that a great historical representation implies definite philosophical presuppositions. How the content of these presuppositions is formed, whether they assume a linear or dialectical development of history, is only of secondary interest. What is important is that without these presuppositions the writing of history as a representation of what actually happened is unthinkable and meaningless.[4]

Our task has thus been pointed out for us—to ascertain and set forth clearly the central presupposition which determined the whole of Baur's historical investigation. On this point Baur leaves us in no doubt of his basic principle. He wanted a purely historical investigation and interpretation of the Christian faith and early Church history. 'My basic principle, is, in short, the *purely historical principle*. It is simply a case of interpreting the historical facts—as far as that is at all possible—in a purely objective manner.'[5] 'I can designate my standpoint only as the purely historical standpoint and the task is thus to interpret Christianity, *especially in its origins*, as a historical event and to understand it as such.'[6]

A *purely historical* interpretation meant, for Baur, that there could be no supernatural or miraculous events in history, because the supernatural realm (if it exists) lies outside of history and is therefore unknowable. Thus, Christianity cannot be rightly understood if its origin is treated as in any way supernatural. 'With a miracle all explanation and understanding ceases, and where the beginning is not explained or understood, no continuing development which proceeds from the beginning is

---

[3] Introduction to volume I of Baur's *Ausgewählte Werke* (ed. Klaus Scholder; 1963), p. xxiv.

[4] 'Ferdinand Christian Baur als Historiker', *Evangelische Theologie*, XXI (1961), p. 458; similarly R. Bultmann, 'Ist voraussetzungslose Exegese möglich?' in *Glauben und Verstehen*, III (Tübingen, 1962), pp. 142–50; ET: 'Is exegesis without presuppositions possible?' in *Existence and Faith*, Shorter Writings of Rudolf Bultmann, selected, translated, and introduced by Schubert M. Ogden (London, 1961), pp. 289–96.

[5] *Das Christenthum* (1st ed. Tübingen, 1853), p. iv.

[6] Ibid. (2nd ed. Tübingen, 1860), p. viii.

possible; there can be no development at all and no historical continuity.'[7]

This statement of Baur's means that even if there were a God who had created the world, this God would be unable to break into history; he would be locked out of his world. But in actuality Baur did not believe that such a God existed, and consequently there could be no miraculous intervention into the history of the world. This, in fact, was the one presupposition which determined the whole of Baur's historical investigation and also that of the Tübingen School. On this point all the members of the School were agreed, and it is just here that the whole on-going critical investigation must give account of itself. *Not the Hegelian philosophy, but the acceptance or rejection of a transcendent personal God determined Baur's dogmatic and historical investigations.*

No one saw this more clearly than Richard Lipsius, Hilgenfeld's sharp-sighted, rationalistic friend and later colleague at Jena. What is the principle of the Tübingen School? asked Lipsius, in a letter to Baur a year before Baur's death.

But what is this principle? You answer: the historical interpretation of Christianity, even more precisely, the historical-critical interpretation. With this everyone is gladly agreed; certainly in the broad and general sense. But I spoke expressly of the *purely* historical interpretation, i.e. of that interpretation which *excludes* the absolute miracle, which comprehends what has happened, therefore (without detriment to the acknowledgement of a causality which holds sway over everything finite), as a real human happening in the context of finite causes and workings: in short, I spoke of those historical considerations which demand for Christianity no special measuring stick but the same one as that which profane history employs everywhere in its field. With regard to *this* consideration of history, which excludes the miracle in the theological sense, my statement was true; to dispute this historical interpretation would be equivalent to renouncing all further scientific investigation: for where miracles occur, scientific investigation ceases.

It is certainly a question whether or not everyone is gladly agreed with this statement. I maintain that no supernaturalist could subscribe to it. Supernaturalism and the purely historical interpretation are opposing viewpoints which exclude each other. On this point both Weisse and Ewald are agreed with you, the former expressly, the latter actually, for it is well known that Ewald acts as if he acknowledges miracles, whereas in reality he stands as far removed from a belief in

---

[7] *Die Tübinger Schule*, p. 45.

miracles as anyone else. For Weisse the miracles in John's Gospel are the reason why he declares the narrative material to be unauthentic. Ewald seems, under a thick cloud of words, to want to indicate that his apostolic author did not mean the miracle narratives in the literal sense, in short, that the miracles in the Gospel of John did *not* happen, that an acknowledgement of the external objectivity of these miracles is irreconcilable with the presupposed historical principle; thus, that an author who considers these miracles as events which actually happened could not have been an apostle. This is a train of thought upon which you, Ewald, and Weisse are all agreed. That Ewald twists the meaning of the miracle narratives in order to be able to acknowledge John as the author is certainly a futile procedure, and that he tries to give the impression that he accepts miracles is dishonesty. But he has the principle itself in common with you and he would certainly have come to the same results regarding John's Gospel as you, if you had not come to them earlier. *Now* the man is certainly under a self-imposed obligation to come to a different view of the matter from you; certainly he is inconsistent, for his criticism of the Pentateuch rests essentially on the same method as you employ in your criticism of the Gospel of John.

As concerns Weisse, his hypothesis is as untenable as possible; but with respect to his denial of miracles he is in accord with you and has the advantage over Ewald in that he honestly acknowledges this. He is also in harmony with your result as regards the authenticity of the fourth Gospel.

How then is the matter now viewed from the supernatural standpoint? In such a way that all differences between you and Weisse appear completely worthless and negligible, because one rejects your common presupposition. If the absolute miracle belongs to the realm of possibility and reality, then all these questions which you, Weisse, and Ewald answer differently could not even arise; for the difficulties which—out of your common presupposition—arise against the apostolic authorship of John's Gospel do not exist for the opposing viewpoint. In this sense is the expression 'cat-fight', which I used, to be understood. I will say: the question of the principle must be so stated: purely historical interpretation or belief in miracles. If the rejection of the second or the acknowledgement of the first makes one a member of the Tübingen School, then both Ewald and Weisse also belong (indeed, even Ritschl too, who certainly skips over this point in silence; but since he has not expressly taken back his former view, one must suppose, until he says otherwise, that he still holds it), and consequently everything that is disputed among those named is a question for discussion inside the Tübingen School. Now since from the orthodox side, i.e. from the side of those who believe in miracles, the whole principle on which the Tübingen perspective as well as the Weissian and Ewaldian rests, is rejected as godless, then our pious theologians have absolutely no need to trouble themselves about the dispute over the Johannine question, which is otherwise so important and has been carried on by the three of you. From the supernaturalistic point of view this dispute is simply a cat-fight, just as is, from the Jesuit standpoint, the dispute between the two Lutheran factions over the *kenosis*,[8] but to a far lesser degree, since Lutherans and Jesuits are not as fundamentally separated as supernaturalism is from the historical principle advocated by the three of you.

The historical principle which Uhlhorn damns as the Tübingen principle, is, therefore, the same principle employed by other investigators—in spite of deviating results. But however this principle may be judged, to declare that all opponents of the miraculous beginning of Christianity are members of the Tübingen School is, at any rate, to go too far, and within this larger circle one must peg off a smaller area for the actual Tübingen School. At the moment *this* distinction appears as the less important. The central issue concerns the defence of the common principle, the right of a purely historical interpretation, i.e. no miraculous beginning. In this defence there are a large number of theologians participating who do not belong to the Tübingen School, and to raise the Uhlhorn terminology—the denial of the miraculous beginning of Christianity generally—to be the criterion of the Tübingen heresy, would mean extending this heretical name to such people as even Ewald and Weisse. That 'Tübingen' and 'damned' are identical concepts is certainly accepted in our pious circles as already settled. But what one here damns under this name is the principle of the purely historical interpretation, i.e. the scientific investigation itself, which cannot begin with miracles.[9]

What Lipsius perceived with such acuteness was that all historical criticism is ultimately determined by its dogmatic presuppositions, and, above all, the existence of God. It is not a question of discussing individual historical details. Historical criticism must be prepared to submit itself to a radical questioning; it must be honest and unflinching enough not to push aside this question of the existence of a transcendent personal God. It is an either/or: if there is no such God then there can be no supernatural intervention in history, and the Tübingen principle is so far correct. But if there is such a God who refuses to allow

[8] The doctrine of Christ's self-emptying (Philippians, 2:7).
[9] Lipsius to Baur, 23 Dec. 1859.

himself to be excluded from his world, then Baur's whole theological and historical viewpoint must be radically re-estimated.

Confronted with this demand Baur would have replied, that while supernatural intervention in history could not be *a priori* excluded as impossible, i.e. Baur would concede the *possibility* of a transcendent personal God, such a God would be *necessarily* excluded, since it would always be impossible to verify the supernatural by historical methods. But the whole matter would then be placed on a different level and it would then be a question of establishing criteria by which a revelation *in history* might be determined. However, Baur never seriously considered this possibility. The supernatural and miraculous were to all intents and purposes excluded from history as *a priori* impossible. In the last analysis Baur started from the presupposition that miracles were impossible, because he rejected the idea of a transcendent personal God.

If one had to sum up the aim and object of the Tübingen School in a single statement it would be that the Tübingen School made the first comprehensive and consequent attempt to interpret the New Testament and the history of the early Church from a non-supernatural (indeed, anti-supernatural) and non-miraculous standpoint. This was expressed clearly by Lipsius in his penultimate letter to Baur.

The main content of your letter is still concerned with the concept of the Tübingen School. You raise the question as to why above all the Tübingen School should be regarded as 'damned', if, as I maintained, the free rivalry of those bound to us in the same endeavour has already made its appearance alongside of the School in the narrower sense. You will find, finally, the reason for the general hate against you and your School lies in the fact that you, first of all, actually carried through the purely historical standpoint within the period of New Testament history by means of a consistent application of the principle to every detail of all the relevant questions. And you were the first to carry through this investigation with the openness and uprightness, the sharpness and precision, without which scientific views and basic axioms have no true significance. In all this I can see nothing with which to disagree. This merit will remain undiminished to you and your direct pupils, and in my opinion the only question is whether or not one must *necessarily* be led in all details to the same conclusions which you have drawn from the principle of a purely historical interpretation.[10]

[10] Lipsius to Baur, Mar. 1860.

The fundamental axiom of Baur's whole historical investigation was that the New Testament writings are not trustworthy historical documents. This axiom followed logically from the rejection of the supernatural and miraculous element in Christianity. For if there is no such element, then its New Testament portrayal is obviously without historical foundation, and all narratives in the New Testament where a supernatural intervention into history is either maintained or presupposed are *ipso facto* historically fictitious. Thus far, all members of the Tübingen School, and sympathizers such as Lipsius, were fully agreed; but beyond this point the adherents of the purely historical interpretation began to differ, the differences finally leading to the break up of the School. To describe all the by-ways taken would lead us too far afield and we shall therefore confine ourselves to the main features of Baur's own total-view, which formed the basis of the original Tübingen perspective.

The first question which Baur had to settle was that of a methodological starting-point. In beginning with the four authentic Pauline epistles, Romans, Galatians, 1 and 2 Corinthians, Baur believed himself to stand on solid historical ground. From these epistles, especially Galatians, Baur concluded that Paul was engaged in a continual conflict, not only with the Judaizers, but also with Peter, James, and the rest of the original apostles. Baur now had to decide whether this dispute was of merely temporary duration or a long-lasting conflict which continued for many decades after Paul's death. This problem in turn could only be settled by discovering whether or not traces of such a conflict were to be found in the later post-apostolic writings. In the book of Acts there was no mention of such a dispute—an omission which could be explained in two ways: either the author considered the disagreement (if there was one) to have been of too little significance to include in his historical portrayal, or he deliberately covered it up for one reason or another. Baur decided that the second alternative was the true explanation, that the dispute was not of temporary duration but lasted well into the second century. The question now was whether or not he could find any evidence to support his hypothesis.

Fundamentally, Baur based his whole argument on the *Clementine Homilies* which he believed to have been written about A.D.

170. In the attack on the person of Simon the magician, Baur perceived a disguised attempt to vilify the apostle Paul. On this identification Baur rested his entire case, that the bitter opposition between Pauline and Jewish Christians continued late into the second century. It is true that in the Clementine writings Paul is nowhere mentioned by name and the whole book is set in time before the conversion of Saul (according to the chronology of Acts 8:4–24). Nevertheless, because Peter followed Simon around from place to place refuting Simon's false teaching, Baur saw this as evidence of the continuing struggle between Pauline and Jewish Christianity. And yet one has only to read through the Clementine writings with an open mind to see that Baur's hypothesis is utterly untenable. For this Simon was portrayed not as an apostate from Judaism who rejected the necessity of keeping the law (as Paul might have been portrayed), but as a Samaritan, an idolater, a blasphemer, a complete perverter of the *Christian* faith who denied the resurrection of Jesus and even God himself. If we set forth the Clementine portrayal of Simon more accurately than Baur did or wanted to do, then we derive the following picture: Simon was a Samaritan, the son of Antonius and Rachel, who lived in the village of the Getones. By profession a magician, Simon wished to be thought of as the Christ. He denied that there was one God, but claimed there were many gods and that he himself possessed a certain power which set him above all gods. He turned air into water and water into blood and by solidifying the blood into human flesh created a boy—a far nobler work than God the Creator of the universe had been able to produce. Simon then turned the boy back into air, but used the soul of the boy as an agent in working his black magic. And what are some of Simon's magic acts? He makes statues walk, rolls himself in fire and is not burned; sometimes he flies through the air, makes loaves of bread from stone, becomes a serpent, transforms himself into a goat, becomes two-faced, and changes himself into gold. Apart from these miraculous Acts Simon denies all the central doctrines of Christianity, including the resurrection of the dead. When confronted by Peter he curses and swears; his crimes are numerous and wickedness characterizes his whole person and life. But we will hear how the author of the *Clementine Recognitions* allows Simon to describe himself.

I am the first power; I am always, and without beginning. But having entered the womb of Rachel, I was born of her as a man, that I might be visible to men. I have flown through the air, I have been mixed with fire, I have been made one body with it; I have made statues move; I have animated lifeless things; I have made stones bread; I have flown from mountain to mountain; I have moved from place to place upheld by angels' hands, and I have lighted on the earth. Not only have I done such things, but even now I am able to do them, that by so doing I may prove to all, that I am the Son of God enduring to eternity, and that I can make those who believe on me endure in like manner for ever.[11]

And this Simon Magus, then, according to Baur, is the apostle Paul in disguise. One would have to say that it was certainly an effective disguise. Whether any one who was not prejudiced in advance would recognize the apostle Paul in this description is indeed doubtful. Baur was able to do so only because he omitted most of Simon's extravagant assertions and claims. Because Peter and Paul disputed at Antioch, and because Peter here disputes with Simon, Baur concluded that Simon was to be identified with Paul. Thus in order to strengthen his case for the historical framework which he had adduced, Baur simply grasped at every straw he could find. The date and authorship of each New Testament book was then determined according to how it fitted into this historical framework (the tendency approach). 'Fitted' is the wrong word. Baur *forced* the books into the framework by manipulating the facts and distorting the evidence, by emphasizing the details which harmonized with his views while omitting everything which did not. One sees that only too clearly from his portrayal of Simon the magician, and his rejection of the final two chapters of the epistle to the Romans. From this letter Baur had deduced that the church at Rome was composed predominantly of Jewish Christians. The fact that all the names of friends which Paul greets in this final chapter are Gentile names might have caused Baur to reconsider his whole conclusion regarding the composition of the church at Rome. But, no, rather than weaken his whole tendency approach, Baur chose simply to reject the final two chapters as unauthentic.

We may conclude with a brief examination of four other central points in Baur's tendency approach, in order to see how

---

[11] *Recognitions*, III, 47; cf. *Homilies*, II, 32.

unscientific his procedure actually was and how invalid his final results and conclusions.

1. The Differences between Acts and the Pauline Epistles

In Baur's view the book of Acts was unhistorical through and through. There were substantially two main grounds for this: first, the miracles stories, which were *ipso facto* unhistorical, and secondly, the omission of any reference to the dispute between Paul and the other apostles. Baur therefore saw the book as a conciliatory attempt to soften the differences between Pauline and Jewish Christianity. This hypothesis of Baur's was certainly quite reasonable; it might well have been so, but the evidence was inconclusive. Baur did not seriously consider the possibility that the dispute between Peter and Paul was confined to a single incident, with no continuing estrangement of the parties involved. Nor did Baur exert himself to ascertain whether the alleged contradictions might not be harmonized; he simply assumed that because he was unable to see any harmonization, therefore none was possible.

What has been demonstrated over the past century, however, is the accurate historical detail in the book.[12] When Sir William Ramsay 'first set out on his archeological work, in the late seventies of the last century, he was firmly convinced of the truth of the then fashionable Tübingen theory, that Acts was a late production of the middle of the second century AD, and he was only gradually compelled to a complete reversal of his views by the inescapable evidence of the facts uncovered in the course of his research'.[13] Some years later Ramsay explained his change of mind.

I may fairly claim to have entered on this investigation without any prejudice in favour of the conclusion which I shall now attempt to justify to the reader. On the contrary, I began with a mind unfavourable to it, for the ingenuity and apparent completeness of the Tübingen theory had at one time quite convinced me. It did not then lie in my

---

[12] See F. F. Bruce. *The New Testament Documents. Are They Reliable?* (5th ed., London, 1960); H. J. Cadbury, *The Book of Acts in History* (London, 1955); perhaps the best modern survey of the date and authorship of Acts is to be found in Donald Guthrie's *New Testament Introduction* (London, 1970), pp. 336-85. It would lie completely beyond the scope of this book to enter into a discussion of the widely differing views concerning the historicity of Acts; for a full and up-to-date survey of the question see W. W. Gasque, *A History of the Criticism of the Acts of the Apostles* (Tübingen, 1974).

[13] F. F. Bruce, op. cit., p. 90.

line of life to investigate the subject minutely; but more recently I found myself often brought into contact with the book of Acts as an authority for the topography, antiquities and society of Asia Minor. It was gradually borne in upon me that in various details the narrative showed marvellous truth. In fact, beginning with a fixed idea that the work was essentially a second century composition, and never relying on its evidence as trustworthy for first century conditions, I gradually came to find it a useful ally in some obscure and difficult investigations.[14]

In Ramsay's opinion, 'Luke's history is unsurpassed in respect of its trustworthiness',[15] and Ramsay summed up his evaluation of Luke's qualities as a historian in the following words:

Luke is a historian of the first rank; not merely are his statements of fact trustworthy; he is possessed of the true historic sense; he fixes his mind on the idea and plan that rules in the evolution of history, and proportions the scale of his treatment to the importance of each incident. He seizes the important and critical events and shows their true nature at greater length, while he touches lightly or omits entirely much that was valueless for his purpose. In short, this author should be placed along with the very greatest of historians.[16]

Not every scholar will be in complete accord with Ramsay's conclusions, but there is a growing consensus of opinion among scholars who are not prejudiced in advance (as Baur was) against the historicity of Acts, that in this book there is a great deal of accurate historical detail. And if the Lucan record is trustworthy in small historical details, the probability of it being an accurate if not exhaustive account of the history of the early Church is greatly increased. F. F. Bruce highlighted this point when he wrote:

Now, all these evidences of accuracy are not accidental. A man whose accuracy can be demonstrated in matters where we are able to test it is likely to be accurate even when the means for testing him are not available. Accuracy is a habit of mind, and we know from happy (or unhappy) experience that some people are habitually accurate just as others can be depended upon to be inaccurate. Luke's record entitles him to be regarded as a writer of habitual accuracy.[17]

[14] *St. Paul the Traveller and Roman Citizen* (London, 1895), pp. 7–8.
[15] *The Bearing of Recent Discovery on the Trustworthiness of the New Testament* (London, 1920), p. 81; quoted Bruce, op. cit., p. 90.
[16] Ibid., p. 222; quoted Bruce, op. cit., p. 91.
[17] Bruce, op. cit., p. 90.

2. *The Authorship of Revelation*

To accept the book of Revelation as Johannine was really quite a concession to the traditional viewpoint, although Baur accepted its apostolic authorship only because it fitted in with his historical framework. For Baur required as many props to support his historical perspective as he could find and he believed that the Apocalypse provided this supporting evidence. If twelve apostles were mentioned (although not by name), then Baur thought himself justified in assuming that John had intended to exclude Paul from the apostolic corpus. The condemnation of the Nicolaitans, according to Baur, was a veiled allusion to the Paulinists, and the testing of false apostles a direct reference to Paul himself. That there was absolutely no sound basis for these suppositions will be scarcely disputed.

3. *The Gospel of John*

This was a key point in Baur's scheme. Because Baur found in the Gospel no trace of the conflict between Pauline and Jewish Christianity, he reckoned it among the conciliatory writings and dated it late in the second century. This hypothesis has been completely overthrown by the finding of a papyrus fragment of the Gospel dating back to about A.D. 130. And as the fragment was found in a remote Egyptian area, there are good grounds for assuming that by this date the Gospel was widely known and that its composition is to be dated even earlier. With this find another cornerstone in Baur's historical framework was removed, demonstrating how unreliable Baur's judgement had been and how fragile his whole tendency approach.

4. *The Ignatian Letters*

The Ignatian Letters were so important in Baur's framework because, were they authentic, then they provided not only a fixed historical date, but also an insight into the situation within the Church during the first two decades of the second century. The letters revealed absolutely no trace of any conflict between Pauline and Jewish-Christian parties; all is at peace—even at Rome. But according to Baur the conflict was raging unabated. If, therefore, the letters were genuine it meant that the ground would be almost completely pulled away from under Baur's total-view. It was an extremely crucial point. Baur was thus compelled to prove that the letters were unauthentic and composed much later in the second century. He therefore set himself with all his powers to demonstrate their unhistorical nature. But his arguments were weak and after his death were demolished by the brilliant work of Theodor Zahn in Germany and J. B. Lightfoot in England. Both established independently of each other the authenticity of the seven letters—a verdict, afterwards, never seriously questioned by any patristic scholar.

What Baur desired was a total-view of history and in particular of the history of the Christian Church. In this desire he was right. Any view of early Church history must be a total-view based on clear historical facts into which the unclear pieces of history are fitted. The tragedy was that Baur chose the wrong total-view and then spent the rest of his lifetime distorting the evidence in order to maintain it. The problem which still confronts the investigation of the historical sources of Christianity is to set forth a total-view which takes full account of its dogmatic premises. For if we learn anything from the procedure of the Tübingen School it is this: that *Biblical exegesis and interpretation without conscious or unconscious dogmatic presuppositions is impossible.* The interpretation of the Bible and Biblical history demands an open, unconcealed, and honest statement of the fundamental historical principles by which it is to be interpreted. The validity of all Biblical exegesis and interpretation rests upon its readiness to set forth clearly and unflinchingly the dogmatic presuppositions on which it is based.

Bibliography

FERDINAND CHRISTIAN BAUR

I. Letters and Manuscripts

THE following is a complete list of all known letters to and from Baur. Unless otherwise stated all letters in the UBT are found under the *Signatur* Md 750.

A. Letters from Baur to:

Academic Senate of the Tübingen University	2 letter(s)	1852	UAT
Bauer, Ludwig Amandus	2 ,,	1822, and without date	SMM
Baur, Albert (Baur's son)	38 ,,	1858–60	UBT
——, Caroline (Baur's sister)	1 ,,	1854	UBT
——, Friedrich August (Baur's brother)	64 ,,	1823–55	UBT
	1 ,,	1860	SBB
——, Pauline (Baur's daughter)	1 ,,	1859	SBB
Becher, Emilie (Baur's fiancée)	1 ,,	1820/1	UBT
——, (Emilie's father) (Baur's proposal of marriage to Emilie; the draft of the letter is also there)	1 ,,	1820	UBT
Elwert, Eduard	1 ,,	1838	ZBZ
Fischer, Adolf	1 ,,	1854 (Md 750 c)	UBT
Fischer, Kuno	1 ,,	1857	UBH
Gaupp, Louise (Baur's sister)	1 ,,	1854	UBT
Grüneisen, Karl von	2 ,,	1833–4	SMM
Heyd, Ludwig Friedrich Copies by Zeller of 30 letters are found under the *Signatur* Md 750. II. 6	32 ,,	1824–42 (Md 619 r)	UBT
Hilgenfeld, Adolf	90 ,,	1847–60	HN
Keller, Adelbert	2 ,,	1858–60 (Md 760[2] 34)	UBT
Märklin, Christian	13 ,,	1837–47	SMM
Mohl, Robert von	1 ,,	1847	SBB

Planck, Karl Christian	3 letter(s)	1848–57	WLS
Rector of the Tübingen University	1 ,,	1842 (Mi II 53)	UBT
Reuss, Jeremias Friedrich (Ephorus at Blaubeuren)	1 ,,	1839	SMM
Schlayer, J. von. (Württemberg Minister of Internal Affairs)	1 ,,	1839 (Md 750 V.4)	UBT
Schwegler, Albert	2 ,,	1853 (Md 753)	UBT
Schweizer, Alexander	20 ,,	1845–59	ZBZ
Strauss, D. F.	3 ,,	1837–42	UBT
Teuffel, W. S.	1 ,,	1859	SMM
Tholuck, August	1 ,,	1836 (draft)	UBT
Ullmann, Karl	11 ,,	1832–8	UBH
Vischer, F. T.	9 ,,	1855–60 (Md 787.51)	UBT
——, Robert (Son of F. T.)	1 ,,	1853 (Md 788.13)	UBT
Zeller, Albert (Son of Eduard)	1 ,,	1859 (Md 747.19)	UBT
——, Eduard	162 ,,	1847–60 (Md 747.19)	UBT
——, Emilie	5 ,,	1856–7 (Md 747.19)	UBT

4 letters to unknown recipients (1834–53) are located in the SMM.

B. Letters to Baur from (All letters under the *Signatur* Md 750, I):

1. Bauer, Bruno	1 letter(s)	1836
2. Baur, Albert	1 ,,	1858
3. Biedermann, A. E. (Prof. of Theology in Zürich)	1 ,,	1860
4. Creuzer, G. F. (Prof. of Philology in Heidelberg)	3 ,,	1823–5
5. Elwert, Eduard	8 ,,	1835–6
6. Ewald, Heinrich	1 ,,	1844
7. Grüneisen, Karl von (Court preacher in Stuttgart)	1 ,,	1834
8. Hasert, Fr. R. (Pastor in Switzerland)	1 ,,	1850
9. Heyd, L. F. (Pastor in Markgröningen)	3 ,,	1833–8
10. Lipsius, R. A. (Prof. of Theology in Leipzig, Kiel, and Jena)	5 ,,	1859–60
11. Märklin, Christian	2 ,,	1846

12. Mohl, Robert von (Prof. of law in Tübingen
and Heidelberg; related to Baur by marriage) 17 letter(s) 1847–60
13. Moser, G. H. (School-inspector)   1   ,,   1836
14. Neander, August   1   ,,   1832
15. Orelli, J. K. von (Prof. of Philology in
Zürich)   1   ,,   1836
16. Osiander, C. N. (Stuttgart schoolmaster)   1   ,,   1826
17. Ritschl, Albrecht   1   ,,   1852
18. Schweizer, Alexander (Prof. of Theology in
Zürich)   1   ,,   1853
19. Strauss, D. F.   20   ,,   1835–60
20. Ullmann, Karl (Prof. of Theology in Halle
and Heidelberg)   1   ,,   1838
21. Volkmar, Gustav   1   ,,   1859
22. Wurm, J. F. (Wurm wrote against Strauss's
Life of Jesus)   1   ,,   1836

A few of the letters have been published in part or in whole in the following sources:

The Strauss–Baur correspondence was published in full with comprehensive footnotes by Ernst Barnikol, 'Der Briefwechsel zwischen Strauss und Baur', *ZKG*, LXXIII (1962), pp. 74–125.

Correspondence between Baur, Strauss, and Zeller is found in Wilhelm Lang, 'Ferdinand Baur und David Friedrich Strauss' (loc. cit.); Ernst Barnikol, 'Das ideengeschichtliche Erbe Hegels bei und seit Strauss und Baur im 19. Jahrhundert' (loc. cit.); Adolf Rapp, 'Baur und Strauss in ihrer Stellung zueinander und zum Christentum' (loc. cit.).

The most detailed evaluation of this correspondence in English is contained in my *David Friedrich Strauss and his Theology* (Cambridge, 1973).

Baur's letter to his brother on Schleiermacher's theology was edited by Heinz Liebing and published in the *ZTK*, LIV (1957), pp. 225–43.

Nineteen letters from Baur to Hilgenfeld are printed in whole or in part by Helmut Pölcher in his dissertation (see under Hilgenfeld).

Baur's letter to Tholuck is printed in my article 'Die Verhandlungen über die Berufung Ferdinand Christian Baurs nach Berlin und Halle', *ZKG*, LXXXIV (1973), pp. 233–48.

Two letters to Ludwig Amandus Bauer are printed by Carl Hester in his 'Gedanken zu Ferdinand Christian Baurs Entwicklung als Historiker anhand zweier unbekannter Briefe', *ZKG*, LXXXIV (1973), pp. 264–9.

An extract from Baur's letter to Schlayer, one letter from Baur to F. T. Vischer (1857), and two letters from Lipsius to Baur (1859–60) were edited by Klaus Schuffels and printed in *BWKG*, 1968/9, pp. 385–408.

The sermon preached by Baur at the wedding of his daughter Emilie to Eduard Zeller is printed in Barnikol, *Ferdinand Christian Baur als rationalistisch-kirchlicher Theologe.*

C. Other material in the Baur *Nachlass* (Md 750) includes:
   III. 8 seminary addresses 1817–54.
   IV. 6 sermons 1813–57.
   V. 4 Gutachten und Voten; 1 letter to J. von Schlayer (1839).
   VI. Poem for the silver wedding aniversary of Baur's sister.
   VII. Manuscript 'Seneca und Paulus'.
   VIII. Seminary certificates and a poem (1816).
   IX. Particulars about Baur's father, Christian Jacob Baur.
   X. Letter from Friedrich August Baur to Eduard Zeller (1861).
   XI. Miscellaneous notes.

D. Sermons and Manuscripts
   8 sermons (1813–26) are found under the *Signatur* Mh 970. 221 sermons preached in the Tübingen Stiftskirche (1826–48) are located in Mh 969. Other manuscripts, lectures from Baur's own hand and others written down by his pupils, are found under the *Signatur* Mh II, 154–66. A detailed oversight of this material is given by Klaus Schuffels, 'Der Nachlass Ferdinand Christian Baurs in der Universitätsbibliothek Tübingen und im Schiller-Nationalmuseum Marbach/Neckar', *ZKG*, LXXIX (1968), pp. 375–84.

II. Published Writings

The following is a complete list of all Baur's published writings arranged in chronological order.
   1818. Review article: G. P. C. Kaiser, *Die biblische Theologie* . . . Bengel's *Archiv für die Theologie und ihre neueste Literatur*, II: 3 (1818), pp. 656–717.
   1824. *Symbolik und Mythologie oder die Naturreligion des Alterthums* (2 vols.; Stuttgart, 1824–5).
   1827. *Primae Rationalismi et Supranaturalismi historiae capita potiora*
       Pars I. *De Gnosticorum Christianismo ideali.* Dissertatio inauguralis historico-theologica, quam Deo juvante Munus Professoris Theologiae Evangelicae Ordinarii (Tubingae, 1827).
       Pars II. *Comparatur Gnosticismus cum Schleiermacherianae theologiae indole* (Tubingae, 1827).
       Pars III. *Exponitur praesertim Arianismi indoles rationalis* (Tubingae, 1828).

1828. 'Anzeige der beiden academischen Schriften von Dr. F. C. Baur: *Primae Rationalismi et Supranaturalismi historiae capita potiora*' (Pars I and II), *TZT*, 1828: I, pp. 220–64.

Review: C. F. Schnurrer, *Universitatis litterarum Tubingensis nuper Cancellarii*. *TZT*, 1828: II, pp. 277–93.

Review: C. Otfried Müller, *Prolegomena zu einer wissenschaftlichen Mythologie*. *Jahrbücher für Philologie und Pädagogik*, VI (1828), pp. 3–30.

1829. *De orationis habitae a Stephano Acta Cap. VII consilio* (Tubingae, 1829).

1830. 'Über den wahren Begriff γλώσσαις λαλεῖν, mit Rücksicht auf die neuesten Untersuchungen hierüber', *TZT*, 1830: II, pp. 75–133.

'Predigt zur Vorbereitung auf das Säcularfest der Übergabe der Augsburgischen Confession . . .', *Feier des dritten Säkularfestes der Übergabe der Augsburgischen Confession auf der Universität Tübingen* (Tübingen, 1830), pp. 93–101.

1831. *Das manichäische Religionssystem nach den Quellen neu untersucht und entwikelt* (Tübingen, 1831); new edition (Hildesheim, 1973).

De Ebionitarum origine et doctrina, ab Essenis repetenda (Tubingae, 1831).

'In Andreae Osiandri de justificatione doctrinam', in *Epistola Gratulatoria ad D. Theophilum Jakobum Planck* (Tubingae, 1831).

'Die Christuspartei in der korinthischen Gemeinde, der Gegensatz des petrinischen und paulinischen Christenthums in der ältesten Kirche, der Apostel Petrus in Rom', *TZT*, 1831: IV, pp. 61–206. Republished in *AW*, I.

1832. 'Über die ursprüngliche Bedeutung des Passahfestes und des Beschneidungsritus', *TZT*, 1832: I, pp. 40–124.

'Der hebräische Sabbat und die Nationalfeste des mosaischen Kultus', *TZT*, 1832: III, pp. 125–92.

'Apollonius von Tyana und Christus, oder das Verhältniss des Pythagoräismus zum Christenthum. Ein Beitrag zur Religionsgeschichte der ersten Jahrhunderte nach Christus', *TZT*, 1832: IV, pp. 3–235. Republished in *Drei Abhandlungen*, 1876; new edition (Hildesheim, 1966).

1833. 'Der Gegensatz des Katholicismus und Protestantismus nach den Principien und Hauptdogmen der beiden Lehrbegriffe. Mit besonderer Rücksicht auf Herrn Dr. Möhler's *Symbolik*', *TZT*, 1833: III, IV, pp. 1–438. Published separately as a book in 1834; reprinted in 1836 *mit einer Übersicht über die neuesten, auf die Symbolik beziehenden Kontroversen*.

1834. *Erwiderung auf Herrn Dr. Möhlers neueste Polemik gegen die protestantische Lehre und Kirche* (Tübingen, 1834).

Comparatur Eusebius Caesariensus historie ecclesiasticae parens cum parente historiarum Herodoto Halicarnassensi (Tubingae, 1834).

Review article: Bretschneider, *Grundlagen des evangelischen Pietismus. JWK,* 1834: I, pp. 513–55.

Review: Lentzen, *De Pelagianorum doctrinae principiis.* Wiggers, *Versuch einer pragmatischen Darstellung des Semipelagianismus. JWK,* 1834: II, pp. 897–931.

1835. Review: Dähne, *Geschichtliche Darstellung der jüdisch-alexandrinischen Religionsphilosophie. JWK,* 1835: II, pp. 737–92.

'Vorrede' to Mac Crie, *Geschichte der Ausbreitung und Unterdrückung der Reformation in Spanien im 16. Jahrhunderte* (Stuttgart, 1835).

Die christliche Gnosis oder die christliche Religionsphilosophie in ihrer geschichtlichen Entwiklung (Tübingen, 1835); new edition Darmstadt, 1967).

Die sogenannten Pastoralbriefe des Apostels Paulus aufs neue kritisch untersucht (Stuttgart and Tübingen, 1835).

1836. 'Über Zweck und Veranlassung des Römerbriefs und die damit zusammenhängenden Verhältnisse der römischen Gemeinde. Eine historisch-kritische Untersuchung', *TZT,* 1836: III, pp.59–178. Reprinted in *AW,* I.

'Abgenöthigte Erklärung gegen einen Artikel der Evangelischen Kirchenzeitung, herausgegeben von D. E. W. Hengstenberg, Prof. der Theol. an der Universität zu Berlin. Mai 1836', *TZT,* 1836: III, pp. 179–232. Also printed separately in 1836 and republished in *AW,* I.

'Einige weitere Bemerkungen über die Christuspartei in Korinth', *TZT,* 1836: IV, pp. 3–32.

Review: Augusti, *Lehrbuch der christlichen Dogmengeschichte. JWK,* 1836: I, pp. 227–40.

Review: Münscher, *Lehrbuch der christlichen Dogmengeschichte. JWK,* 1836: I, pp. 753–72.

1837. Review: Heigl, *Der Bericht des Porphyrios über Origenes.* Lommatzsch, *Origenis opera omnia.* Schnitzer, *Origenes über die Grundlehre . . . JWK,* 1837: I, pp. 652–86.

'Über den Begriff der christlichen Religions-Philosophie, ihren Ursprung und ihre ersten Formen', *Zeitschrift für spekulative Theologie* (ed. Bruno Bauer), 1837, pp. 354–402.

'Kritische Studien über den Begriff der Gnosis', *TSK,* 1837, pp. 511–79.

'Der Prophet Jonas, ein assyrisch-babylonisches Symbol', *Zeitschrift für die historische Theologie,* 1837: I, pp. 88–114.

'Das Christliche des Platonismus oder Sokrates und Christus',

TZT, 1837: III, pp. 1–154. Published separately in 1837 and republished in *Drei Abhandlungen*, 1876.

1838. 'Über den Ursprung des Episcopats in der christlichen Kirche. Prüfung der neuesten von Hrn. Dr. Rothe hierüber aufgestellten Ansicht', *TZT*, 1838: III, pp. 1–185. Reprinted in *AW*, III.

Review: Rothe, *Die Anfänge der christlichen Kirche*. *JWK*, 1838: I, pp. 416–48.

'Kritische Übersicht über die neuesten, das γλώσσαις λαλεῖν in der ersten christlichen Kirche betreffenden Untersuchungen', *TSK*, 1838, pp. 618–702.

Die christliche Lehre von der Versöhnung in ihrer geschichtlichen Entwicklung von der ältesten Zeit bis auf die neueste (Tübingen, 1838).

1839. 'Tertullians Lehre vom Abendmahl, und Herr Dr. Rudelbach, nebst einer Übersicht über die Hauptmomente der Geschichte der Lehre vom Abendmahl', *TZT*, 1839: II, pp. 56–144.

Review article: C. H. Weisse, *Die evangelische Geschichte* . . . *JWK*, 1839: I, pp. 161–99; 585–621.

Review: Twesten, *Vorlesungen über die Dogmatik der evangelisch-lutherischen Kirche*. *JWK*, 1839: II, pp. 73–108.

Review: Schenkel, *De ecclesia Corinthia primaeva factionibus turbata*. *JWK*, 1839: II, pp. 702–19.

1841. Review: Matthies, *Erklärung der Pastoralbriefe*. *JWK*, 1841: I, pp. 93–117.

Review: Schneckenburger, *Über den Zweck der Apostelgeschichte*. *JWK*, 1841: I, pp. 361–81.

'Über die geschichtliche Bedeutung der fünfundzwanzig Jahre 1816–1841'. Rede zur Feier des Gedächtnisses der fünfundzwanzigjährigen Regierung seiner Majestät des Königs Wilhelm von Württemberg am 31. Oktober 1841 auf der Universität zu Tübingen. *Gratulationsschrift des Gymnasiums zu Tübingen für die vierte Säcularfeier der Universität Tübingen, 9–11 August 1877* (Tübingen, 1877).

Die christliche Lehre von der Dreieinigkeit und Menschwerdung Gottes in ihrer geschichtlichen Entwicklung.

Vol. I: *Das Dogma der alten Kirche bis zur Synode von Chalcedon* (Tübingen, 1841).

Vol. II: *Das Dogma des Mittelalters* (Tübingen, 1843).

Vol. III: *Die neuere Geschichte des Dogma, von der Reformation bis in die neuesten Zeit* (Tübingen, 1843).

1842. *Worte der Erinnerung an Friedrich Heinrich Kern* (Tübingen, 1842).

Review: G. F. Frank, *Anselm von Canterbury*. *TJ*, 1842, pp. 556–74.

1843. Review: H. Martensen, *Meister Eckart*. *TJ*, 1843, pp. 146–53.

1844. 'Über die Composition und den Charakter des johanneischen Evangeliums', *TJ*, 1844, pp. 1–191; 397–475; 615–700.
Review: A. Schliemann, *Die Clementinen* ... *TJ*, 1844, pp. 536–85.

1845. Review: Köllner, *Symbolik der heiligen apostolischen katholischen römischen Kirche*. Buchmann, *Populärsymbolik*. *TJ*, 1845, pp. 120–45.
Review: Wilken, *Andreas Osianders Leben, Lehre und Schriften*. *TJ*, 1845, pp. 371–6.
'Kritische Beiträge zur Kirchengeschichte der ersten Jahrhunderte, mit besonderer Rücksicht auf die Werke von Neander und Gieseler', *TJ*, 1845, pp. 207–314.
Paulus, der Apostel Jesu Christi. Sein Leben und Wirken, seine Briefe und seine Lehre (Stuttgart, 1845); 2nd ed. 1866–7; reprinted (Osnabrück, 1968). E. T. *Paul, the Apostle of Jesus Christ, His Life and Work, His Epistles and His Doctrine* (2 vols.; London and Edinburgh, 1875; 2nd ed. 1876).

1846. 'Der Begriff der christlichen Philosophie und die Hauptmomente ihrer Entwicklung mit Rücksicht auf Ritters Geschichte der christlichen Philosophie', *TJ*, 1846, pp. 29–115; 183–233.
Der Kritiker und der Fanatiker in der Person des Herrn Heinrich W. J. Thiersch. Zur Charakteristik der neuesten Theologie (Stuttgart, 1846).
'Der Ursprung und Charakter des Lukasevangeliums, mit Rücksicht auf die neuesten Untersuchungen', *TJ*, 1846, pp. 453–615.

1847. 'Bemerkungen zur johanneischen Frage, besonders in betreff des Todestages Jesu und der Passahfeier der ältesten Kirche. Gegen Herrn Dr. Bleek', *TJ*, 1847, pp. 89–136.
'Über Prinzip u. Charakter des Lehrbegriffs der reformierten Kirche, in seinem Unterschied von der lutherischen, mit Rücksicht auf Schweizers Darstellung der reformierten Glaubenslehre', *TJ*, 1847, pp. 309–89.
'Kritische Studien über das Wesen des Protestantismus. I. Der deutsche Protestantismus von einem deutschen Theologen', *TJ*, 1847, pp. 506–81.
Kritische Untersuchungen über die kanonischen Evangelien, ihr Verhältnis zu einander, ihren Charakter und Ursprung (Tübingen, 1847).
Lehrbuch der christlichen Dogmengeschichte (Stuttgart, 1847; 2nd ed., Tübingen, 1858; 3rd ed., Leipzig, 1867; new ed., Darmstadt, 1968).

1848. 'Über den Charakter und die geschichtliche Bedeutung des calixtinischen Synkretismus', *TJ*, 1848, pp. 163–97.

'Das johanneische Evangelium und die Passahfeier des zweiten Jahrhunderts. Gegen Weitzel', *TJ*, 1848, pp. 264–86.

'Die johanneischen Briefe. Ein Beitrag zur Geschichte des Kanons', *TJ*, 1848, pp. 293–337.

Die ignatianischen Briefe und ihr neuester Kritiker. Eine Streitschrift gegen Herrn Bunsen (Tübingen, 1848).

'Die evangelisch-theologische Fakultät vom Jahr 1777 bis 1812', and 'Die evangelisch-theologische Fakultät vom Jahr 1812 bis 1848', in *Geschichte und Beschreibung der Universität Tübingen* (ed. K. Klüpfel; Tübingen, 1849), pp. 216–47; 389–426.

'Noch ein Wort über das Prinzip des reformierten Lehrbegriffs', *TJ*, 1848, pp. 419–43.

'Zur Geschichte der protestantischen Mystik; die neueste Litteratur derselben', Part I, *TJ*, 1848, pp. 453–528.

1849. Part II, *TJ*, 1849, pp. 85–143.

'Zur neutestamentlichen Kritik. Übersicht über die neuesten Erscheinungen auf ihrem Gebiet', *TJ*, 1849, pp. 299–370; 455–534.

1850. 'Beiträge zur Erklärung der Korintherbriefe', Part I, *TJ*, 1850, pp. 139–85.

'Die Einleitung in das neue Testament als theologische Wissenschaft. Ihr Begriff und ihre Aufgabe, ihr Entwicklungsgang und ihr innerer Organismus', Part I, *TJ*, 1850, pp. 463–566.

1851. Part II, *TJ*, 1851, pp. 70–94; 222–53; 291–329.

'Das Wesen des Montanismus nach den neuesten Forschungen', *TJ*, 1851, pp. 538–94.

'Ehrenrettung Calvins gegen eine katholische Verunglimpfung', *TJ*, 1851, pp. 595–8.

Das Markusevangelium nach seinem Ursprung und Charakter. Nebst einem Anhang über das Evangelium Marcions (Tübingen, 1851).

1852. 'Beiträge zur Erklärung der Korintherbriefe', Part II, *TJ*, 1852, pp. 1–40; 535–74.

'Über Phil. 2, 6 ff.', *TJ*, 1852, pp. 133–44.

'Kritik der neuesten Erklärung der Apokalypse', *TJ*, 1852, pp. 305–400; 441–69.

Die Epochen der kirchlichen Geschichtsschreibung (Tübingen, 1852). Republished in *AW*, II. E. T. *Ferdinand Christian Baur on the Writing of Church History* (ed. Hodgson; New York, 1968).

1853. *Das Christenthum und die christliche Kirche der drei ersten Jahrhunderte* (Tübingen, 1853; 2nd ed., 1860; 3rd ed., published under the title: *Kirchengeschichte der drei ersten Jahrhunderte*, 1863 = *Geschichte der Christlichen Kirche*, Vol. I. Republished in *AW*,

III. E. T. *The Church History of the First Three Centuries* (2 vols.; London and Edinburgh, 1878–9).

'Rückblick auf die neuesten Untersuchungen über das Markusevangelium', *TJ*, 1853, pp. 54–93.

'Über die Philosophumena Origenis, insbesondere ihren Verfasser', *TJ*, 1853, pp. 152–61.

'Die Hippolytus-Hypothese des Herrn Ritter Bunsen', *TJ*, 1853, pp. 428–42.

1854. 'Die johanneische Frage und ihre neuesten Bearbeitungen', *TJ*, 1854, pp. 196–287.

'Caius und Hippolytus. Mit Rücksicht auf Döllinger, Hippolytus und Calixtus', *TJ*, 1854, pp. 330–66.

1855. 'Das Prinzip des Protestantismus und seine geschichtliche Entwicklung, mit Rücksicht auf die neuesten Werke von Schenkel, Schweizer, Heppe, und die neuesten Verhandlungen über die Unionsfrage', *TJ*, 1855, pp. 1–137.

'Die beiden Briefe an die Thessalonicher, ihre Echtheit und Bedeutung für die Lehre von der Parusie Christi', *TJ*, 1855, pp. 141–68.

'Die reichsgeschichtliche Auffassung der Apokalypse', *TJ*, 1855, pp. 283–314.

'Über die Stelle Jak. 4, 5', *TJ*, 1855, pp. 573–6.

An Herrn Dr. Karl Hase. Beantwortung des Sendschreibens 'Die Tübinger Schule' (Tübingen, 1855).

1856. 'Das System des Gnostikers Basilides und die neuesten Auffassungen desselben', *TJ*, 1856, pp. 121–62.

'Der erste petrinische Brief, mit besonderer Beziehung auf das Werk: "Der petrinische Lehrbegriff... von Dr. B. Weiss"', *TJ*, 1856, pp. 193–240.

1857. 'Über Zweck und Gedankengang des Römerbriefs nebst der Erörterung einiger paulinischer Begriffe, mit besonderer Rücksicht auf die Kommentare von Tholuck und Philippi', *TJ*, 1857, pp. 60–108; 184–209.

'Zur johanneischen Frage: 1. über Justin d. Märt., gegen Luthardt; 2. über den Passahstreit, gegen Steitz', *TJ*, 1857, pp. 209–57.

'Das Verhältnis des ersten johanneischen Briefs zum johanneischen Evangelium', *TJ*, 1857, pp. 315–31.

'Die Lehre vom Abendmahl, nach Dr. Rückert: Das Abendmahl... 1856', *TJ*, 1857, pp. 533–76.

1858. 'Bemerkungen über die Bedeutung des Wortes Κανών', *ZWT*, 1858, pp. 141–50.

'Seneca und Paulus, das Verhältnis des Stoizismus zum Christentum nach den Schriften Senecas', *ZWT*, 1858, pp. 161–246; 441–70.

'Entgegnung gegen Herrn Dr. G. E. Steitz über den Paschastreit der alten Kirche', *ZWT*, 1858, pp. 298–312.

1859. 'Die Lehre des Apostels Paulus vom erlösenden Tode Christi, mit Rücksicht auf Dr. Schweizers Abhandlung in den Theol. Stud. u. Krit. 1858', *ZWT*, 1859, pp. 225–51.

'Kritisch-exegetische Bemerkungen über einige Stellen der Evangelien, namentlich des Markusevangeliums', *ZWT*, 1859, pp. 364–81.

Die Tübinger Schule und ihre Stellung zur Gegenwart (Tübingen, 1859; 2nd ed., 1860).

Die christliche Kirche von Anfang des vierten bis zum Ende des sechsten Jahrhunderts in den Hauptmomenten ihrer Entwicklung (Tübingen, 1859; 2nd ed., 1863 = *Geschichte der christlichen Kirche*, vol. II).

1860. 'Die Bedeutung des Ausdrucks: ὁ υἱὸς τοῦ ἀνθρώπου', *ZWT*, 1860, pp. 274–92.

1861. *Die christliche Kirche des Mittelalters in den Hauptmomenten ihrer Entwicklung* (ed. F. F. Baur; Tübingen, 1861; 2nd ed., 1869 = *Geschichte der christlichen Kirche*, vol. III).

1862. *Kirchengeschichte des neunzehnten Jahrhunderts* (ed. E. Zeller; Tübingen, 1862; 2nd ed., 1877 = *Geschichte der christlichen Kirche*, vol. V). Republished in *AW*, IV.

1863. *Kirchengeschichte der neueren Zeit, von der Reformation bis zum Ende des achtzehnten Jahrhunderts* (ed. F. F. Baur; Tübingen, 1863 = *Geschichte der christlichen Kirche*, vol. IV).

1864. *Vorlesungen über neutestamentliche Theologie* (ed. F. F. Baur; Leipzig, 1864); new edition with an introduction by W. G. Kümmel (Darmstadt, 1973).

1865. *Vorlesungen über die christliche Dogmengeschichte*, ed. F. F. Baur. Vol. I/1: *Das Dogma der alten Kirche von der apostolischen Zeit bis zur Synode in Nicäa* (Leipzig, 1865).

1866. Vol. I/2: *Das Dogma der alten Kirche von der Synode in Nicäa bis zum Ende des sechsten Jahrhunderts* (Leipzig, 1866).

Vol. II: *Das Dogma des Mittelalters* (Leipzig, 1866).

1867. Vol. III: *Das Dogma der neueren Zeit* (Leipzig, 1867).

1963. Ausgewälte Werke in Einzelausgaben (ed. Klaus Scholder; Stuttgart-Bad Cannstatt, 1963–70).

Vol. I. *Historisch-kritische Untersuchungen zum Neuen Testament*. Introduction by Ernst Käsemann, 1963.

   1. 'Die Christuspartei in der korinthischen Gemeinde...' (1831), pp. 1–146.

2. 'Über Zweck und Veranlassung des Römerbriefs' (1836), pp. 147–266.
3. 'Abgenötigte Erklärung' (1836), pp. 267–320.
4. 'Über den Ursprung des Episkopats in der christlichen Kirche' (1838), pp. 321–505.
Vol. II. *Die Epochen der kirchlichen Geschichtschreibung* (1852). Introduction by Ernst Wolf, 1963.
Vol. III. *Das Christenthum und die christliche Kirche der drei ersten Jahrhunderte* (2nd ed., 1860). Introduction by Ulrich Wickert, 1966.
Vol. IV. *Kirchengeschichte des neunzehnten Jahrhunderts* (1862). Introduction by Heinz Liebing, 1970.
Vol. V. *Für und wider die Tübingen Schule*, Introduction by Klaus Scholder (forthcoming).
1969. Geschichte der christlichen Kirche (5 vols; Leipzig, 1969).

III. Secondary Literature

BARNIKOL, ERNST. 'Das ideengeschichtliche Erbe Hegels bei und seit Strauss und Baur im 19. Jahrhundert', *Wissenschaftliche Zeitschrift der Martin-Luther-Universität Halle-Wittenberg*, Gesellschafts- und sprachwissenschaftliche Reihe, X: I (1961), pp. 281–328.
——. *Ferdinand Christian Baur als rationalistisch-kirchlicher Theologe* (Berlin, 1970).
BARTH, KARL. *Die protestantische Theologie im 19. Jahrhundert* (Zürich, 1947). E.T. *Protestant Theology in the Nineteenth Century* (London, 1972).
BAUER, KARL. 'Ferdinand Christian Baur als Kirchenhistoriker', *Blätter für württembergische Kirchengeschichte*, N. F. XXV (1921), pp. 1–38; XXVI (1922), pp. 1–60.
——. 'Zur Jugendgeschichte von Ferdinand Christian Baur (1805–1807)', *TSK*, XCV (1923/4), pp. 303–13.
BAUR, AUGUST. 'Ferdinand Christian Baur', *PK*, XXXIX (1892), pp. 661–7; 691–9.
FRAEDRICH, G. *Ferdinand Christian Baur: der Begründer der Tübinger Schule als Theologe, Schriftsteller und Charakter* (Gotha, 1909).
GEIGER, WOLFGANG. *Spekulation und Kritik: Die Geschichtstheologie Ferdinand Christian Baurs* (Munich, 1964).
HARRIS, HORTON. *David Friedrich Strauss and his Theology* (Cambridge, 1973).
——. 'Die Verhandlungen über die Berufung Ferdinand Christian Baurs nach Berlin und Halle', *ZKG*, LXXXIV (1973), pp. 233–48.
HERINGA, S. P. *Ferdinand Christian Baur. Volledig en kritiesch overzicht van zijn werkzaamheid op theologiesch gebied* (Haarlem, 1869).
HESTER, CARL. 'Gedanken zu Ferdinand Christian Baurs Entwicklung

als Historiker anhand zweier unbekannter Briefe', *ZKG*, LXXXIV (1973), pp. 249–69.

HILGENFELD, A. 'Ferdinand Christian Baur nach seiner wissenschaftlichen Entwickelung und Bedeutung', *ZWT*, XXXVI (1893), pp. 222–44.

HODGSON, P. C. *The Formation of Historical Theology: A Study of Ferdinand Christian Baur* (New York, 1966).

——. *Ferdinand Christian Baur on the Writing of Church History*, edited and translated by Peter C. Hodgson (New York, 1968).

KÖSTLIN, JULIUS. Review: *Vorlesungen über neutestamentliche Theologie*, *TSK*, 1866, pp. 719-68.

LANDERER, M. A. 'Rede bei der akademischen Gedächtnisfeier in der Aula zu Tübingen, 7 February 1861', in *Worte der Erinnerung an Ferdinand Christian von Baur* (Tübingen, 1861), pp. 32–83.

LANG, WILHELM. 'Ferdinand Baur und David Friedrich Strauss', *PJ*, CLX (1915), pp. 474–504; CLXI (1915), pp. 123–44.

LIEBING, H. 'Ferdinand Christian Baurs Kritik an Schleiermachers Glaubenslehre', *ZTK*, LIV (1957), pp. 225–43.

——. 'Historisch-kritische Theologie: zum 100. Todestag Ferdinand Christian Baurs am 2. Dezember 1960', *ZTK*, LVII (1960), pp. 302–17.

PENZEL, K. 'Will the Real Ferdinand Christian Baur Please Stand Up?', *Journal of Religion*, XLVIII (1968), pp. 310–23.

PFLEIDERER, O. *The Development of Theology in Germany Since Kant and Its Progress in Great Britain since 1825* (London, 1890).

——. 'Zu Ferdinand Christian Baurs Gedächtnis', *PK*, XXXIX (1892), pp. 565–73.

RAPP, ADOLF. 'Baur und Strauss in ihrer Stellung zueinander und zum Christentum', *BWKG*, 3. Folge LII (1952), pp. 95–149; LIII (1953), p. 157; LIV (1954), pp. 182–5.

SCHNEIDER, E. *Ferdinand Christian Baur in seiner Bedeutung für die Theologie* (Munich, 1909).

SCHOLDER, K. 'Albert Schweitzer und Ferdinand Christian Baur', in *Albert Schweitzer: Sein Denken und sein Weg*, ed. H. W. Bähr (Tübingen, 1962), pp. 184–92.

——. 'Ferdinand Christian Baur als Historiker', *Evangelische Theologie*, XXI (1961), pp. 435–58.

SEYERLEN, R. 'Ferdinand Christian Baur als akademischer Lehrer und Mensch', *ZWT*, XXXVI (1893), pp. 244–54.

Worte der Erinnerung an Ferdinand Christian Baur (Tübingen, 1861).

ZELLER, E. 'Ferdinand Christian Baur', *ADB*, II, pp. 172–9.

——. 'Ferdinand Christian Baur', *Vorträge und Abhandlungen geschichtlichen Inhalts*, 1st ed. (1865), I, pp. 354–434; 2nd ed. (1875), I, pp. 390–479.

EDUARD ZELLER

I. *Letters*

From Zeller to:

Baur, Ferdinand Christian	263 letters	1841–60.
Fischer, Kuno	71 ,,	1855–1904.
Haack, Adolf	3 ,,	1831–2.
Schwegler, Albert	23 ,,	1841–9.
Strauss, D. F.	42 ,,	1837–73.
Vatke, Wilhelm	15 ,,	1842–74.
Vischer, F. T.	25 ,,	1854–82.
Zeller, Gustav (brother)	276 ,,	1829–86.
—— (mother)	50 ,,	1831–50.
—— (parents)	33 ,,	1827–37.

All letters are found in the Universitätsbibliothek Tübingen under the *Signatur* Md 747; 6 letters from Zeller to Schwegler under Md 753. I.

II. *Writings*

A complete list of Zeller's writings is found in Edward Zeller's *kleine Schriften*, III (Berlin, 1911), pp. 518–58.

1841. Review: *Hegels Vorlesungen über die Philosophie der Religion. HJ*, February 1841, Nrs. 50–5.

1842. 'Die Annahme einer Perfektibilität des Christenthums historisch und dogmatisch untersucht', *TJ*, 1842, pp. 1–50.

'Über einige Fragen in Betreff der neutestamentlichen Christologie', *TJ*, 1842, pp. 51–101.

'Erinnerung an Schleiermachers Lehre von der Persönlichkeit Gottes', *TJ*, 1842, pp. 263–87.

'Einige weitere Beiträge zur Einleitung in die Apokalypse', *TJ*, 1842, pp. 654–717.

1844. 'Aphorismen über Christenthum, Urchristenthum und Unchristenthum', *JG*, 1844, pp. 491–528.

1845. 'Über das Wesen der Religion', *TJ*, 1845, pp. 26–75; 393–430.

Review: K. R. Köstlin, *Der Lehrbegriff des Evangeliums. TJ*, 1845, pp. 75–100.

'Die äußeren Zeugnisse über das Dasein und den Ursprung des vierten Evangeliums', *TJ*, 1845, pp. 579–656.

'Zur Charakteristik der modernen Bekehrungen', *JG*, 1845, pp. 14–32.

'Wanderbuch für Dr. H. Merz als Antwort auf seine Broschüre: "Die Jahrbücher der Gegenwart und ihre Helden"', *JG*, 1845, pp. 415–25.

1846. 'Die Theologie der Gegenwart und die theologischen Jahr-
bücher', *TJ*, 1846, pp. 1–28.
1847. 'Einige weitere Bemerkungen über die äußere Bezeugung des
vierten Evangeliums', *TJ*, 1847, pp. 136–74.
'Die Lehre des neuen Testaments vom Zustand nach dem
Tode', *TJ*, 1847, pp. 390–409.
1848. 'Die älteste Überlieferung über die Schriften des Lukas', *TJ*,
1848, pp. 528–73.
1854. *Die Apostelgeschichte nach ihrem Inhalt und Ursprung kritisch
untersucht* (Stuttgart, 1854). E. T. *The Contents and Origin of the
Acts of the Apostles, critically investigated* (2 vols.; London, 1875–
6).
1860. 'Die Tübinger historische Schule', *HZ*, IV (1860), pp. 90–173
(anonymous). Republished in *VA*, I, pp. 267–353; 2nd ed.,
pp. 294–389.
'Ferdinand Christian Baur', *PJ*, VII (1861), pp. 495–512;
VIII (1861), pp. 206–24; 283–314. Republished in *VA*, I,
pp. 354–434; 2nd ed., pp. 390–479.
1861. 'Die historische Kritik und das Wunder', *HZ*, VI (1861), pp.
356–73. Reprinted in *Kleine Schriften*, III, pp. 348–65.
'Ewald's neueste Äußerungen über Baur', *ZWT*, 1861, pp.
319–29.
1862. 'Zur Würdigung der Ritschl'schen "Erläuterungen"', *HZ*, VIII
(1862), pp. 100–116. Reprinted in *Kleine Schriften*, III, pp. 366–
84.
1865. *Vorträge und Abhandlungen*, I–II (Leipzig, 1865); 2nd ed., 1875/7;
Vol. III (Leipzig, 1884).
1910. *Kleine Schriften* (3 vols.; ed. Leuze; Berlin, 1910–11).

III. Secondary Literature

DIEHLS, H. 'Gedächtnisrede auf Eduard Zeller', in Zeller's *Kleine
Schriften*, III, pp. 465–511.
DILTHEY, W. 'Aus Eduard Zellers Jugendjahren', *Deutsche Rundschau*,
XC (1897), pp. 280–95. Also in Dithey's *Gesammelte Schriften*, IV,
pp. 433–50.
FELLER, R. *Die Universität Bern 1834–1934* (Bern and Leipzig, 1935).
LANG, WILHELM. 'Eduard Zeller: Erinnerungen', *Deutsche Rundschau*,
CXXXV (1908), pp. 173–91; alternatively pp. 186–204.
WIEGAND, FR. 'Eduard Zeller's Berufung nach Marburg und August
Vilmar', *HZ*, CV (3.F.9) (1910), pp. 285–95.
ZELLER, ED. *Erinnerungen eines Neunzigjährigen* (Stuttgart, 1904).
ZIEGLER, TH. 'Eduard Zeller', *Protestantische Monatshefte*, XII (1908),
pp. 203–14.

Pamphlets relating to Zeller's calling to Bern are found in the Tübingen Universitätsbibliothek under the title 'Schriften betreffend die Berufung des Dr. Zellers' (*Signatur* Fo V 198).

ALBERT SCHWEGLER

I. Letters

Schwegler to Zeller. 17 letters, 1841–53. UBT Md 747. 704.

Zeller to Schwegler. 23 letters, 1841–9. UBT Md 747. 704; Md 753, I.

II. Writings

1841. *Der Montanismus und die christliche Kirche des zweiten Jahrhunderts* (Tübingen, 1841).

1842. 'Die neueste Johanneische Literatur', *TJ*, 1842, pp. 140–70; 288–309.

1843. 'Über den Charakter des nachapostolischen Zeitalters. Gegen L. Georgii', *TJ*, 1843, pp. 176–94.

'Die Hypothese vom schöpferischen Urevangelisten (zugleich Anzeige von Wilkes Urevangelist und B. Bauers Kritik der Synoptiker', *TJ*, 1843, pp. 203–78.

1846. 'Polemisches und apologetisches gegen Dorner', *TJ*, 1846, pp. 133–82.

Das nachapostolische Zeitalter in den Hauptmomenten seiner Entwicklung (2 vols.; Tübingen, 1846).

'Zur Charakteristik eines heutigen Theologen', *JG*, 1846, pp. 881–94.

III. Secondary Literature

ACKERKNECHT, E. 'Albert Schwegler: Historiker und Philosoph', *Schwäbische Lebensbilder*, IV (Stuttgart, 1948), pp. 312–40.

PRESSEL, TH. *Worte am Grabe des Dr. F. C. Albert Schwegler* (Tübingen, 1857).

TEUFFEL, W. S. 'Fr. Karl Albert Schwegler', in Teuffel's *Studien und Charakteristiken*, pp. 503–15.

ZELLER, E. 'Albert Schwegler', in Schwegler's *Römische Geschichte*, vol. III, pp. VII–XXXVI. Reprinted in Zeller's *Vorträge und Abhandlungen*, II, pp. 329–63.

KARL CHRISTIAN PLANCK

I. Letters

Planck to Schwegler. 11 letters, 1843–8. UBT, Md 753, I, IV.

II. Writings

1841. Review: Schwegler, *Montanismus*. *JWK*, 1841: II, pp. 588–600.

1842. Review article: Bruno Bauer, *Kritik der evangelischen Geschichte der Synoptiker*. *JWK*, 1842: I, pp. 851–912.

1843. 'Das Princip des Ebionitismus', *TJ*, 1843, pp. 1–34.
'Über die religionsphilosophische Stellung des Judenthums',
TJ, 1843, pp. 429–42.
Review: Bruno Bauer, *Die gute Sache der Freiheit und meine
eigene Angelegenheit. JG*, September 1843, pp. 139–68.
1845. Review: Ebrard, *Wissenschaftliche Kritik der evangelischen Geschichte.*
TJ, 1845, pp. 145–71; 315–45.
'Der Ursprung des Mosaismus', *TJ*, 1845, pp. 450–519; 656–
721.
1847. 'Judenthum und Urchristenthum' *TJ*, 1847, pp. 258–93; 409–
34; 448–506.
1851. 'Die Grundlagen des Erlösungsbegriffes. Ein Wort über das
Endergebnis der "Tübinger Kritik"', *TJ*, 1851, pp. 27–70.
1881. *Testament eines Deutschen* (Tübingen, 1881).

III. Secondary Literature
Collected Articles 'zum Karl Christian Plancks 50. jährigen Todestag,
1930', UBT, L XVI, 254 b.
GAESE, K. H. *Materialen zu einer Karl-Christian-Planck-Biographie* (Diss.
Tübingen, 1958).
PLANCK, MATHILDE, *Karl Christian Planck. Leben und Werk* (Stuttgart,
1950).
PLANCK, MAX. 'Lebensabriss', in *Zur Erinnerung an Karl Christian Planck*
(Tübingen, 1880).
RAYHRER, ANNEMARIE, 'Karl Christian Planck', *Schwäbische Lebens-
bilder*, IX (Lebensbilder aus Schwaben und Franken; Stuttgart,
1969), pp. 263–95.

KARL REINHOLD KÖSTLIN
I. Letters

Köstlin to F. T. Vischer	19 letters	1851–82. UBT
,, to Zeller	15 ,,	1844–93. UBT
,, to Hilgenfeld	33 ,,	1849–91. Hilgenfeld *Nachlass*
,, to Planck	266 ,,	1848–80 WLS

II. Writings
1843. *Der Lehrbegriff des Evangeliums und der Briefe Johannis und die
verwandten neutestamentlichen Lehrbegriffe* (Berlin, 1843).
1850. 'Zur Geschichte des Urchristenthums', *TJ*, 1850, pp. 1–62;
235–302.
1851. 'Die pseudonyme Litteratur der ältesten Kirche, ein Beitrag zur
Geschichte der Bildung des Kanons', *TJ*, 1851, pp. 149–221.

1853. *Der Ursprung und die Komposition der synoptischen Evangelien* (Stuttgart, 1853).
'Über den Hebräerbrief, mit Rücksicht auf die neueren Untersuchungen desselben', *TJ*, 1853, pp. 410–28; 1854, pp. 366–446; 463–83.

III. Secondary Literature

ANONYMOUS. 'Karl Reinhold Köstlin' (obituary), SMSK, 17 April 1894, pp. 761–2.

SCHNEIDER, E. 'Karl Reinhold Köstlin', *ADB*, LI, pp. 343–4.

ALBRECHT RITSCHL

I. Letters

Extracts from letters to and from Ritschl are contained in Ritschl's biography (see below, III). Three letters to Zeller (1847–52) are found in the Zeller *Nachlass* in Tübingen, nine letters to Hilgenfeld are in the Hilgenfeld *Nachlass* in Munich.

II. Writings

1845. Review: Dietlein, *Das Urchristenthum*. *TJ*, 1845, pp. 547–61.
1846. *Das Evangelium Marcions und das kanonische Evangelium des Lucas* (Tübingen, 1846).
1847. 'Das Verhältnis der Schriften des Lukas zu der Zeit ihrer Entstehung', *TJ*, 1847, pp. 293–304.
      Review: Baur, *Paulus, der Apostel Jesu Christi*. *Allgemeine Literatur-Zeitung* (Halle), 1847, Nr. 124–127.
1850. *Die Entstehung der altkatholischen Kirche* (Bonn, 1850).
1851. 'Über den gegenwärtigen Stand der Kritik der synoptischen Evangelien', *TJ*, 1851, pp. 480–538.
1856. Review: K. Schwarz, *Zur Geschichte der neuesten Theologie. Literarisches Centralblatt*, 1856, Nr. 17.
1857. *Die Entstehung der altkatholischen Kirche* (2nd ed., Bonn, 1857).
1861. 'Über geschichtliche Methode in der Erforschung des Urchristenthums', *JDT*, 1861, pp. 429–59.
1862. 'Einige Erläuterungen zu dem Sendschreiben: Die historische Kritik und das Wunder', *HZ*, VIII (1862), pp. 85–99.

III. Secondary Literature

RITSCHL, OTTO. *Albrecht Ritschls Leben* (2 vols.; Freiburg i/B, 1892/6).

ADOLF HILGENFELD

I. Letters

Hilgenfeld's letters to his father, wife, and other members of his family are found in the Hilgenfeld *Nachlass*, at present in possession of Herr Dr. Helmut Pölcher of the Goethe Institute in Munich. The greatest part of Hilgenfeld's letters to friends, and theological acquaintances are now missing. 107 letters to Zeller (1846–99) are in the Tübingen Universitätsbibliothek; 51 letters to Lagarde are found in the Göttingen Universitätsbibliothek. The most important letters to Hilgenfeld from such people as Baur, Zeller, Köstlin, Ritschl, Strauss, Lipsius, Volkmar, Holtzmann, and Schenkel are printed by Pölcher in vol. IV of his dissertation (see below, III).

II. *Writings*

1848. *Die Clementinischen Recognitionen und Homilien nach ihrem Ursprung und Inhalt dargestellt* (Jena, 1848).

1849. *Das Evangelium und die Briefe Johannis, nach ihrem Lehrbegriff dargestellt* (Halle, 1849).

'Der Paschastreit und das Evangelium Johannis mit Rücksicht auf Weitzels Darstellung', *TJ*, 1849, pp. 209–81.

1850. 'Über die Composition der klementinischen Rekognitionen', *TJ*, 1850, pp. 63–93.

Das Markus-Evangelium (Leipzig, 1850).

1851. *Die Göttingische Polemik gegen meine Forschungen in sittlicher und wissenschaftlicher Hinsicht gewürdigt* (Leipzig, 1851).

1852. 'Neue Untersuchung über das Markusevangelium, mit Rücksicht auf Dr. Baurs Darstellung', *TJ*, 1852, pp. 102–32; 259–93; 304.

Der Galaterbrief (Leipzig, 1852).

1853. *Die apostolischen Väter: Untersuchungen über Inhalt und Ursprung der unter ihrem Namen erhaltenen Schriften* (Halle, 1853).

1854. *Die Evangelien nach ihrer Entstehung und geschichtlichen Bedeutung.* (Leipzig, 1854).

'Der Ursprung der pseudoclementinischen Recognitionen und Homilien, nach dem neuesten Stand der Untersuchung', *TJ*, 1854, pp. 483–535.

1855. *Das Urchristenthum in den Hauptwendepunkten seines Entwicklungsganges mit besonderer Rücksicht auf die neuesten Verhandlungen der HH. DD. Hase und Baur* (Jena, 1855).

'Die johanneischen Briefe', *TJ*, 1855, pp. 471–526.

1857. 'Die Evangelienfrage und ihre neuesten Behandlungen von Weisse, Volkmar und Meyer', *TJ*, 1857, pp. 381–440; 498–532.

1858. 'Das Urchristenthum und seine neuesten Bearbeitungen von Lechler und Ritschl', *ZWT*, 1858, pp. 54–140; 377–440; 562–602.

1859. 'Einige Bemerkungen zu Dr. Baur's neuester Schrift über "die Tübinger Schule"', *ZWT*, 1859, pp. 276–80.

1860. *Der Paschastreit der alten Kirche* (Halle, 1860).

1863. 'Die Theologie des neunzehnten Jahrhunderts nach ihrer Stellung zu Religion und Christenthum und mit besonderer Rücksicht auf Baur's Darstellung', *ZWT*, 1863, pp. 1–40.

1864. 'Baur's kritische Urgeschichte des Christenthums und ihre neueste Bestreitung', *ZWT*, 1864, pp. 113–45.

1868. 'Der Magier Simon', *ZWT*, 1868, pp. 357–96.

1875. *Historisch-kritische Einleitung in das neue Testament* (Leipzig, 1875).

1884. *Die Ketzergeschichte des Urchristenthums* (Leipzig, 1884).

1893. 'F. C. Baur nach seiner wissenschaftlichen Entwickelung und Bedeutung', *ZWT*, 1893, pp. 222–44.

III. Secondary Literature

HILGENFELD, HEINRICH. 'Zu Hilgenfelds wissenschaftlicher Thätigkeit', *ZWT*, 1907–8, pp. 14–24.

——. 'Der Fall Hilgenfeld in Osterburg', *ZWT*, 1907–8, pp. 297–323.

PÖLCHER, HELMUT. *Adolf Hilgenfeld und das Ende der Tübinger Schule* (Parts I, II, IV; Diss. Erlangen, 1962).

GUSTAV VOLKMAR

I. Letters

The whereabouts of Volkmar's correspondence–*Nachlass* is now unknown. Thirty-two letters to Hilgenfeld (1852–72) are found in the Hilgenfeld *Nachlass*; one letter to Baur (1859) in the UBT under the *Signatur* Md 750. I. 21; seven letters to Zeller (1862–9) in the Zeller *Nachlass Signatur* Md 747, 804.

II. Writings

1846. 'Über einen historischen Irrthum in den Evangelien', *TJ*, 1846, pp. 363–83.

1850. 'Über das Lucasevangelium nach seinem Verhältnis zu Marcion und seinem dogmatischen Charakter, mit besonderer Beziehung auf die kritischen Untersuchungen Ferd. Chr. Baurs und A. Ritschls', *TJ*, 1850, pp. 110–38; 185–235.

1854. 'Ein neu entdecktes Zeugnis für das Johannesevangelium', *TJ*, 1854, pp. 446–62.

1855. 'Die Zeit Justins d.M. kritisch untersucht', *TJ*, 1855, pp. 227–83.

1856. 'Über den Simon Magus der Apostelgeschichte und den Ursprung der Simonie', *TJ*, 1856, pp. 279–86.

1857. *Die Religion Jesu und ihre erste Entwicklung nach dem gegenwärtigen Stande der Wissenschaft* (Leipzig, 1857).

'Über Euodia, Euodius und Anaclet', *TJ*, 1857, pp. 147–51.

1882. *Jesus Nazarenus* (Zürich, 1882).

III. Secondary Literature

JÜLICHER, ADOLF. 'Gustav Volkmar', *ADB*, LIV, pp. 764–75.

THE TÜBINGEN SCHOOL

BECKH, H. 'Die Tübinger Schule kritisch beleuchtet', *Zeitschrift für Protestantismus und Kirche*, N. F. LXXIV (1864), pp. 1–57; 69–95; 133–78; 203–44.

BERGER, SAMUEL. F. C. *Baur: les origines de l'école de Tubingue et ses principes, 1826–1844* (Strasbourg, 1867).

GEORGII, L. Review: Schwegler, *Montanismus. DJWK*, 1842, pp. 45–59; 129–51.

——. 'Über den Charakter der christlichen Geschichte in den ersten zwei Jahrhunderten', *DJWK*, 1842, pp. 913–27.

HASE, K. *Die Tübinger Schule. Ein Sendschreiben an Herrn Dr. Ferdinand Christian von Baur* (Leipzig, 1855).

LIPSIUS, R. A. 'Ferdinand Christian Baur und die Tübinger Schule', *Unsere Zeit*, VI (1862), pp. 229–54.

MACKAY, R. W. *The Tübingen School and its Antecedents* (London, 1863).

MERZ, HEINRICH. *Die Jahrbücher der Gegenwart und ihre Helden* (Stuttgart, 1845).

SCHMIDT, H/HAUSSLEITER, J. 'Ferdinand Christian Baur und die neuere Tübinger Schule', *RE* (3rd ed.), II, pp. 467–83.

UHLHORN, G. 'Die älteste Kirchengeschichte in der Darstellung der Tübinger Schule', *JDT*, III (1858), pp. 280–349.

ZELLER, E. 'Die Tübinger historische Schule', *HZ*, IV (1860), pp. 356–73. Reprinted in revised form in *Vorträge und Abhandlungen geschichtlichen Inhalts*, pp. 267–353.

Index of Names